Alexander Sutherland, George Sutherland

The History of Australia and New Zealand from 1606 to 1890

Alexander Sutherland, George Sutherland

The History of Australia and New Zealand from 1606 to 1890

ISBN/EAN: 9783337312176

Printed in Europe, USA, Canada, Australia, Japan

Cover: Foto ©ninafisch / pixelio.de

More available books at **www.hansebooks.com**

THE
HISTORY
OF
AUSTRALIA AND NEW ZEALAND

FROM 1606 TO 1890

BY

ALEXANDER SUTHERLAND, M.A.

AND

GEORGE SUTHERLAND, M.A.

LONDON
LONGMANS, GREEN, AND CO.
AND NEW YORK: 15 EAST 16th STREET
GEORGE ROBERTSON AND CO.
MELBOURNE, SYDNEY, ADELAIDE, AND BRISBANE
1894

THE ABERDEEN UNIVERSITY PRESS.

LIST OF ILLUSTRATIONS.

	PAGE
Captain Cook,	*frontispiece*.
William Dampier,	6
Rocks, South Heads, Sydney,	13
Town and Cove of Sydney, in 1798,	17
Matthew Flinders,	21
Cook's Monument, Botany Bay,	24
The Explorers' Tree, Katoomba, N.S.W.,	26
Governor Collins,	33
Governor Macquarie,	39
Blue Mountain Scenery, Wentworth Falls, N.S.W.,	41
St. Andrew's Cathedral, Sydney,	46
Captain Charles Sturt,	51
The First House Built in Victoria,	56
The First Hotel in Victoria,	57
Edward Henty,	61
John Pascoe Fawkner,	62
Governor Latrobe,	65
Collins Street, Melbourne, in 1840,	66
First Settlement at Adelaide, 1836,	69
Governor Hindmarsh,	71
Proclamation Tree, Glenelg,	74
Colonial Secretary's Office, Sydney,	81
Edward Hargraves,	92
Perth, Western Australia, in 1838,	114
Perth, 1890,	115
Boomerangs, or Kylies,	122
Parliament House, Brisbane,	123
Victoria Bridge, Brisbane,	126

LIST OF ILLUSTRATIONS.

	PAGE
Government House, Brisbane,	130
Robert O'Hara Burke,	144
William John Wills,	145
Sir John Franklin,	156
Queen Truganina, the last of the Tasmanians,	163
King William Street, Adelaide,	167
George Street, Sydney,	169
The Lithgow Zigzag, the Blue Mountains,	172
The Town Hall, Sydney,	174
Collins Street, Melbourne,	177
Town Hall, Melbourne,	182
Port of Melbourne,	183
A Maori Dwelling,	185
Milford Sound, South Island, New Zealand,	191
Rev. S. Marsden, "the Apostle of New Zealand,"	195
Auckland, from the Wharf,	206
Stronghold of the Maoris at Rangiriri,	222
Sir George Grey,	224
Knox Church, Dunedin,	228
Christchurch Cathedral,	230
The Maori King,	232
Rangiriri, from the Waikato,	236
The Cargill Fountain,	243
Victoria Defence Fleet,	245

CONTENTS.

CHAPTER	PAGE
I.—The Early Discoverers,	1
II.—Convict Settlement at Sydney, 1788 to 1850,	11
III.—Discoveries of Bass and Flinders,	18
IV.—New South Wales, 1800 to 1808,	25
V.—Tasmania, 1803 to 1836,	31
VI.—New South Wales, 1808 to 1837,	38
VII.—Discoveries in the Interior, 1817 to 1836,	48
VIII.—Port Phillip, 1800 to 1840,	55
IX.—South Australia, 1836 to 1841,	67
X.—New South Wales, 1836 to 1850,	75
XI.—South Australia, 1841 to 1850,	81
XII.—The Discovery of Gold,	89
XIII.—Victoria, 1851 to 1855,	98
XIV.—New South Wales, 1851 to 1860,	107
XV.—West Australia, 1829 to 1890,	111
XVI.—Queensland, 1823 to 1890,	119
XVII.—Explorations in the Interior, 1840 to 1860,	131
XVIII.—Discoveries in the Interior, 1860 to 1886,	143
XIX.—Tasmania, 1837 to 1890,	155
XX.—South Australia, 1850 to 1890,	163
XXI.—New South Wales, 1860 to 1890,	168
XXII.—Victoria, 1855 to 1890,	175
XXIII.—The Times of the Maoris,	184
XXIV.—New Zealand Colonised,	200
XXV.—White Men and Maoris,	215
XXVI.—New Zealand, 1843 to 1890,	227

HISTORY OF AUSTRALIA AND NEW ZEALAND.

CHAPTER I.

THE EARLY DISCOVERERS.

1. To the people who lived four centuries ago in Europe only a very small portion of the earth's surface was known. Their geography was confined to the regions lying immediately around the Mediterranean, and including Europe, the north of Africa, and the west of Asia. Round these there was a margin, obscurely and imperfectly described in the reports of merchants; but by far the greater part of the world was utterly unknown. Great realms of darkness stretched all beyond, and closely hemmed in the little circle of light. In these unknown lands our ancestors loved to picture everything that was strange and mysterious. They believed that the man who could penetrate far enough would find countries where inexhaustible riches were to be gathered without toil from fertile shores, or marvellous valleys; and though wild tales were told of the dangers supposed to fill these regions, yet to the more daring and adventurous these only made the visions of boundless wealth and enchanting loveliness seem more fascinating.

Thus, as the art of navigation improved, and long voyages became possible, courageous seamen were tempted to venture out into the great unknown expanse. Columbus carried his trembling sailors over great tracts of unknown ocean, and discovered the two continents of America; Vasco di Gama penetrated far to the south, and rounded the Cape of Good Hope; Magellan, passing through the straits now called by his name, was the first to enter the Pacific Ocean; and so in the case of a hundred others, courage and skill carried the hardy seaman over many seas and into many lands that had lain unknown for ages.

Australia was the last part of the world to be thus visited and explored. In the year 1600, during the times of Shakespeare, the region to the south of the East Indies was still as little known as ever; the rude maps of those days had only a great blank where the islands of Australia should have been. Most people thought there was nothing but the ocean in that part of the world; and as the voyage was dangerous and very long—requiring several years for its completion—scarcely any one cared to run the risk of exploring it.

2. De Quiros.—There was, however, an enthusiastic seaman who firmly believed that a great continent existed there, and who longed to go in search of it. This was De Quiros, a Spaniard, who had already sailed with a famous voyager, and now desired to set out on an expedition of his own. He spent many years in beseeching the King of Spain to furnish him with ships and men so that he might seek this southern continent. King Philip for a long time paid little attention to his entreaties, but was at last overcome by his perseverance, and told De Quiros that, though he himself had no money for such purposes, he would order the Governor of Peru to provide the necessary vessels. De Quiros carried the king's instructions to Peru, and two ships were soon prepared and filled with suitable crews—the *Capitana* and the *Almiranta*, with a smaller vessel called the *Zabra* to act as tender. A nobleman named Torres was appointed second in command, and they set sail from Peru, on a prosperous voyage across the Pacific, discovering many small islands on their way, and seeing for the first time the Coral Islands of the South Seas. At length (1606) they reached a shore which stretched as far as they could see both north and south, and De Quiros thought he had discovered the great Southern Continent. He called the place " Tierra Australis del Espiritu Santo," that is, the "Southern Land of the Holy Spirit". It is now known that this was not really a continent, but merely one of the New Hebrides Islands, and more than a thousand miles away from the mainland. The land was filled by high mountains, verdure-clad to their summits, and sending down fine streams, which fell in hoarse-sounding waterfalls from the edges of the rocky shore, or wandered amid tropical luxuriance of plants down to the golden sands that lay within the coral barriers. The inhabitants came down to the edge of the green and shining waters making signs of peace, and twenty soldiers went ashore, along with an officer, who made friends with them, exchanging cloth for pigs and fruit. De Quiros coasted along the islands for a day or two till he entered a fine bay, where his vessels anchored, and Torres went ashore. A chief came down to meet him, offering him a present of fruit, and making signs to show that he did not wish the Spaniards to intrude upon his land. As Torres paid no attention, the chief drew a line upon the sand, and defied the Spaniards to cross it. Torres immediately stepped over it, and the natives launched some arrows at him, which dropped harmlessly from his iron armour. Then the Spaniards fired their muskets, killing the chief and a number of the naked savages. The rest stood for a moment, stupefied at the noise and flash; then turned and ran for the mountains.

The Spaniards spent a few pleasant days among the fruit plantations, and slept in cool groves of overarching foliage; but subsequently they had quarrels and combats with the natives, of whom they killed a considerable number. When the Spaniards had taken on board a sufficient supply of wood and of fresh water they set sail, but had scarcely got out to sea when a fever spread among the crew, and became a perfect plague. They returned and anchored in the bay, where the vessels lay like so many hospitals. No one died, and after a few days they again put to sea, this time to be driven back again by bad weather. Torres, with two ships, safely reached the sheltering bay, but the vessel in which De Quiros sailed was unable to enter it, and had to stand out to sea and weather the storm. The sailors then refused to proceed further with the voyage, and, having risen in mutiny, compelled De Quiros to turn the vessel's head for Mexico, which they reached after some terrible months of hunger and thirst.

3. Torres.—The other ships waited for a day or two, but no signs being seen of their consort, they proceeded in search of it. In this voyage Torres sailed round the land, thus showing that it was no continent, but only an island. Having satisfied himself that it was useless to seek for De Quiros, he turned to the west, hoping to reach the Philippine Islands, where the Spaniards had a colony, at Manila. It was his singular fortune to sail through that opening which lies between New Guinea and Australia, to which the name of "Torres Strait" was long afterwards applied. He probably saw Cape York rising out of the sea to the south, but thought it only another of those endless little islands with which the strait is studded. Poor De Quiros spent the rest of his life in petitioning the King of Spain for ships to make a fresh attempt. After many years he obtained another order to the Governor of Peru, and the old weather-beaten mariner once more set out from Spain full of hope; but at Panama, on his way, death awaited him, and there the fiery-souled veteran passed away, the last of the great Spanish navigators. He died in poverty and disappointment, but he is to be honoured as the first of the long line of Australian discoverers. In after years, the name he had invented was divided into two parts; the island he had really discovered being called Espiritu Santo, while the continent he thought he had discovered was called Terra Australis. This last name was shortened by another discoverer—Flinders—to the present term Australia.

4. The Duyfhen.—De Quiros and Torres were Spaniards, but the Dutch also displayed much anxiety to reach the great South Continent. From their colony at Java they sent out a small vessel, the *Duyfhen*, or *Dove*, which sailed into the Gulf of Carpentaria, and passed half-way down along its eastern side. Some sailors landed, but so many of them were killed by the natives that the captain was glad to embark again and sail for home, after calling the place of their disaster Cape Keer-weer, or Turnagain. These Dutch sailors were the first Europeans, as far as can now be known, who landed on Australian soil; but as they never published any account of their voyage, it is only by the merest chance that we know anything of it.

5. Other Dutch Discoverers.—During the next twenty years various Dutch vessels, while sailing to the settlements in the East Indies, met with the coast of Australia. In 1616 Dirk Hartog landed on the island in Shark Bay which is now called after him. Two years later Captain Zaachen is said to have sailed along the north coast, which he called Arnhem

Land. Next year (1619) another captain, called Edel, surveyed the western shores, which for a long time bore his name. In 1622 a Dutch ship, the *Leeuwin*, or *Lioness*, sailed along the southern coast, and its name was given to the south-west cape of Australia. In 1627 Peter Nuyts entered the Great Australian Bight, and made a rough chart of some of its shores; in 1628 General Carpenter sailed completely round the large gulf to the north, which has taken its name from this circumstance. Thus, by degrees, all the northern and western, together with part of the southern shores, came to be roughly explored, and the Dutch even had some idea of colonising this continent.

6. Tasman.—During the next fourteen years we hear no more of voyages to Australia; but in 1642 Antony Van Diemen, the Governor of the Dutch possessions in the East Indies, sent out his friend Abel Jansen Tasman, with two ships, to make new discoveries in the South Seas. Tasman first went to the Island of Bourbon, from which he sailed due south for a time; but finding no signs of land, he turned to the east, and three months after setting out he saw a rocky shore in the distance. Stormy weather coming on, he was driven out to sea, and it was not till a week later that he was able to reach the coast again. He called the place Van Diemen's Land, and sent some sailors on shore to examine the country. These men heard strange noises in the woods, and saw trees of enormous height, in which notches were cut seven feet apart. These they believed to be the steps used by the natives in climbing the trees, and they therefore returned to report that the land was exceedingly beautiful, but inhabited by men of gigantic size. Tasman, next day, allowed the carpenter to swim ashore and set up the Dutch flag; but having himself seen, from his ship, what he thought to be men of extraordinary stature moving about on the shore, he lost no time in taking up his anchor and setting sail. Farther to the east he discovered the islands of New Zealand, and after having made a partial survey of their coasts, he returned to Batavia. Two years after he was sent on a second voyage of discovery, and explored the northern and western shores of Australia itself; but the results do not seem to have been important, and are not now known. His chief service in the exploration of Australia was the discovery of

Tasmania, as it is now called, after his name. This he did not know to be an island; he drew it on his maps as if it were a peninsula belonging to the mainland of Australia.

7. Dampier.—The discoveries that had so far been made were very imperfect, for the sailors generally contented themselves with looking at the land from a safe distance. They made no surveys such as would have enabled them to draw correct charts of the coasts; they seldom landed, and even when they did, they never sought to become acquainted with the natives, or to learn anything as to the nature of the interior of the country. The first who took the trouble to obtain information of this more accurate kind was the Englishman, William Dampier.

When a young man Dampier had gone out to Jamaica to manage a large estate; but not liking the slave-driving business,

WILLIAM DAMPIER.

he crossed over to Campeachy, and lived for a time in the woods, cutting the more valuable kinds of timber. Here he became acquainted with the buccaneers who made the lonely coves of Campeachy their headquarters. Being persuaded to join them, he entered upon a life of lawless daring, constantly fighting and plundering, and meeting with the wildest adventures. He was often captured by the American natives, still more often by the Spaniards, but always escaped to enter upon exploits of fresh danger. In 1688 he joined a company of buccaneers, who proposed to make a voyage round the world and plunder on their way. It took them more than a year to reach the East Indies, where they spent a long time, sometimes attacking Spanish ships or Dutch fortresses, sometimes leading an easy luxurious life among the natives, often quarrelling among themselves, and even going so far as to leave their captain with forty men on the island of Mindanao. But at length the time came when it was necessary to seek some quiet spot where they should be able to clean and repair the bottoms of their ships. Accordingly, they landed on the north-west coast of Australia, and lived for twelve days at the place now called "Buccaneers' Archipelago". They were the first Europeans who held any communication with the natives of Australia, and the first to publish a detailed account of their voyage thither. Growing tired of a lawless life, and having become wealthy, Dampier bought an estate in England, where he lived some years in retirement, till his love of adventure led him forth again. The King of England was anxious to encourage discovery, and fitted out a vessel called the *Roebuck*, to explore the southern seas. Dampier was the only man in England who had ever been to Australia, and to him was given the command of the little vessel, which sailed in the year 1699. It took a long time to reach Australia, but at last the *Roebuck* entered what Dampier called Shark Bay, from an enormous shark he caught there. He then explored the north-west coast as far as Roebuck Bay, in all about nine hundred miles; of which he published a full and fairly accurate account. He was a man of keen observation, and delighted to describe the habits and manners of the natives, as well as peculiarities in the plants and animals, of the various places he visited. During the time he was in Australia he frequently met with the blacks and became well acquainted with them. He gives this description of their appearance:—

"The inhabitants are the most miserable wretches in the universe, having no houses nor garments. They feed upon a few fish, cockles, mussels, and periwinkles. They are without religion and without government. In figure they are tall, straight-bodied and thin, with small, long limbs."

The country itself, he says, is low and sandy, with no fresh water and scarcely any animals except one which looks like a racoon, and jumps about on its long hind legs. Altogether, his description is not prepossessing; and he says that the only pleasure he had found in this part of his voyage was the satisfaction of having discovered the most barren spot on the face of the earth.

This account is, in most respects, correct, so far as regards the portion of Australia visited by Dampier. But, unfortunately, he saw only the most inhospitable part of the whole continent. There are many parts whose beauty would have enchanted him, but as he had sailed along nearly a thousand miles without seeing any shore that was not miserable, it is not to be wondered at that he reported the whole land to be worthless. He was subsequently engaged in other voyages of discovery, in one of which he rescued the famous Alexander Selkirk from his lonely island; but, amid all his subsequent adventures, he never entertained the idea of returning to Australia.

Dampier published a most interesting account of all his travels in different parts of the world, and his book was for a long time the standard book of travels. Defoe used the materials it contained for his celebrated novel, *Robinson Crusoe*. But it turned away the tide of discovery from Australia; for those who read of the beautiful islands and rich countries Dampier had elsewhere visited would never dream of incurring the labour and expense of a voyage to so dull and barren a spot as Australia seemed to be from the description in his book. Thus we hear of no further explorations in this part of the world until nearly a century after; and, even then, no one thought of sending out ships specially for the purpose.

8. Captain Cook.—But in the year 1770 a series of important discoveries was indirectly brought about. The Royal Society of London, calculating that the planet Venus would cross the disc of the sun in 1769, persuaded the English Government to send out an expedition to the Pacific Ocean for the purpose of making observations which would enable astronomers to calculate the distance of the earth from the sun. A small vessel, the *Endeavour*, was chosen; astronomers with their instruments embarked, and the whole placed under the charge of James Cook, a sailor whose admirable character fully merited this distinction. At thirteen he had been a shopkeeper's assistant, but, preferring the sea, he had become an apprentice in a coal vessel. After many years of rude life in this trade, during which he contrived to carry on his education in mathematics and navigation, he entered the Royal Navy, and by diligence and honesty rose to the rank of master. He had completed so many excellent surveys in North America, and, besides, had made himself so well acquainted with astronomy, that the Government had no hesitation in making their choice. That it was a wise one, the care and success of Cook fully showed. He carried the expedition safely to Tahiti, built fortifications, and erected instruments for the observations, which were admirably made. Having finished this part of his task, he thought it would be a pity, with so fine a ship and crew, not to make some discoveries in these little-known seas. He sailed south for a time without meeting land; then, turning west, he reached those islands of New Zealand which had been first seen by Tasman. But Cook made a far more complete exploration than had been possible to Tasman. For six months he examined their shores, sailing completely round both islands and making excellent maps of them.

Then, saying good-bye to these coasts at what he named Cape Farewell, he sailed westward for three weeks, until his outlook man raised the cry of "land," and they were close to the shores of Australia at Cape Howe. Standing to the northeast, he sailed along the coast till he reached a fine bay, where he anchored for about ten days. On his first landing he was opposed by two of the natives, who seemed quite ready to encounter more than forty armed men. Cook endeavoured to gain their goodwill, but without success. A musket fired between them startled, but did not dismay them; and when some small shot was fired into the legs of one of them, though he turned and ran into his hut, it was only for the purpose of putting on a shield and again facing the white men. Cook made many subsequent attempts to be friendly with the natives, but always without success. He examined the country for a few miles inland, and two of his scientific friends—Sir Joseph Banks and Dr. Solander—made splendid collections of botanical specimens. From this circumstance the place was called Botany Bay, and its two headlands received the names of Cape Banks and Cape Solander. It was here that Captain Cook, amid the firing of cannons and volleys of musketry, took possession of the country on behalf of His Britannic Majesty, giving it the name, "New South Wales," on account of the resemblance of its coasts to the southern shores of Wales.

Shortly after they had set sail from Botany Bay they observed a small opening in the land; but Cook did not stay to examine it, merely marking it on his chart as "Port Jackson," in honour of his friend Sir George Jackson. The vessel still continued her course northward along the coast, till they anchored in Moreton Bay. After a short stay, they again set out towards the north, making a rough chart of the shores they saw. In this way they had sailed along thirteen hundred miles without serious mishap, when one night, at about eleven o'clock, they found the sea grow very shallow; all hands were quickly on deck, but before the ship could be turned she struck heavily on a sunken rock. No land was to be seen, and they therefore concluded that it was upon a bank of coral they had struck. The vessel seemed to rest upon the ridge; but, as the swell of the ocean rolled past, she bumped very heavily. Most of the cannons and other heavy articles were thrown overboard, and, the ship being thus lightened, they tried to float her off at daybreak. This they were unable to do; but, by working hard all next day, they prepared everything for a great effort at the evening tide, and had the satisfaction of seeing the rising waters float the vessel off. But now the sea was found to be pouring in through the leaks so rapidly that, even with four pumps constantly going, they could scarcely keep her afloat. They worked hard day and night, but the ship was slowly sinking, when, by the ingenious device of passing a sail beneath her and pulling it tightly, it was found that the leakage was sufficiently decreased to keep her from foundering. Shortly after, they saw land, which Captain Cook called "Cape Tribulation". He took the vessel into the mouth of a small river, which they called the Endeavour, and there careened her. On examining the bottom, it was found that a great sharp rock had pierced a hole in her timbers, such as must inevitably have sent her to the bottom in spite of pumps and sails, had it not been that the piece of coral had broken off and remained firmly fixed in the vessel's side, thus itself filling up the greater part of the hole it had caused. The ship was fully repaired; and, after a delay of two months, they proceeded northward along the coast to Cape York. They then sailed through Torres Strait, and made it clear that New Guinea and Australia are not joined.

9. Subsequent Visits.—Several ships visited Australia during the next few years, but their commanders contented themselves with merely viewing the coasts which had already been discovered, and returned without adding anything new. In 1772 Marion, a Frenchman, and next year Furneaux, an Englishman, sailed along the coasts of Van Diemen's Land. In 1777 Captain Cook, shortly before his death, anchored for a few days in Adventure Bay, on the east coast of Van Diemen's Land. La Perouse, Vancouver, and D'Entrecasteaux also visited Australia, and, though they added nothing of importance, they assisted in filling in the details. By this time nearly all the coasts had been roughly explored, and the only great point left unsettled was, whether Van Diemen's Land was an island or not.

CHAPTER II.

THE CONVICT SETTLEMENT AT SYDNEY, 1788-1800.

1. Botany Bay.—The reports brought home by Captain Cook completely changed the beliefs current in those days with regard to Australia. From the time of Dampier it had been supposed that the whole of this continent must be the same flat and miserable desert as the part he described. Cook's account, on the other hand, represented the eastern coast as a country full of beauty and promise. Now, it so happened that, shortly after Cook's return, the English nation had to deal with a great difficulty in regard to its criminal population. In 1776 the United States declared their independence, and the English then found they could no longer send their convicts over to Virginia, as they had formerly done. In a short time the gaols of England were crowded with felons. It became necessary to select a new place of transportation; and, just as this difficulty arose, Captain Cook's voyages called attention to a land in every way suited for such a purpose, both by reason of its fertility and of its great distance. Viscount Sydney, therefore, determined to send out a party to Botany Bay, in order to found a convict settlement there; and in May, 1787, a fleet was ready to sail. It consisted of the *Sirius* war-ship, its tender the *Supply*, together with six transports for the convicts, and three ships for carrying the stores. Of the convicts, five hundred and fifty were men and two hundred and twenty were women. To guard these, there were on board two hundred soldiers. Captain Phillip was appointed Governor of the colony, Captain Hunter was second in command, and Mr. Collins went out as judge-advocate, to preside in the military courts, which it was intended to establish for the administration of justice. On the 18th, 19th, and 20th of January, 1788, the vessels arrived, one after another, in Botany Bay, after a voyage of eight months, during which many of the convicts had died from diseases brought on by so long a confinement.

2. Port Jackson.—As soon as the ships had anchored in Botany Bay, convicts were landed and commenced to clear the timber from a portion of the land; but a day or two was sufficient to show the unsuitability of Botany Bay for such a settlement. Its waters were so shallow that the ships could not enter it properly, and had to lie near the Heads, where the great waves of the Pacific rolled in on them by night and day. Governor Phillip, therefore, took three boats, and sailed out to search for some more convenient harbour. As he passed along the coast he turned to examine the opening which Captain Cook had called Port Jackson, and soon found himself in a winding channel of water, with great cliffs frowning overhead. All at once a magnificent prospect opened on his eyes. A harbour, which is, perhaps, the most beautiful and perfect in the world, stretched before him far to the west, till it was lost on the distant horizon. It seemed a vast maze of winding waters, dotted here and there with lovely islets; its shores thickly wooded down to the strips of golden sand which lined the most charming little bays; and its broad sheets of rippling waters bordered by lines of dusky foliage. The scene has always been one of surpassing loveliness; but to those who filled the first boats that ever threw the foam from its surface, who felt themselves the objects of breathless attention to groups of natives who stood gazing here and there from the projecting rocks, it must have had an enchanting effect. To Captain Phillip himself, whose mind had been filled with anxiety and despondency as to the future prospects of his charge, it opened out like the vision of a world of new hope and promise.

Three days were spent in examining portions of this spacious harbour, and in exploring a few of its innumerable bays. Captain Phillip selected, as the place most suitable for the settlement, a small inlet, which, in honour of the Minister of State, he called Sydney Cove. It was so deep as to allow vessels to approach to within a yard or two of the shore, thus avoiding the necessity of spending time and money in building wharves or piers.

ROCKS, SOUTH HEADS, SYDNEY.

After a few days the fleet was brought round and lay at anchor in this little cove which is now the crowded Circular Quay. The convicts were landed, and commenced to clear away the trees on the banks of a small stream which stole silently through a very dense wood. When an open space had been obtained, a flagstaff was erected near the present battery on Dawe's Point ; the soldiers fired three volleys, and the Governor read his commission to the assembled company. Then began a scene of noise and bustle. From dawn to sunset, nothing could be heard but the sound of axes, hammers, and saws, with the crash of trees and the shouts of the convict overseers. They lost no time in preparing their habitations on shore; for the confinement of the overcrowded ships had become intolerably hateful.

3. Early Sufferings.—More than a third of their number were ill with scurvy and other diseases—sixty-six lay in the little hospital which had been set up, and many of them never recovered. Those who were well enough to work began to clear the land for cultivation; but so soon as everything was ready for the ploughing to begin, the amazing fact was discovered that no one knew anything of agriculture; and had it not been that Governor Phillip had with him a servant who had been for a time on a farm, their labour would have been of little avail. As it was, the cultivation was of the rudest kind; one man, even if he had been a highly experienced person, could do very little to instruct so many. The officers and soldiers were smart enough on parade, but they were useless on a farm; the convicts, instead of trying to learn, expended all their ingenuity in picking each other's pockets, or in robbing the stores. They would do no work unless an armed soldier was standing behind them, and if he turned away for a moment, they would deliberately destroy the farm implements in their charge, hide them in the sand or throw them into the water. Thus, only a trifling amount of food was obtained from the soil; the provisions they had brought with them were nearly finished, and when the news came that the *Guardian* transport, on which they were depending for fresh supplies, had struck on an iceberg and had been lost, the little community was filled with the deepest dismay. Soon after, a ship arrived with a number of fresh convicts, but no provisions; in great haste the *Sirius* was sent to the Cape of Good Hope, and the *Supply* to Batavia; these vessels brought back as much as they could get, but it was all used in a month or two. Starvation now lay before the settlement; every one, including the officers and the Governor himself, was put on the lowest rations which could keep the life in a man's body, and yet there was not enough of food, even at this miserable rate, to last for any length of time.

Numbers died of starvation; the Governor stopped all the works, as the men were too weak to continue them. The sheep and cattle which they had brought with so much trouble to become the origin of flocks and herds were all killed for food, with the exception of two or three which had escaped to the woods and had been lost from sight.

4. Norfolk Island.—Under these circumstances, Governor Phillip sent two hundred convicts, with about seventy soldiers, to Norfolk Island, where there was a moderate chance of their being able to support themselves; for, immediately after his arrival in New South Wales, he had sent Lieutenant King to take possession of that island, of whose beauty and fertility Captain Cook had spoken very highly. Twenty-seven convicts and soldiers had gone along with King, and had cleared away the timber from the rich brown soil. They had little trouble in raising ample crops, and were now in the midst of plenty, which their less fortunate companions came to share. But the *Sirius*, in which they had been carried over, was wrecked on a coral reef near the island before she could return, and with her was lost a considerable quantity of provisions.

5. The Second Fleet.—The prospects of the colony at Sydney had grown very black, when a store-ship suddenly appeared off the Heads. Great was the rejoicing at first; but when a storm arose and drove the vessel northward among the reefs of Broken Bay, their exultation was changed to a painful suspense. For some hours her fate was doubtful; but, to the intense relief of the expectant people on shore, she managed to make the port and land her supplies. Shortly after, two other store-ships arrived, and the community was never again so badly in want of provisions. Matters were growing cheerful, when a fresh gloom was caused by the arrival of a fleet filled to overflowing with sick and dying convicts. Seventeen hundred had been embarked, but of these two hundred had died on the way, and their bodies had been thrown overboard. Several hundreds were in the last stages of emaciation and exhaustion; scarcely one of the whole fifteen hundred who landed was fit for a day's work. This brought fresh misery and trouble, and the deaths were of appalling frequency.

6. Escape of Prisoners.—Many of the convicts sought

to escape from their sufferings by running away; some seized the boats in the harbour and tried to sail for the Dutch colony in Java; others hid themselves in the woods, and either perished or else returned, after weeks of starvation, to give themselves up to the authorities. In 1791 a band of between forty and fifty set out to walk to China, and penetrated a few miles into the bush, where their bleached and whitened skeletons some years after told their fate.

7. Departure of Governor Phillip.—Amid these cares and trials the health of Governor Phillip fairly broke down, and, in 1792, forced him to resign. He was a man of energy and decision; prompt and skilful, yet humane and just in his character; his face, though pinched and pale with ill-health, had a sweet and benevolent expression; no better man could have been selected to fill the difficult position he held with so much credit to himself. He received a handsome pension from the British Government, and retired to spend his life in English society. Major Grose and Captain Patterson took charge of the colony for the next three years; but in 1795 Captain Hunter, who, after the loss of his ship, the *Sirius*, had returned to England, arrived in Sydney to occupy the position of Governor.

8. Governor Hunter.—By this time affairs had passed their crisis, and were beginning to be favourable. About sixty convicts, whose sentences had expired, had received grants of land, and, now that they were working for themselves, had become successful farmers. Governor Hunter brought out a number of free settlers, to whom he gave land near the Hawkesbury; and, after a time, more than six thousand acres were covered with crops of wheat and maize. There was now no fear of famine, and the settlement grew to be comfortable in most respects. Unfortunately, the more recent attempts to import cattle with which to stock the farms had proved more or less unsuccessful; so that the discovery of a fine herd of sixty wandering through the meadows of the Hawkesbury was hailed with great delight. These were the descendants of the cattle which had been lost from Governor Phillip's herd some years before.

9. State of the Settlement.—Twelve years after the foundation of the colony, its population amounted to between six

CONVICT SETTLEMENT AT SYDNEY.

and seven thousand persons. These were all settled near Sydney, which was a straggling town with one main street 200 feet wide, running up the valley from Sydney Cove, while on the slopes at either side the huts of the convicts were stationed far apart and each in a fenced-in plot of ground. On the little hills overlooking the cove, a number of big, bare, stone buildings were the Government quarters and barracks for the soldiers.

Attempts had been made to penetrate to the west, though without success. The rugged chain of the Blue Mountains was an

Town and Cove of Sydney in 1798.
(Compare with page 169.)

impassable barrier. Seventy miles north of Sydney a fine river—the Hunter—had been discovered by Lieutenant Shortland while in pursuit of some runaway convicts who had stolen a boat. Signs of coal having been seen near its mouth, convicts were sent up to open mines, and, these proving successful, the town of Newcastle rapidly formed. In 1800 Governor Hunter returned to England on business, intending to come out again; but he was appointed to the command of a war-ship, and Lieutenant King was sent out to take his place.

CHAPTER III.

THE DISCOVERIES OF BASS AND FLINDERS.

1. No community has ever been more completely isolated than the first inhabitants of Sydney. They were three thousand miles away from the nearest white men; before them lay a great ocean, visited only at rare intervals, and, for the greater part, unexplored; behind them was an unknown continent, a vast, untrodden waste, in which they formed but a speck. They were almost completely shut out from intercourse with the civilised world, and few of them could have any hope of returning to their native land. This made the colony all the more suitable as a place of punishment; for people shrank with horror at the idea of being banished to what seemed like a tomb for living men and women. But, for all that, it was not desirable that Australia should remain always as unknown and unexplored as it then was; and, seven years after the first settlement was made, two men arrived who were determined not to suffer it so to remain.

When Governor Hunter came in 1795, he brought with him, on board his ship the *Reliance*, a young surgeon, George Bass, and a midshipman called Matthew Flinders. They were young men of the most admirable character, modest and amiable, filled with a generous and manly affection for one another, and fired by a lofty enthusiasm which rejoiced in the wide field for discovery and fame that spread all around them. Within a month after their arrival they purchased a small boat about eight feet in length, which they christened the *Tom Thumb*. Its crew consisted of themselves and a boy to assist,—truly a poor equipment with which to face a great and stormy ocean like the Pacific. They sailed out, and after tossing for some time like a toy on the huge waves, they succeeded in entering Botany Bay, which they thoroughly explored, making a chart of its shores and rivers. On their return, Governor Hunter was so highly pleased with their work, that, shortly after, he gave them a holiday, which they spent in making a longer expedition to the south. It was said that a very large river fell into the sea south of Botany Bay, and they went out to search for its mouth.

2. Boat Excursion.—In this trip they met with some adventures which will serve to illustrate the dangers of such a voyage. On one occasion, when their boat had been upset on the shore, and their powder was wetted by the seawater, about fifty natives gathered round them, evidently with no friendly intention. Bass spread the powder out on the rocks to dry, and procured a supply of fresh water from a neighbouring pond. But they were in expectation every moment of being attacked and speared, and there was no hope of defending themselves till the powder was ready. Flinders, knowing the fondness of the natives for the luxury of a shave, persuaded them to sit down one after another on a rock, and amused them by clipping their beards with a pair of scissors. As soon as the powder was dry the explorers loaded their muskets and cautiously retreated to their boat, which they set right, and pushed off without mishap.

Once more on the Pacific, new dangers awaited them. They had been carried far to the south by the strong currents, and the wind was unfavourable. There was therefore no course open to them but to row as far as they could during the day, and at night throw out the stone which served as an anchor, and lie as sheltered as they could, in order to snatch a little sleep. On one of these nights, while they lay thus asleep, the wind suddenly rose to a gale, and they were roughly wakened by the splashing of the waves over their boat. They pulled up their stone anchor and ran before the tempest—Bass holding the sail and Flinders steering with an oar. As Flinders says: "It required the utmost care to prevent broaching to; a single wrong movement or a moment's inattention would have sent us to the bottom. The task of the boy was to bale out the water, which, in spite of every care, the sea threw in upon us. The night was perfectly dark, and we knew of no place of shelter, and the only direction by which we could steer was the roar of the waves upon the neighbouring cliffs." After an hour spent in this manner, they found themselves running straight for the breakers. They pulled down their mast and got out the oars, though without much hope of escape. They rowed desperately, however, and had the satisfaction of rounding the long line of boiling surf. Three minutes after they were in smooth water, under the lee of the rocks, and soon they discovered a well-sheltered cove, where they anchored for the rest of the night.

It was not till two days later that they found the place they were seeking. It turned out not to be a river at all, but only the little bay of Port Hacking, which they examined and minutely described. When they reached Sydney they gave information which enabled accurate maps to be constructed of between thirty and forty miles of coast.

3. Clarke.—On arriving at Port Jackson, they found that an accident had indirectly assisted in exploring that very coast on which they had landed. A vessel called the *Sydney Cove*, on its way to Port Jackson, had been wrecked on Furneaux Island, to the north of Van Diemen's Land. A large party, headed by Mr. Clarke, the supercargo, had started in boats, intending to sail along the coasts and obtain help from Sydney. They were thrown ashore by a storm at Cape Howe, and had to begin a dreary walk of three hundred miles through dense and unknown country. Their small store of provisions was soon used, and they could find no food and little fresh water on their path. Many dropped down, exhausted by hunger and fatigue, and had to be abandoned to their fate. Of those who contrived to approach within thirty miles of Sydney, the greater part were murdered by the same tribe of blacks from whom Bass and Flinders had apprehended danger. Clarke and one or two others reached Port Jackson; their clothes in tatters, their bodies wasted almost to the bones, and in such a state that, when a boat was brought to carry them over the bay to Sydney, they had to be lifted on board like infants. Mr. Clarke, on his recovery, was able to give a very useful account of a great tract of land not previously explored. The crew of the *Sydney Cove* were meanwhile living on one of the Furneaux Group, and several small ships were sent down from Sydney to rescue the crew and cargo; these also served to make the coast better known. Flinders was very anxious to go in one of them, in order to make a chart of the places he might pass; but his ship, the *Reliance*, sailed for Norfolk Island, and he had to be a long time absent.

4. Discovery of Bass Straits.—His friend Bass was

more fortunate; for Governor Hunter gave him an open whaleboat, together with provisions for six weeks, and six men to manage the boat. With these he discovered the harbour and river of Shoalhaven; entered and mapped out Jervis Bay; discovered Twofold Bay, then rounded Cape Howe, and discovered the country now called Victoria. After sailing along the Ninety-mile Beach, he saw high land to the south-west; and, standing out towards it, discovered the bold headland which was afterwards named Wilson's Promontory. Bad weather drove him to seek for shelter, and this led to the discovery of Western Port, where he remained thirteen days. But as his provisions were running short, he was forced, with a heavy heart, to turn homeward. He had again to seek shelter, however, from strong head winds, and in doing so discovered what is called Corner Inlet. In all he prolonged his voyage to eleven weeks, before he again reached Sydney: during that time he had explored six hundred miles of coast, and had discovered four important bays, as well as what is perhaps the most important cape in Australia. His greatest service, however, was the proof that Van Diemen's Land is not joined to Australia, but is divided from it by the wide strait to which Bass's name is now so justly given. All this, effected in an open whaleboat on a great ocean,

MATTHEW FLINDERS.

may well fill us with admiration for the courage and skill of the young surgeon.

5. Flinders.—When Flinders returned from Norfolk Island, he obtained leave to join the next vessel that should start for the wreck of the *Sydney Cove*. Having arrived at Furneaux Island, during the time that the wreckage and remaining cargo were being gathered, he obtained the loan of a small boat for five days, and in it made careful surveys of the islands and straits to the north of Van Diemen's Land. It was in this trip that he made the first discovery of that peculiar Australian animal, the wombat.

6. Circumnavigation of Van Diemen's Land. —Next year (1798) Governor Hunter gave to the two ardent young men a small sloop—the *Norfolk*—in which to prosecute their discoveries. They received three months' leave of absence, in which time they proposed to sail round Van Diemen's Land. This they did, and discovered during their voyage the river Tamar and its estuary, Port Dalrymple. It was not in discovery alone that they were successful. Flinders made the most beautiful and exact charts of all the coasts; he sometimes spent whole days in careful and laborious observations and measurements, in order to have the latitude and longitude of a single place correctly marked.

7. Fate of Bass.—On their return to Sydney Bass met some friends, who persuaded him to join them in making their fortune by carrying contraband goods into South America, in spite of the Spaniards. What became of Bass is not known, but it is supposed that he was captured by the Spaniards and sent to the silver mines, where he was completely lost from sight. He who entered those dreary mines was lost for ever to human knowledge; and Bass may have perished there after years of wearisome and unknown labour. After all his hardships and adventures, his enthusiasm and his self-devotion, he passed away from men's eyes, and no one was curious to know whither he had gone; but Australians of these days have learnt to honour the memory of the man who first, in company with his friend, laid the foundation of so much of their geography.

8. The Publication of Flinders' Charts.—Flinders remained in His Majesty's service, and in the following year was raised to the rank of lieutenant. With his little ship, the

Norfolk, he examined the coasts of New South Wales, from Sydney northward as far as Hervey Bay. Next year (1800) he went to London, where his charts were published, containing the first exact accounts of the geography of Australia. They were greatly praised, and the English Government resolved to send out an expedition to survey all the coasts of Australia in like manner. Flinders was placed at the head of it; a vessel was given to him, which he called the *Investigator*; a passport was obtained for him from the French Government, so that, though England and France were then at war, he might not be obstructed by French war-ships. Sailing to the south coast of Australia, he discovered Kangaroo Island and Spencer's Gulf, and then entered Port Phillip under the impression that he was the discoverer of that inlet, but afterwards learnt that Lieutenant Murray, in his ship the *Lady Nelson*, had discovered it ten weeks before.

9. Baudin.—As Flinders sailed down towards Bass Strait he met with a French expedition, under M. Baudin, who had been sent out by Napoleon to make discoveries in Australia. He had loitered so long on the coast of Tasmania that Flinders had been able to complete the examination of the southern coast before he even approached it. Yet Baudin sailed into the very bays which had already been mapped out, gave them French names, and took to himself the honour of their discovery. Some months later the two expeditions met one another again in Port Jackson. Flinders showed his charts, and the French officers allowed that he had carried off the honours of nearly all the discoveries on the south coast; but, in spite of that, a report was published in France in which Flinders' claims were quite ignored, and Baudin represented as the hero of Australian discovery. The colonists at Port Jackson, however, treated the French sailors with much kindness. Many of them were suffering from scurvy, and these were carried to the Sydney hospital and carefully tended; and though the colonists had themselves eaten only salt meat for months before, in order to preserve their cattle, yet they killed these very cattle to provide fresh meat for the sick sailors. Baudin and his officers were feasted, and everything was done both by Flinders and the people of Sydney to make their stay agreeable.

10. Imprisonment of Flinders.—Flinders continued

his voyage northwards, rounded Cape York, and examined the northern coasts, making an excellent chart of Torres Strait; but his vessel becoming too rotten to be longer used, he was forced to return to Sydney. Desiring to carry his charts and journals to England, he took his passage in an old store-ship, but she had not sailed far before she struck on a coral reef; the crew with difficulty reached a small sandbank, from which they were not released till two months after. Flinders saved his papers, and brought them back to Sydney. A small schooner, the *Cumberland*, was given him in which to sail for England; but she was too leaky, and too small a vessel to carry food for so long a voyage; so that he was forced to put into the Mauritius, which then belonged to France. He fancied that his passport from Napoleon would be his protection; but the Governor, De Caen, a low and ignorant fellow, seized him, took his papers from him, and cast him into prison.

Cook's Monument, Botany Bay.

Baudin soon after called at the Mauritius, and would probably have procured the release of his brother-mariner had he not died immediately after his arrival. The charts of Flinders, however, were all sent to France, where they were published with altered names, as if they were the work of Frenchmen. Meanwhile, Flinders was spending the weary months in close confinement at the Mauritius.

11. Death of Flinders.—Nearly six years passed away before the approach of an English fleet compelled the French to release him; and when he went to England he found that people knew all about those very places of which he thought he was bringing the first tidings. He commenced, however, to write his great book, and worked with the utmost pains to make all his maps scrupulously accurate. After about four years of incessant labour, the three volumes were ready for the press; but he was doomed never to see them. So many years of toil, so many nights passed in open boats or on the wet sands, so many shipwrecks and weeks of semi-starvation, together with his long and unjust imprisonment, had utterly destroyed his constitution; and on the very day when his book was being published, the wife and daughter of Flinders were tending his last painful hours. He was, perhaps, our greatest maritime discoverer: a man who worked because his heart was in his work; who sought no reward, and obtained none; who lived laboriously, and did honourable service to mankind; yet died, like his friend Bass, almost unknown to those of his own day, but leaving a name which the world is every year more and more disposed to honour.

CHAPTER IV.

NEW SOUTH WALES, 1800-1808.

1. Governor King.—Governor Hunter, who left Sydney in the year 1800, was succeeded by Captain King, the young officer who has been already mentioned as the founder of the settlement at Norfolk Island. He was a man of much ability, and was both active and industrious; yet so overwhelming at this time were the difficulties of Governorship in New South Wales, that his term of office was little more than a distressing failure. The colony consisted chiefly of convicts, who were—many of them —the most depraved and hardened villains to be met with in the history of crime. To keep these in check, and to maintain order, was no easy task; but to make them work, to convert them into industrious and well-behaved members of the community, was far beyond any Governor's power. King made an effort, and did his very best; but after a time he grew disheartened, and, in his disappointment, complained of the folly which expected him to make farmers out of pickpockets. His chances of success would have been much increased had he been properly seconded by his subordinates. But, unfortunately, circumstances had arisen which caused the officers and soldiers not only to render him no assistance whatever, but even to thwart and frustrate his most careful plans.

2. The New South Wales Corps.

In 1790 a special corps had been organised in the British army for service in the colony; it was called the New South Wales Corps, and was intended to be permanently settled in Sydney. Very few high-class officers cared to enter this service, so far from home and in the midst of the lowest criminals. Those who joined it generally came out with the idea of quickly gathering a small fortune, then resigning their commissions and returning to England. The favourite method of making money was to import goods into the settlement and sell them at high rates of profit; and, in their haste to become rich, many resorted to unscrupulous devices for obtaining profits. A trade in which those who commanded were the sellers, whilst the convicts and settlers under their charge were the purchasers, could hardly fail to ruin discipline and introduce grave evils, more especially when ardent

THE EXPLORERS' TREE, KATOOMBA, N.S.W.

spirits began to be the chief article of traffic. It was found that nothing sold so well among the convicts as rum, their favourite liquor; and, rather than not make money, the officers began to import large quantities of that spirit, thus deliberately assisting to demoralise still further the degraded population which they had been sent to reform. So enormous were the profits made in this debasing trade that very few of the officers could refrain from joining it. Soon the New South Wales Corps became like one great firm of spirit merchants, engaged in the importing and retailing of rum. The most enterprising went so far as to introduce stills and commence the manufacture of spirits in the colony. By an order of the Governor in Council this was forbidden, but many continued to work their stills in secret. This system of traffic, demoralising to every one engaged in it, was shared even by the highest officials in the colony. In the year 1800 the chief constable was a publican, and the head gaoler sold rum and brandy opposite the prison gates.

3. State of the Colony.—Under these circumstances, drunkenness became fearfully prevalent; the freed convicts gave themselves up to unrestrained riot, and, when intoxicated, committed the most brutal atrocities; the soldiers also sank into the wildest dissipation; and many of the officers themselves led lives of open and shameless debauchery. This was the community Governor King had to rule. He made an effort to effect some change, but failed; and we can hardly wonder at the feeling of intense disgust which he entertained and freely expressed.

4. Mutiny of Convicts.—Most of the convicts, on their arrival in the colony, were "assigned"—that is, sent to work as shepherds or farm-labourers for the free settlers in the country; but prisoners of the worst class were chained in gangs and employed on the roads, or on the Government farms. One of these gangs, consisting of three or four hundred convicts, was stationed at Castlehill, a few miles north of Parramatta. The prisoners, emboldened by their numbers and inflamed by the oratory of a number of political exiles, broke out into open insurrection. They flung away their hoes and spades, removed their irons, seized about two hundred and fifty muskets, and marched towards the Hawkesbury, expecting to be there reinforced by so many additional convicts that they would be able to overpower the military. Major Johnstone, with twenty-four soldiers of the New South Wales Corps, pursued them; they halted and turned round to fight, but he charged with so much determination into their midst that they were quickly routed, and fled in all directions, leaving several of their number dead on the spot. Three or four of the ringleaders were caught and hanged; the remainder returned quickly to their duty.

5. Origin of Wool-growing.—During Governor King's term of office a beginning was made in what is now an industry of momentous importance to Australia. In the New South Wales Corps there had been an officer named Macarthur, who had become so disgusted with the service that, shortly after his arrival in Sydney, he resigned his commission, and, having obtained a grant of land, became a settler in the country. He quickly perceived that wool-growing, if properly carried on, would be a source of much wealth, and obtained a number of sheep from the Dutch colony at the Cape of Good Hope, with which to make a commencement. These were of a kind which did not suit the climate, and his first attempt failed; but in 1803, when he was in England on a visit, he spoke so highly of New South Wales as a country adapted for wool-growing, that King George III. was interested in the proposal, and offered his assistance. Now, the sheep most suitable for Macarthur's purpose were the merino sheep of Spain; but these were not to be obtained, as the Spaniards, desirous of keeping the lucrative trade of wool-growing to themselves, had made it a capital crime to export sheep of this kind from Spain. But it so happened that, as a special favour, a few had been given to King George, who was an enthusiastic farmer; and when he heard of Macarthur's idea, he sent him one or two from his own flock to be carried out to New South Wales. They were safely landed at Sydney, Governor King made a grant of ten thousand acres to Mr. Macarthur, at Camden, and the experiment was begun. It was not long before the most marked success crowned the effort, and in the course of a few years the meadows at Camden were covered with great flocks of sheep, whose wool yielded annually a handsome fortune to their enterprising owner.

6. Governor Bligh.—In 1806 Governor King was succeeded by Captain Bligh, whose previous adventures have made his name so well known. In his ship, the *Bounty*, he had been sent by the British Government to the South Sea Islands for a cargo of bread-fruit trees. But his conduct to his sailors was so tyrannical that they mutinied, put him, along with eighteen others, into an open boat, then sailed away, and left him in the middle of the Pacific Ocean. Bligh was a skilful sailor, and the voyage he thereupon undertook is one of the most remarkable on record. In an open boat he carried his little party over 3,500 miles of unknown ocean to the island of Timor, where they found a vessel that took them home.

In appointing Captain Bligh to rule the colony, the English Government spoiled an excellent seaman to make a very inefficient Governor. It was true that New South Wales contained a large convict population, who required to be ruled with despotic rigour; yet there were many free settlers who declined to be treated like slaves and felons, and who soon came to have a thorough dislike to the new Governor. Not that he was without kindly feeling; his generous treatment of the Hawkesbury farmers, who were ruined by a flood in 1806, showed him to have been warm-hearted in his way; he exerted himself to the utmost, both with time and money, to alleviate their distress, and received the special thanks of the English Government for his humanity. And yet his arbitrary and unamiable manners completely obscured all these better qualities. He caused the convicts to be flogged without mercy for faults which existed only in his own imagination; he bullied his officers, and, throughout the colony, repeated the same mistakes which had led to the mutiny of the *Bounty*. At the same time, he was anxious to do what he conceived to be his duty to his superiors in England. He had been ordered to put a stop to the traffic in spirits, and, in spite of the most unscrupulous opposition on the part of those whose greed was interested, he set himself to effect this reform by prompt and summary measures, and with a contemptuous disregard of the hatred he was causing; but, in the end, the officers were too strong for him, and in the quarrel that ensued the Governor was completely defeated.

7. Expulsion of Bligh.—Month after month Bligh

became more and more unpopular; those whom he did not alienate in the course of his duty he offended by his rudeness, until, at last, there was scarcely any one in the colony who was his friend. Many were inflamed by so bitter a hatred that they were ready to do anything for revenge, and affairs seemed to be in that critical state in which a trifling incident may bring about serious results.

This determining cause was supplied by a quarrel which took place between Mr. Macarthur and Mr. Atkin, the new judge-advocate of the colony. Mr. Macarthur was condemned to pay a heavy fine for neglect, in having permitted a convict to escape in a vessel of which he was partly the owner. He refused to pay, and was summoned before the court, of which Atkin was the president. He declined to appear, on the ground that Atkin was his personal enemy. Thereupon Atkin caused him to be seized and put in gaol. Bligh appointed a special court to try him, consisting of six officers, together with Atkin himself. Macarthur was brought before it, but protested against being judged by his enemy, stating his willingness, however, to abide by the decision of the six officers. The officers supported his protest, and the trial was discontinued. Bligh was exceedingly angry, and, by declaring he would put the six officers in gaol, brought matters to a crisis. The officers of the New South Wales Corps all took part with their comrades; they assisted Mr. Macarthur to get up a petition, asking Major Johnstone, the military commander, to depose Governor Bligh, and himself take charge of the colony. Major Johnstone was only too glad of the opportunity. He held a council of officers, at which Mr. Macarthur and several others were present. Their course of action was decided upon, and next morning the soldiers marched, with colours flying and drums beating, to the gate of the Governor's house. Here they were met by Bligh's daughter, who endeavoured to persuade them to retire; but they made her stand aside and marched up the avenue. Meantime the Governor had hidden himself in the house; the soldiers entered and searched everywhere for him, till at length they discovered him behind a bed, where he was seeking to hide important papers. He was arrested, and sentinels were posted to prevent his escape. Major Johnstone assumed the Governor's position, and appointed his friends to the most important offices in the Government service. He continued to direct affairs for some time, until Colonel Foveaux superseded him. Foveaux, in his turn, was superseded by Colonel Patterson, who came over from Tasmania to take charge of the colony until a new Governor should be sent out from home. Patterson offered Bligh his liberty if he would promise to go straight to England, and not seek to raise a disturbance in the colony. This promise was given by Bligh, and yet no sooner was he free than he began to stir up the Hawkesbury settlers in his behalf. They declined to assist him, however, and Bligh went over to Tasmania, where the settlement to be described in the next chapter had been formed. Here he was received with great good-will, until the news arrived from Sydney that, according to the solemn promise he had given, he ought at that time to have been on his way to England. An attempt was made to capture him, but he escaped to England, where his adventures in New South Wales were soon forgotten, and he rose to be an admiral in the English navy. When the news of the rebellion reached the authorities in England, Major Johnstone was dismissed from the service, and Major-General Lachlan Macquarie was sent out to be Governor of the colony. Major Johnstone retired to a farm in New South Wales, where he lived and prospered till his death in 1817.

CHAPTER V.

TASMANIA, 1803-1836.

1. First Settlement.—After the departure of Baudin from Sydney it was discovered that there was an inclination on the part of the French to settle in some part of Australia. It was known that the inlet called Storm Bay, in the island then known as Van Diemen's Land, had especially attracted their notice, its shores having been so green and leafy. It was now known that Van Diemen's Land was severed by a broad strait from the mainland, and the Governor at Sydney thought that if the French proposed to make a settlement anywhere they would be certain to appropriate this island, and deny that the English had any claim to it. He, therefore, prepared an expedition to proceed to Storm Bay and take possession of its shores. For that purpose he chose Lieutenant John Bowen, who had recently arrived as an officer of a ship of war, and appointed him commandant of the proposed settlement. The colonial ship called the *Lady Nelson* was chosen as the means of conveying him and eight soldiers, while a whaling ship called the *Albion* was chartered for the purpose of carrying twenty-four convicts and six free persons, who were to found the new colony. This was a very small number with which to occupy a large country; but Governor King thought that in the meantime they would be sufficient to assert a prior claim, and that the authorities in England could subsequently decide whether the settlement should be increased or withdrawn.

Governor King saw also another object in founding this new colony. He had some most unruly convicts in Sydney, who were only a source of trouble and annoyance to all the rest. It seemed to him an advantage to be able to send these off to a place by themselves, under specially severe discipline. In September, 1803, the two ships sailed up Storm Bay and into the mouth of the river Derwent. Lieutenant Bowen caused them to anchor on the right side of the estuary, in a little bay called Risdon Cove. The people were soon on shore, and pitched their tents on a grassy hill a little back from the water. Bowen went out to survey the country, while the convicts set to work to build huts for themselves; a little village soon appeared, and in the long grass that surrounded it a few sheep and goats were pastured for the use of the rising colony. The place was named Hobart Town, after Lord Hobart, who was then Secretary of State for the Colonies. A month later Governor King sent forty-two convicts and fifteen soldiers to increase the strength of the settlement; and the little village was beginning to look populous, when, unexpectedly, there came a great accession from another source.

2. Collins.—During this same year, 1803, the British Government, moved by fears of a French occupation, had resolved to form a settlement on the shores of Port Phillip. Accordingly David Collins, who had been judge-advocate at Sydney, but had taken a trip to England, was chosen to be Lieutenant-Governor of the new colony, and was despatched with 307 convicts, 24 wives of convicts, 51 soldiers, and 13 free settlers, on board two ships, the *Calcutta* and the *Ocean*. Collins had made an effort to form a settlement at Port Phillip, on a sandy shore, near the site of Sorrento, but had grown disgusted with the place; and early in 1804 he carried off all the people, and resolved to abandon Port Phillip in favour of the Derwent. He landed at Risdon on the 15th February, and, after a short examination, came to the conclusion that the situation was unsuitable. Next day he went in search of a better place, and chose a little bay on the opposite side, some six miles nearer the mouth of the estuary, and thither the whole settlement was soon after removed. There, at the very foot of the lofty Mount Wellington, Hobart Town began to grow in its new situation. Houses were rapidly erected; most of them consisted of posts stuck in the ground, interwoven with twigs of wattle trees, and then daubed over

GOVERNOR COLLINS.

with mud. The chimneys were built of stones and turf, and the roofs were thatched with grass. Whilst the new town was growing, a party of convicts and soldiers was still busy on the little farms at Risdon, and early in May they had a most unfortunate affray with the natives. A party of two or three hundred blacks, who were travelling southward, came suddenly in sight of the white men and their habitations. These were the first Europeans whom they had seen, and they became much excited at the strange spectacle. While they were shouting and gesticulating, the Englishmen thought they were preparing for an attack and fired upon them. The blacks fled and the white men pursued them, killing about thirty of the unfortunate natives. Thus was begun a long warfare, which ended only with the complete extinction of the native races.

3. Patterson.—Next year, 1804, the Sydney Government sent another party of convicts, under Colonel Patterson, to found a colony in the north of Tasmania. The position selected was near the entrance to Port Dalrymple; and here, for eight years, a small settlement continued to exist in an independent state, until, in 1812, it was placed under the charge of the Governor at Hobart Town.

4. Death of Collins.—The colony at the latter place was meanwhile slowly establishing itself; and in 1808, when Bligh visited it after his expulsion from Sydney, he found the little township with quite a settled and comfortable appearance. In 1810 it lost its amiable and warm-hearted Governor. While calmly and cheerfully conversing with a friend, Mr. Collins fell back dead in his chair. He was a man of a good and kindly nature, a little vain and self-important, but earnest and upright, and possessed of very fair abilities. The distinguished part he played in the early colonisation of Australia will always render him a prominent person in our history.

5. Governor Davey.—It took some time for the news of the Governor's death to reach England, and during the three years that elapsed before his successor could be sent out, the place was filled in turn by three gentlemen, named Lord, Murray, and Geils, till, in 1813, the new Governor, Davey, arrived. He had been a colonel of marines, and had shown himself a good soldier, but he had few of the qualities of a Governor. He was rough and excessively coarse in his manners, and utterly regardless of all decorum. He showed his defiance of all conventional rules by the manner of his entry. The day being warm, he took off his coat and waistcoat, and marched into the town in a costume more easy than dignified; he listened to the address of welcome with careless indifference, and throughout showed little respect either for himself or for the people he had come to govern. Yet, under his rule, the colony made progress. In his first year he opened the port to ordinary merchant ships; for, previously, as the town was a convict settlement of the most severe type, no free person was allowed to land without special permission. From this time commerce began to spring up; free settlers spread over the country, and cultivated it with such success that, in 1816, besides supplying all the necessities of their own community, they were able to export grain to Sydney.

6. New Norfolk.—In 1807 the settlement of Norfolk Island had been abandoned by the British Government, on account of its expense, and the convicts, of whom many had there grown to be decent, orderly farmers, were brought to Tasmania. They formed a new settlement on the Derwent, about fifteen miles above Hobart Town, at a place which they called "New Norfolk," in affectionate memory of their former island home.

7. Bushranging.—About this time the colony began to be greatly annoyed by bushrangers. From twenty to forty convicts generally escaped every year and betook themselves to the wild country around the central lakes of Tasmania. There, among the fastnesses of the western mountains, they led a desperate and daring life, sometimes living with the natives, whom they quickly taught all the wickedness they themselves knew. Their ordinary lives were wretchedly debased; and, in search of booty, or in revenge for fancied injuries, they often committed the most savage crimes. They treated their native companions like beasts, to be used for a while, and then shot or mangled when no longer wanted; and it is not surprising that the blacks soon became filled with intense hatred of all the white invaders of their land. Frequently the aboriginal tribes united to attack the lonely farm-house and murder all its inhabitants. Hence, every settler in the country districts was well supplied with arms, and taught all his household to use them; the walls were pierced here and there with holes, through which a musket might be directed in safety against an advancing enemy. The fear of bushrangers who might attack them for the sake of plunder, and of natives who might massacre them in revenge, kept the scattered settlers in constant terror and trouble.

8. Governor Sorell.—But in 1817, when Governor Davey grew tired of his position and resigned it, choosing rather to live an easy-going life on his estate near Hobart Town, than be troubled with the cares of office, Colonel Sorell, the new Governor, set himself with vigour to suppress these ruthless marauders. He was to some extent successful, and the young colony enjoyed an interval of peace. Farming was profitable, and the exports of wheat began to assume large dimensions. The best breeds of sheep were brought into the island, and Van Diemen's Land wool, which at first had been despised in England, and used only for stuffing mattresses, grew into favour, and was bought by the manufacturers at high prices. Thus many of the settlers became wealthy, and the estates from which their wealth was derived began to have a correspondingly high value, so as to give the colony an assured prosperity which was certainly remarkable in the sixteenth year from its foundation. Another industry was added, which indirectly contributed to the wealth of Tasmania. The captain of a merchant vessel, on his way to Sydney, had seen a great shoal of whales off the south coast of Tasmania, and, along with the Governor of New South Wales, secretly formed a scheme to fit out a whaling expedition. But his crew also had seen the whales, and soon made the fact widely known; so that, by the time the captain's party was ready to sail, there were several other whaling vessels on the point of starting. They were all successful, and very soon a large number of ships was engaged in whale fishing. Now, as Hobart Town was the nearest port, the whalers found that it saved time to go thither with their oil, and to buy their provisions and refit their ships there; so that the trade and importance of the little city received a very material impetus in this way.

Much of the progress was due to the sensible management of Governor Sorell, who spared no effort to reform the convicts, as well as to elevate and refine the free settlers. Hence it was with great regret that the colonists saw his term of office expire in 1824. They petitioned the English Government to allow him to stay for other six years; and when the reply was given that this could not be done, as Colonel Sorell was required elsewhere, they presented him with a handsome testimonial, and settled on him an income of £500 a year from their own revenues.

9. Governor Arthur.—After Colonel Sorell had left,

bushranging became as troublesome as ever. Governor Arthur arrived in 1824, and found the colony fast relapsing into its former unsettled state. He learnt that, shortly before, some thirteen or fourteen convicts had succeeded in escaping from the penal settlement in an open boat, and had landed on a lonely part of the coast. They were joined by a great crowd of concealed convicts, and, under the leadership of Crawford and Brady, formed a dangerous horde of robbers, who, for years, kept the whole colony in terror. For a while they plundered without hindrance, till a party of about a dozen attacked the house of an old gentleman named Taylor, who had the courage to fight and defeat them. With his three sons, his carpenter, and his servant, he fired upon the advancing ruffians, whilst his daughters rapidly reloaded the muskets. The robbers retreated, leaving their leader —Crawford—and two or three others, who had been wounded, to be captured by Mr. Taylor and sent to Hobart Town, where they were executed. Brady then became chief leader of the band, and though his encounter with Mr. Taylor had taken away all his ardour for fighting, he contrived to plunder and annoy for a long time. Deep in the woods, along the silent banks of the Shannon, the outlaws lived securely; for, even when the soldiers ventured to penetrate into these lonely regions, the outlaws could easily escape to the rugged mountain sides, where they could hide or defend themselves. Governor Arthur's task was not an easy one, for Brady could command a powerful force, and his was not the only one of the kind; the result was that, for a long time, the country was unsettled and trade was paralysed. Seeing no other course open, Governor Arthur offered a pardon and a free passage home to those who surrendered. So many were thus induced to submit peaceably that, at length, Brady was almost alone; and whilst he wandered in a secluded valley, without followers, he was surprised by John Batman, who, several years after, assisted in the settlement of Victoria. Brady surrendered and was executed; the bushrangers, by degrees, disappeared, and the colonists once more breathed freely.

10. Separation.—Hitherto Tasmania had only been a dependency of New South Wales, but in 1825 it was made a separate colony, with a Supreme Court of its own. In 1829 it received its first legislative body, fifteen gentlemen being appointed to consult with the Governor and make laws for the colony. For some years after, the history of Tasmania is simply an account of quiet industry and steady progress. Hobart Town, by degrees, grew to be a fine city, with handsome buildings and well kept streets The country districts were fenced in and well tilled, good roads and bridges were made, and everything looked smiling and prosperous. The only serious difficulty was the want of coin for the ordinary purposes of trade. So great was the scarcity of gold and silver money that pieces of paper, with promises to pay a certain sum—perhaps a sixpence or a shilling —were largely used in the colony, in place of the money itself. At the request of Governor Arthur, coins to the value of a hundred thousand pounds were sent out from England for the use of the colonists.

Governor Arthur's period of office expired in 1836, and he left the colony, greatly to the regret of the colonists, who subscribed £1,500 to present him with a testimonial. He was succeeded by Sir John Franklin, the famous voyager, whose history will be related in a subsequent chapter.

CHAPTER VI.

NEW SOUTH WALES, 1808-1837.

1. Governor Macquarie.— In 1808 the English Government held an inquiry as to the circumstances which had caused the expulsion of Governor Bligh; and though they cashiered Major Johnstone, and indeed ordered the whole of the New South Wales Corps to be disbanded, yet, as it was clear that Bligh had been himself very much to blame, they yielded to the wishes of the settlers in so far as to appoint a new Governor in his place, and therefore despatched Major-General Macquarie to take the position. He was directed to reinstate Bligh for a period of twenty-four hours, in order to indicate that the authorities in England would not suffer the colonists to dictate to them in these matters; but that they reserved completely to themselves the right to appoint and dismiss the Governors. However, as Bligh had by this time gone to Tasmania, Macquarie was forced to content himself, on his arrival, with merely proclaiming what had been his instructions.

In the early days of the colonies their destinies were, to a great extent, moulded by the Governors who had charge of them. Whether for good or for evil, the influence of the Governor was decisive; and it was, therefore, a matter of great good fortune to Sydney that, during the long administration of Governor Lachlan Macquarie, this influence was almost wholly on the side of good. Not that Macquarie had no faults. He was a man full of vanity and self-conceit; a man who, instead of sober despatches to his superiors in England, wrote flowery accounts of himself and his wonderful doings; a man who, in his egoism, affixed the names of himself and of his family to nearly every place discovered in the colony during his term of office. Yet, apart from this weakness, Macquarie may be characterised as an exemplary man and an admirable Governor. He devoted himself heartily to his work; his chief thought for twelve years was how to improve the state of the little colony, and how to raise the degraded men who had been sent thither. An ardent feeling of philanthropy gave a kindly tone to his restless activity. Once every year he made a complete tour of the settled portions of the colony, to observe their condition and discover what improvements were needed. He taught the farmers to build for themselves neat houses, in place of the rude huts they had previously been content with; he encouraged them to improve their system of farming, sometimes with advice, sometimes with money, but more often with loans from the Government stores. He built churches and schools; he took the warmest interest in the progress of religion and of education; and neglected nothing that

Governor Macquarie.

could serve to elevate the moral tone of the little community. Certainly, no community has ever been in greater need of elevation. The fact that the British Government thought it necessary to send out 1,100 soldiers to keep order among a population of only 10,000 indicates very plainly what was the character of these people, and almost justifies the sweeping assertion of Macquarie, that the colony consisted of those " who had been transported, and those who ought to have been ". Yet Macquarie uniformly showed a kindly disposition towards the convicts; he settled great numbers of them as free men on little farms of their own; and if they did not succeed as well as they might have done, it was not for want of advice and assistance from the Governor.

2. Road over the Blue Mountains.

The most important result of Macquarie's activity was the opening up of new country. He had quite a passion for road-making; and though, on his arrival in the colony, he found only forty-five miles of what were little better than bush tracks, yet, when he left, there were over three hundred miles of excellent and substantial roads spreading in all directions from Sydney. He marked out towns —such as Windsor, Richmond, and Castlereagh—in suitable places; then, by making roads to them, he encouraged the freed convicts to leave Sydney and form little communities inland. But his greatest achievement in the way of road-making was the highway across the Blue Mountains. This range had for years presented an insurmountable barrier. Many persons—including the intrepid Bass—had attempted to cross it, but in vain; the only one who succeeded even in penetrating far into that wild and rugged country was a gentleman called Caley, who stopped at the edge of an enormous precipice, where he could see no way of descending. But in 1813 three gentlemen—named Wentworth, Lawson, and Blaxland—succeeded in crossing. After laboriously piercing through the dense timber which covers some of the ranges, they traversed a wild and desolate country, sometimes crawling along naked precipices, sometimes fighting their way through wild ravines, but at length emerging on the beautiful plains to the west. On their return they found that by keeping constantly on the crest of a long spur, the road could be made

Blue Mountain Scenery, Wentworth Falls, New South Wales.

much easier, and Governor Macquarie, stimulated by their report, sent Surveyor Evans to examine the pass. His opinion was favourable, and Macquarie lost no time in commencing to construct a road over the mountains. The difficulties in his way were immense; for fifty miles the course lay through the most rugged country, where yawning chasms had to be bridged, and often-times the solid rock had to be cut away. Yet, in less than fifteen months, a good carriage highway stretched from Sydney across the mountains; and the Governor was able to take Mrs. Macquarie on a trip to the fine pasture lands beyond, where he founded a town and named it Bathurst, after Lord Bathurst, the Secretary of State. This was a measure of great importance to the colony, for the country between the mountains and the sea was too limited and too much subject to droughts to maintain the two hundred and fifty thousand sheep which the prosperous colony now possessed. Many squatters took their flocks along the road to Bathurst, and settled down in the spacious pasture lands of the Macquarie and Lachlan Rivers.

3. Governor Brisbane.—In 1821 Governor Macquarie left for England, much regretted by the colonists. The only serious mistake of his policy had been that he had quietly dis-couraged the introduction of free settlers, "because," as he said, "the colony is intended for convicts, and free settlers have no business here". His successor—Sir Thomas Brisbane—and, afterwards, Sir Ralph Darling—adopted a more liberal policy, and offered every inducement to free immigrants to make their homes in the colony. It was never found possible, however, to obtain many of that class which has been so successful in America, consisting of men who, having with difficulty gathered sufficient money for their passages, landed in their adopted country without means and with no resources beyond the cheer-ful labour of themselves and of their families, yet settled down in the deep, untrodden forests, and there made for themselves happy and prosperous homes. This was not the class of im-migrants who arrived in New South Wales during the times of Brisbane and Darling. For in 1818 free passages to Australia had been abolished, and the voyage was so long and so expensive that a poor man could scarcely hope to accomplish it. Hence, those who arrived in Sydney were generally young men of good education, who brought with them a few hundred pounds, and not only were willing to labour themselves, but were able to employ the labour of others. In America, the "squatter" was a man who farmed a small piece of land. In Australia, he was one who bought a flock of sheep and carried them out to the pasture lands, where, as they increased from year to year, he grew rich with the annual produce of their wool. Sir Thomas Brisbane was pleased with the advent of men of this class: he gave them grants of land and assigned to them as many convicts as they were able to employ. Very speedily the fine lands of the colony were covered with flocks and herds; and the applications for convicts became so numerous that, at one time, two thousand more were demanded than could be supplied. Hence began an important change in the colony. The costly Government farms were, one after another, broken up, and the convicts assigned to the squatters. Then the unremunerative public works were abandoned; for many of these had been begun only for the purpose of occupying the prisoners. All this tended for good; as the convicts, when thus scattered, were much more manageable, and much more likely to reform, than when gathered in large and corrupting crowds. In Macquarie's time, not one convict in ten could be usefully employed; seven or eight years after, there was not a convict in the colony whose services would not be eagerly sought for at a good price by the squatters.

This important change took place under Governors Brisbane and Darling, and was in a great measure due to those Governors; yet, strange to say, neither of them was ever popular. Brisbane, who entered upon office in 1821, was a fine old soldier, a thorough gentleman, honourable and upright in all his ways. Yet it could not be doubted that he was out of his proper sphere when conducting the affairs of a young colony, and in 1825 the British Government found it necessary to recall him.

4. Governor Darling.— He was succeeded by Sir Ralph Darling, who was also a soldier, but was, at the same time, a man well adapted for business. Yet he, too, failed to give satisfaction. He was precise and methodical, and his habits were painfully careful, exhibiting that sort of diligence which takes infinite trouble and anxiety over details, to the neglect of larger and more important matters. His administration lasted six years, from 1825 to 1831. During this period an association was formed in England, consisting of merchants and members of Parliament, who subscribed a capital of one million pounds, and received from Government a grant of one million acres in New South Wales. They called themselves the Australian Agricultural Company, and proposed to improve and cultivate the waste lands of Australia, to import sheep and cattle for squatting purposes, to open up mines for coal and metals, and, in general, to avail themselves of the vast resources of the colony. Sir Edward Parry, the famous Polar navigator, was sent out as manager. The servants and *employés* of the association formed quite a flourishing colony on the Liverpool Plains, at the head of the Darling River; and though, at first, it caused some confusion in the financial state of New South Wales, yet, in the end, it proved of great benefit to the whole colony.

5. The Legislative Council.—In 1824 a small Executive Council had been formed to consult with Governor Brisbane on colonial matters. In 1829 this was enlarged and became the Legislative Council, consisting of fifteen members, who had power to make laws for the colony. But as their proceedings were strictly secret, and could be completely reversed by the Governor whenever he chose, they formed but a very imperfect substitute for a truly legislative body. Yet this Council was of some service to the colony : one of its first acts was to introduce the English jury system, in place of arbitrary trials by Government officials.

6. The Newspaper War.—Governor Darling was never popular. During the greater part of his period of office intrigues were continually on foot to obtain his recall; and from this state of feeling there arose what has been called the newspaper war, which lasted for four years with great violence. The first Australian newspaper had been established in 1803 by a convict named Howe. It was in a great measure supported by the patronage of the Government, and the Governors always exercised the right of forbidding the insertion of what they disliked. Hence this paper, the *Sydney Gazette*, was considered to be the Government organ, and, accordingly, its opinions of the Governors and their acts were greatly distrusted. But, during the time of Brisbane, an independent newspaper, the *Australian*, was established by Mr. Wentworth and Dr. Wardell. A second of the same kind soon followed, and was called the *Monitor*. These papers found it to their advantage, during the unpopularity of Darling, to criticise severely the acts of that Governor, who was defended by the *Gazette* with intemperate zeal. This altercation had lasted for some time, when, in the third year of Darling's administration, a very small event was sufficient to set the whole colony in an uproar.

A dissipated soldier named Sudds persuaded his companion, Thompson, that their prospects were not hopeful so long as they remained soldiers; but that, if they became convicts, they had a fair chance of growing rich and prosperous. Accordingly, they entered a shop and stole a piece of cloth. They were tried, convicted, and sentenced to be transported to Tasmania for seven years. This was what they wished; but Governor Darling, having heard of the scheme they were so successfully carrying out, took it upon himself to alter the course of the law, and directed them to be chained together with heavy spiked collars of iron about their necks, and to be set to labour on the roads. Sudds was suffering from liver disease; he sank beneath the severity of his punishment, and in a few days he died—while Thompson, about the same time, became insane. This was an excellent opportunity for the opposition papers, which immediately attacked the Governor for what they called his illegal interference and his brutality. The *Gazette* filled its columns with the most fulsome flattery in his defence, and Darling himself was so imprudent as to mingle in the dispute, and to do what he could to annoy the editors of the two hostile papers. Very soon the whole colony was divided into two great classes—the one needlessly extolling the Governor, the other denouncing him as the most cowardly and brutal of men. For four years this abusive warfare lasted, till at length the opponents of Darling won the day; and in 1831 he was recalled by the English Government.

7. Governor Bourke.—Sir Richard Bourke, who succeeded him, was the most able and the most popular of all the Sydney Governors. He had the talent and energy of Macquarie;

but he had, in addition, a frank and hearty manner, which insensibly won the hearts of the colonists, who, for years after his departure, used to talk affectionately of him as the "good old Governor Bourke". During his term of office the colony continued in a sober way to make steady progress. In 1833 its population numbered 60,000, of whom 36,000 were free persons. Every year there arrived three thousand fresh convicts; but as

St. Andrew's Cathedral, Sydney.

an equal number of free immigrants also arrived, the colony was benefited by its annual increase of population.

8. The Land Question.—Governor Bourke, on his landing, found that much discontent existed with reference to what was called the Land Question. It was understood that any one who applied for land to the Government, and showed that he would make a good use of it, would receive a suitable area as a free grant. But many abuses crept in under this system. In theory, all men had an equal right to obtain the land they required; but, in practice, it was seldom possible for one who had no friends among the officials at Sydney to obtain a grant. An immigrant had often to wait for months, and see his application unheeded; while, meantime, a few favoured individuals were calling day by day at the Land Office, and receiving grant after grant of the choicest parts of the colony. Governor Bourke, under instructions from the English Parliament, made a new arrangement. There were to be no more free grants. In the settled districts all land was to be put up for auction; if less than five shillings an acre was offered, it was not to be sold; when the offers rose above that price, it was to be given to the highest bidder. This was regarded as a very fair arrangement; and, as a large sum of money was annually received from the sale of land, the Government was able to resume the practice, discontinued in 1818, of assisting poor people to emigrate from Europe to the colony.

9. The Squatters.—Beyond the surveyed districts the land was occupied by squatters, who settled down where they pleased, but had no legal right to their "runs," as they were called. With regard to these lands new regulations were urgently required: for the squatters, who were liable to be turned off at a moment's notice, felt themselves in a very precarious position. Besides, as their sheep increased rapidly, and the flocks of neighbouring squatters interfered with one another, violent feuds sprang up, and were carried on with much bitterness. To put an end to these evils Governor Bourke ordered the squatters to apply for the land they required. He promised to have boundaries marked out; but gave notice that he would, in future, charge a rent in proportion to the number of sheep the land could support. In return, he would secure to each squatter the peaceable occupation of his run until the time came when it should be required for sale. This regulation did much to secure the stability of squatting interests in New South Wales.

After ruling well and wisely for six years, Governor Bourke retired in the year 1837, amid the sincere regrets of the whole colony.

CHAPTER VII.

DISCOVERIES IN THE INTERIOR, 1817-1836.

1. Oxley.—After the passage over the Blue Mountains had been discovered—in 1813—and the beautiful pasture land round Bathurst had been opened up to the enterprise of the squatters, it was natural that the colonists should desire to know something of the nature and capabilities of the land which stretched away to the west. In 1817 they sent Mr. Oxley, the Surveyor-General, to explore the country towards the interior, directing him to follow the course of the Lachlan and discover the ultimate "fate," as they called it, of its waters. Taking with him a small party, he set out from the settled districts on the Macquarie, and for many days walked along the banks of the Lachlan, through undulating districts of woodland and rich meadow. But, after a time, the explorers could perceive that they were gradually entering upon a region of totally different aspect; the ground was growing less and less hilly; the tall mountain trees were giving place to stunted shrubs; and the fresh green of the grassy slopes was disappearing. At length they emerged on a great plain, filled with dreary swamps, which stretched as far as the eye could reach, like one vast dismal sea of waving reeds. Into this forbidding region they penetrated, forcing their way through the tangled reeds and over weary miles of oozy mud, into which they sank almost to the knees at every step. Ere long they had to abandon this effort to follow the Lachlan throughout its course; they therefore retraced their steps, and, striking to the south, succeeded in going round the great swamp which had opposed their progress. Again they followed the course of the river for some distance, entering, as they journeyed, into regions of still greater desolation; but again they were forced to desist by a second swamp of the same kind. The Lachlan here seemed to lose itself in interminable marshes, and as no trace could be found of its further course, Oxley concluded that they had reached the end of the river. As he looked around on the dreary expanse, he pronounced the country to be "for ever uninhabitable"; and, on his return to Bathurst, he reported that, in this direction at least, there was no opening for enterprise.

The Lachlan, he said, flows into an extensive region of swamps, which are perhaps only the margin of a great inland sea.

Oxley was afterwards sent to explore the course of the Macquarie River, but was as little successful in this as in his former effort. The river flowed into a wide marsh, some thirty or forty miles long, and he was forced to abandon his purpose; he started for the eastern coast, crossed the New England Range, and descended the long woodland slopes to the sea, discovering on his way the river Hastings.

2. Allan Cunningham.—Several important discoveries were effected by an enthusiastic botanist named Allan Cunningham, who, in his search for new plants, succeeded in opening up country which had been previously unknown. In 1825 he found a passage over the Liverpool Range, through a wild and picturesque gap, which he called the Pandora Pass; and on the other side of the mountains he discovered the fine pastoral lands of the Liverpool Plains and the Darling Downs, which are watered by three branches of the Upper Darling—the Peel, the Gwydir, and the Dumaresq. The squatters were quick to take advantage of these discoveries; and, after a year or two, this district was covered with great flocks of sheep. It was here that the Australian Agricultural Company formed their great stations already referred to.

3. Hume and Hovell.—The southern coasts of the district now called Victoria had been carefully explored by Flinders and other sailors, but the country which lay behind these coasts was quite unknown. In 1824 Governor Brisbane suggested a novel plan of exploration; he proposed to land a party of convicts at Wilson's Promontory, with instructions to work their way through the interior to Sydney, where they would receive their freedom. The charge of the party was offered to Hamilton Hume, a young native of the colony, and a most expert and intrepid bushman. He was of an energetic and determined, though somewhat domineering disposition, and was anxious to distinguish himself in the work of exploration. He declined to undertake the expedition in the manner proposed by Governor Brisbane, but offered to conduct a party of convicts from Sydney to the southern coasts. A sea-captain named Hovell asked permission to accompany him. With these two as leaders, and six convict servants to make up the party, they set out from Lake George, carrying their provisions in two carts, drawn by teams of oxen. As soon as they met the Murrumbidgee their troubles commenced; the river was so broad and swift that it was difficult to see how they could carry their goods across. Hume covered the carts with tarpaulin, so as to make them serve as punts. Then he swam across the river, carrying the end of a rope between his teeth; and with this he pulled over the loaded punts. The men and oxen then swam across, and once more pushed forward. But the country through which they had now to pass was so rough and woody that they were obliged to abandon their carts and load the oxen with their provisions. They journeyed on, through hilly country, beneath the shades of deep and far-spreading forests; to their left they sometimes caught a glimpse of the snow-capped peaks of the Australian Alps, and at length they reached the banks of a clear and rapid stream, which they called the Hume, but which is now known as the Murray. Their carts being no longer available, they had to construct boats of wicker-work and cover them with tarpaulin. Having crossed the river, they entered the lightly timbered slopes to the north of Victoria, and holding their course south-west, they discovered first the river Ovens, and then a splendid stream which they called the Hovell, now known as the Goulburn. Their great object, however, was to reach the ocean, and every morning when they left their camping-place they were sustained by the hope of coming, before evening, in view of the open sea. But day after day passed, without any prospect of a termination to their journey. Hume and Hovell, seeing a high peak at some little distance, left the rest of the party to themselves for a few days, and with incredible labour ascended the mountain, in the expectation of beholding from its summit the great Southern Ocean in the distance. Nothing was to be seen, however, but the waving tops of gum trees rising ridge after ridge away to the south. Wearily they retraced their steps to the place where the others were encamped. They called this peak Mount Disappointment. Having altered the direction of their course a little, in a few days they were rejoiced by the sight of a great expanse of water. Passing through country which they declared to resemble, in its freshness and beauty, the well-kept park of an English nobleman, they reached a bay, which the natives called Geelong. Here a dispute took place between the leaders, Hovell asserting that the sheet of water before them was Western Port, Hume that it was Port Phillip. Hume expressed the utmost contempt for Hovell's ignorance; Hovell retorted with sarcasms on Hume's dogmatism and conceit; and the rest of the journey was embittered by so great an amount of ill-feeling that the two explorers were never again on friendly terms. Hume's careful and sagacious observations of the route by which they had come enabled him to lead the party rapidly and safely back to Sydney, where the leaders were rewarded with grants of land and the convicts with tickets-of-leave.

4. **Captain Sturt.**—The long drought which occurred between 1826 and 1828 suggested to Governor Darling the idea that, as the swamps which had impeded Oxley's progress would be then dried up, the exploration of the river Macquarie would not present the same difficulties as formerly. The charge of organising an expedition was given to Captain Sturt,

CAPTAIN CHARLES STURT.

who was to be accompanied by Hume, with a party of two soldiers and eight convicts. They carried with them portable boats; but when they reached the Macquarie they found its waters so low as to be incapable of floating them properly. Trudging on foot along the banks of the river they reached the place where Oxley had turned back. It was no longer a marsh; but, with the intense heat, the clay beneath their feet was baked and hard; there was the same dreary stretch of reeds, now withered and yellow under the glare of the sun. Sturt endeavoured to penetrate this solitude, but the physical exertion of pushing their way through the reeds was too great for them. If they paused to rest, they were almost suffocated in the hot and pestilent air; the only sound they could hear was the distant booming of the bittern, and a feeling of the most lonely wretchedness pervaded the scene. At length they were glad to leave this dismal region and strike to the west through a flat and monotonous district where the shells and claws of crayfish told of frequent inundations. Through this plain there flowed a river, which Sturt called the Darling, in honour of the Governor. They followed this river for about ninety miles, and then took their way back to Sydney, Sturt being now able to prove that the belief in the existence of a great inland sea was erroneous.

5. The Murray.—In 1829, along with a naturalist named Macleay, Sturt was again sent out to explore the interior, and on this occasion carried his portable boats to the Murrumbidgee, on which he embarked his party of eight convicts. They rowed with a will, and soon took the boat down the river beyond its junction with the Lachlan. The stream then became narrow, a thick growth of overhanging trees shut out the light from above, while, beneath, the rushing waters bore them swiftly over dangerous snags and through whirling rapids, until they were suddenly shot out into the broad surface of a noble stream which flowed gently over its smooth bed of sand and pebbles. This river they called the Murray; but it was afterwards found to be only the lower portion of the stream which had been crossed by Hume and Hovell several years before.

Sturt's manner of journeying was to row from sunrise to sunset, then land on the banks of the river and encamp for the night. This exposed the party to some dangers from the suspicious natives, who often mustered in crowds of several hundreds; but Sturt's kindly manner and pleasant smile always converted them into friends, so that the worst mishap he had to record was the loss of his frying pan and other utensils, together with some provisions, which were stolen by the blacks in the dead of night. After twilight the little encampment was often swarming with dark figures; but Sturt joined in their sports, and Macleay especially became a great favourite with them by singing comic songs, at which the dusky crowds roared with laughter. The natives are generally good-humoured, if properly managed; and throughout Sturt's trip the white men and the blacks contrived to spend a very friendly and sociable time together.

After following the Murray for about two hundred miles below the Lachlan they reached a place where a large river flowed from the north into the Murray. This was the mouth of the river Darling, which Sturt himself had previously discovered and named. He now turned his boat into it, in order to examine it for a short distance; but after they had rowed a mile or two they came to a fence of stakes, which the natives had stretched across the river for the purpose of catching fish. Rather than break the fence, and so destroy the labours of the blacks, Sturt turned to sail back. The natives had been concealed on the shore to watch the motions of the white men, and seeing their considerate conduct, they came forth upon the bank and gave a loud shout of satisfaction. The party in the boat unfurled the British flag, and answered with three hearty cheers, as they slowly drifted down with the current. This humane disposition was characteristic of Captain Sturt, who, in after life, was able to say that he had never—either directly or indirectly—caused the death of a black fellow.

When they again entered on the Murray they were carried gently by the current—first to the west, then to the south; and, as they went onward, they found the river grow deeper and wider, until it spread into a broad sheet of water, which they called Lake Alexandrina, after the name of our present Queen, who was then the Princess Alexandrina Victoria. On crossing this lake they found the passage to the ocean blocked up by a great bar of sand, and were forced to turn their boat round and face the current, with the prospect of a toilsome journey of a thousand miles before they could reach home. They had to work hard at their oars, Sturt taking his turn like the rest. At length they entered the Murrumbidgee; but their food was now failing, and the labour of pulling against the stream was proving too great for the men, whose limbs began to grow feeble and emaciated. Day by day they struggled on, swinging more and more wearily at their oars, their eyes glassy and sunken with hunger and toil, and their minds beginning to wander as the intense heat of the midsummer sun struck on their heads. One man became insane; the others frequently lay down, declaring that they could not row another stroke, and were quite willing to die. Sturt animated them, and, with enormous exertions, he succeeded in bringing the party to the settled districts, where they were safe. They had made known the greatest river of Australia and traversed one thousand miles of unknown country, so that this expedition was by far the most important that had yet been made into the interior; and Sturt, by land, with Flinders, by sea, stands first on the roll of Australian discoverers.

6. Mitchell.—The next traveller who sought to fill up the blank map of Australia was Major Mitchell. Having offered, in 1831, to conduct an expedition to the north-west, he set out with fifteen convicts and reached the Upper Darling; but two of his men, who had been left behind to bring up provisions, were speared by the blacks, and the stores plundered. This disaster forced the company soon after to return. In 1835, when the major renewed his search, he was again unfortunate. The botanist of the party, Richard Cunningham, brother of the Allan Cunningham already mentioned, was treacherously killed by the natives; and, finally, the determined hostility of the blacks brought the expedition to an ignominious close.

In 1836 Major Mitchell undertook an expedition to the south, and in this he was much more successful. Taking with him a party of twenty-five convicts, he followed the Lachlan to its junction with the Murrumbidgee. Here he stayed for a short time to explore the neighbouring country; but the party was attacked by hordes of natives, some of whom were shot. The major then crossed the Murray; and, from a mountain top in the Lodden district, he looked forth on a land which he declared to be like the Garden of Eden. On all sides rich expanses of woodland and grassy plains stretched away to the horizon, watered by abundant streams. They then passed along the slopes of the Grampians and discovered the river Glenelg, on which they embarked in the boats which they had carried with them. The scenery along this stream was magnificent; luxurious festoons of creepers hung from the banks, trailing downwards in the eddying current, and partly concealing the most lovely grottos which the current had wrought out of the pure white banks of limestone. The river wound round abrupt hills and through verdant valleys, which made the latter part of their journey to the sea most agreeable and refreshing. Being stopped by the bar at the mouth of the Glenelg, they followed the shore for a short distance eastward, and then turned towards home. Portland Bay now lay on their right, and Mitchell made an excursion to explore it. What was his surprise to see a neat cottage on the shore, with a small schooner in front of it at anchor in the bay. This was the lonely dwelling of the brothers Henty, who had crossed from Tasmania and founded a whaling station at Portland Bay. On Mitchell's return he had a glorious view from the summit of Mount Macedon, and what he saw induced him, on his return to Sydney, to give to the country the name "Australia Felix". As a reward for his important services he received a vote of one thousand pounds from the Council at Sydney, and he was shortly afterwards knighted; so that he is now known as Sir Thomas Mitchell.

CHAPTER VIII.
PORT PHILLIP, 1800-1840.

1. Discovery of Port Phillip.—The discovery of Bass Strait in 1798 had rendered it possible for the captains of ships bound for Sydney to shorten somewhat their voyage thither; and as this was recognised by the English Government to be a great advantage, a small vessel, the *Lady Nelson*, was sent out under the command of Lieutenant Grant, in order to make a thorough exploration of the passage. She reached the Australian coast at the boundary between the two present colonies of Victoria and South Australia. Grant called the cape he first met with Cape Northumberland. He saw and named Cape Nelson, Portland Bay, Cape Schanck, and other features of the coast. When he arrived in Sydney he called the attention of Governor King to a small inlet which he had not been able to examine, although it seemed to him of importance. In 1802 the Governor sent back the *Lady Nelson*, now under the command of Lieutenant Murray, to explore this inlet. Lieutenant Murray entered it, and found that a narrow passage led to a broad sheet of water, thoroughly landlocked, though of very considerable extent. He reported favourably of the beauty and fertility of its shores, and desired to name it Port King, in honour of the Governor; but Governor

King requested that this tribute should be paid to the memory of his old commander, the first Australian Governor, and thus the bay received its present name, Port Phillip. Only sixty days later Flinders also entered the bay; but when he arrived, some time afterwards, in Sydney, he was surprised to find he was not the first discoverer.

It was at this time that the Governor in Sydney was afraid of the intrusion of the French upon Australian soil, and when he heard how favourable the appearance of this port was for settlement he resolved to have it more carefully explored. Accordingly he sent a small schooner, the *Cumberland*, under the charge of Mr. Robbins, to make the examination. The vessel carried Charles Grimes, the Surveyor-General of New South Wales, and his assistant, Mechan; also a surgeon named M'Callum, and a liberated convict named Flemming, who was to report on the agricultural capabilities of the district.

THE FIRST HOUSE BUILT IN VICTORIA.

On arriving at Port Phillip they commenced a systematic survey, Robbins sounding the bay, and making a careful chart, while the other four were every morning landed on the shore to examine the country. They walked ten or fifteen miles each day, and in the evening were again taken on board the schooner. Thus they walked from the site of Sorrento round by Brighton till they reached the river Yarra, which they described as a large fresh-water stream, but without naming it. Then they went round the bay as far as Geelong. They carried a good chart and several long reports to the Governor at Sydney, who would probably have sent a party down to settle by the Yarra, had it not been that an expedition had already set sail from England for the purpose of occupying the shores of Port Phillip.

2. Governor Collins.

This was the expedition of David Collins, already mentioned. He brought out nearly 400 persons, of whom over 300 were convicts. There is good reason to believe that Collins from the first would have preferred to settle at the Derwent, in Tasmania, but at any rate he carried out his work at Port Phillip in a very half-hearted manner. Tuckey chose for the settlement a sandy shore at Sorrento, where scarcely a drop of fresh water was to be had, and where the blazing sun of midsummer must have been unusually trying to a crowd of people fresh from colder climates.

It soon became apparent that the site selected would never prove suitable, and Collins sent Lieutenant Tuckey in search of a better place. That officer seems to have made a very inefficient search. He found no river, and no stream better than the little one on which the town of Frankston now stands. Here he was attacked by a great crowd of blacks, and had

THE FIRST HOTEL IN VICTORIA.

a conflict with them sufficiently severe to prevent his landing again. He was thus debarred from exploration by land, and the stormy weather prevented him from remaining long in the open bay. Tuckey therefore returned with a very gloomy report, and increased the despondency of the little community. Every one was dull and dispirited, except the two or three children who had been allowed to accompany their convict parents. Among these, the leader of all their childish sports, was a little lad named John Pascoe Fawkner, who was destined to be afterwards of note in the history of Port Phillip. Everybody grew dispirited under the heat, the want of fresh water, and the general wretchedness of the situation; and very soon all voices were unanimous in urging the Governor to remove. Collins then sent a boat, with letters, to Sydney, and Governor King gave him permission to cross over to Tasmania. He lost not a moment in doing so, and founded the settlement at the Derwent, to which reference has already been made.

Before he left, there were four convicts who took advantage of the confusion to escape into the bush, hoping to make their way to Sydney. One returned, footsore and weary, just in time to be taken on board; the other three were not again seen. Two are believed to have perished of hunger, and thirty-two years passed away before the fate of the third was discovered.

3. Western Port.—When Hume and Hovell returned to Sydney after their exploring expedition, Hovell insisted that the fine harbour he had seen was Western Port. He had really been at Geelong Harbour, but was all that distance astray in his reckoning. Induced by his report, the Government sent an expedition under Captain Wright to form a settlement at Western Port. Hovell went with him to give the benefit of his experience. They landed on Phillip Island; but the want of a stream of permanent water was a disadvantage, and soon after they crossed to the mainland on the eastern shore, where they founded a settlement, building wooden huts and one or two brick cottages. Hovell had now to confess that the place he had formerly seen was not Western Port, and he went off in search of the fine country he had previously seen, but came back disappointed. The settlement struggled onward for about a year, and was then withdrawn.

It is not easy to explain in a few words why they abandoned their dwellings and the land they had begun to cultivate. It seems to have been due to a general discontent. However, there were private settlers in Tasmania who would have carried out the undertaking with much more energy. For in Tasmania the sheep had been multiplying at a great rate, while the amount of clear and grassy land in that island was very limited. One of the residents in Tasmania, named John Batman, who has been already mentioned, conceived the idea of forming an association among the Tasmanian sheep-owners, for the purpose of crossing Bass Strait and occupying with their flocks the splendid grassy lands which explorers had seen there.

4. Batman.—John Batman was a native of Parramatta,

but when he was about twenty-one years of age he had left his home to seek his fortune in Tasmania. There he had taken up land and had settled down to the life of a sheep-farmer in the country around Ben Lomond. But he was fond of a life of adventure, and found enough of excitement for a time in the troubled state of the colony. It was he who captured Brady, the leader of the bushrangers, and he became well known during the struggle with the natives on account of his success in dealing with them and in inducing them to surrender peaceably. But when all these troubles were over, and he had to settle down to the monotonous work of drafting and driving sheep, he found his land too rocky to support his flocks. Knowing that others in Tasmania were in the same difficulty, he and his friend Gellibrand, a lawyer in Hobart, in the year 1827 asked permission to occupy the grassy lands supposed to be round Western Port, but the Governor in Sydney refused. In 1834 some of them resolved to go without permission, and an association of thirteen members resolved to send sheep over to Port Phillip, which was now known to be the more suitable harbour.

Before they sent the sheep, they resolved to send some one to explore and report. John Batman naturally volunteered, and the association chartered for him a little vessel, the *Rebecca*, in which, after nineteen days of sea-sickness and miserable tossing in the strait, he succeeded in entering Port Phillip on the 29th of May, 1835. Next morning he landed near Geelong and walked to the top of the Barrabool Hills, wading most of the way through grass knee-deep. On the following day he went in search of the aboriginals, and met a party of about twenty women, together with a number of children. With these he soon contrived to be on friendly terms; and after he had distributed among them looking-glasses, blankets, handkerchiefs, apples and sugar, he left them very well satisfied.

5. The Yarra.— A day or two later the *Rebecca* anchored in Hobson's Bay, in front of the ti-tree scrub and the lonely shores where now the streets of Williamstown extend in all directions. Batman again started on foot to explore that river whose mouth lay there in front of him. With fourteen men, all well armed, he passed up the river banks; but, being on the left side, he naturally turned up that branch which is called the Saltwater, instead of the main stream. After two days of walking through open grassy lands, admirably suited for sheep, they reached the site of Sunbury. From a hill at that place they could see fires about twenty miles to the south-east; and, as they were anxious to meet the natives, they bent their steps in that direction till they overtook a native man, with his wife and three children. To his great satisfaction, he learnt that these people knew of his friendly meeting with the women in the Geelong district. They guided him to the banks of the Merri Creek, to the place where their whole tribe was encamped. He stayed with them all night, sleeping in a pretty grassy hollow beside the stream. In the morning he offered to buy a portion of their land, and gave them a large quantity of goods, consisting of scissors, knives, blankets, looking-glasses, and articles of this description. In return, they granted him all the land stretching from the Merri Creek to Geelong. Batman had the documents drawn up, and on the Northcote Hill, overlooking the grass-covered flats of Collingwood and the sombre forests of Carlton and Fitzroy, the natives affixed their marks to the deeds, by which Batman fancied he was legally put in possession of 600,000 acres. Trees were cut with notches, in order to fix the boundaries, and in the afternoon Batman took leave of his black friends. He had not gone far before he was stopped by a large swamp, and so slept for the night under the great gum trees which then spread their shade over the ground now covered by the populous streets of West Melbourne. In the morning he found his way round the swamp, and in trying to reach the Saltwater came upon a noble stream, which was afterwards called the Yarra. In the evening he reached his vessel in the bay. Next day he ascended the Yarra in a boat; and when he came to the Yarra Falls, he wrote in his diary, "This will be the place for a village," unconscious that he was gazing upon the site of a great and busy city. Returning to Indented Head, near the heads of Port Phillip, he left three white men and his Sydney natives to cultivate the soil and retain possession of the land he supposed himself to have purchased. Then he set sail for Tasmania, where he and his associates began to prepare for transporting their households, their sheep and their cattle, to the new country.

6. The Henty Brothers.

—But even earlier than this period a quiet settlement had been made in the western parts of Victoria. There, as early as 1828, sealers had dwelt at Portland Bay, had built their little cottages and formed their little gardens. But they were unauthorised, and could only be regarded by the British Government as intruders, having no legal right to the land they occupied. In 1834, however, there came settlers of another class—Edward, Stephen, and Frank Henty. Their father—a man of some wealth—had in 1828 emigrated with all his family to Western Australia, carrying with him large quantities of fine stock. But the settlement at Swan River proving a failure, he had removed to Tasmania, where his six sons all settled. Very soon they found the pastoral lands of Tasmania too limited, and as Edward Henty had in one of his coasting voyages seen the sealers at Portland Bay and noticed how numerous the whales were in that bay, and how fine the grassy lands that lay within, he chartered a vessel, the *Thistle*, and crossed in her to settle at Portland Bay with servants, sheep, cattle, and horses.

EDWARD HENTY.

The land was all that had been anticipated, and soon Frank, and then Stephen, arrived, with more stock and more men to tend them. Houses and stores were put up, and fields were ploughed. Ere long other settlers followed, and in the course of five or six years all the district lying inland from Portland Bay was well settled and covered with sheep, while at Portland Bay itself so many whales were caught that there were not tanks enough to hold the oil, and much of it was wasted. The English Government after some delay agreed to sell land to the settlers, and before 1840 a thriving little town stood on the shores of Portland Bay.

7. Fawkner.

John Pascoe Fawkner, who, as a boy, had landed at Sorrento in 1803, had grown up to manhood in Tasmania through stormy times, and had at length settled down as an innkeeper in Launceston; with that business, however, combining the editing and publishing of a small newspaper. For he was always a busy and active-minded worker, and had done a great deal to make up for the defective education of his earlier years. When Batman arrived in Launceston with the news of the fine pastoral country across the water, Fawkner became quite excited at the prospects that seemed possible over there. He accordingly began to agitate for the formation of another association, and five members joined him. At his expense, the schooner *Enterprise* was chartered and loaded with all things necessary for a small settlement. On the 27th July, 1835, he set sail from Launceston; but the weather was so rough that, after three days and two nights of inexpressible sickness, Fawkner found himself still in sight of the Tasmanian coast. He therefore asked to be put ashore, and left Captain Lancey to manage the trip as he thought best. The captain took the vessel over to Western Port, as had been originally arranged; but the land there was not nearly so good as they understood it to be in the Port Phillip district. So they sailed round and safely anchored in Hobson's Bay, bringing with them horses and ploughs, grain, fruit trees, materials for a house, boats, provisions, and, indeed, everything that a small settlement could want. Getting out their boat, they entered upon the stream which they saw before them; but, unfortunately, they turned up the wrong arm, and, after rowing many miles, were forced to turn back, the water all the way being salt and

JOHN PASCOE FAWKNER.

unfit for drinking. For this reason they called this stream the Saltwater; but next morning they started again and tried the other branch. After pulling for about an hour and a half they reached a basin in the river whose beauty filled them with exultation and delight. A rocky ledge over which the river flowed kept the water above it fresh; the soil was rich, and covered with splendid grass, and they instantly came to the conclusion to settle in this favoured spot. Next day they towed the vessel up, and landed where the Custom House now is. At night they slept beside the falls, where the air was fragrant with the sweet scent of the wattle trees just bursting into bloom.

They had not been on the river many days before Mr. Wedge —one of Batman's party—in crossing the country from Indented Head to the Yarra, was astonished to see the masts of a vessel rising amid the gum trees. On reaching the river bank, what was his surprise to find, in that lonely spot, a vessel almost embedded in the woods, and the rocks and glades echoing to the sound of hammer and saw and the encouraging shouts of the ploughmen! Wedge informed Fawkner's party that they were trespassers on land belonging to John Batman and Company. Captain Lancey, having heard the story of the purchase, declared that such a transaction could have no value. When Wedge was gone, the settlers laid their axes to the roots of the trees, and began to clear the land for extensive cultivation. A fortnight later Wedge brought round all his party from Indented Head in order to occupy what Batman had marked as the site for a village, and the two rival parties were encamped side by side where the western part of Collins Street now stands. A little later Fawkner arrived with further settlers and with a wooden house, which he soon erected by the banks of the Yarra, the first regularly built house of Melbourne. He placed it by the side of the densely wooded stream, which was afterwards turned into Elizabeth Street. Great crowds of black and white cockatoos raised their incessant clamour at the first strokes of the axe; but soon the hillside was clear, and man had taken permanent possession of the spot.

8. William Buckley.—Meanwhile a circumstance had happened which favoured Batman's party in no small degree. The men left at Indented Head were surprised one morning to see an extremely tall figure advancing towards them. His hair was thickly matted; his skin was brown, but not black, like that of the natives; he was almost naked, and he carried the ordinary arms of the aborigines. This was William Buckley, the only survivor of the three convicts who had escaped from Governor Collins's expedition. He had dwelt for thirty-two years among the natives. During this long time he had experienced many strange adventures, but had not exercised the smallest influence for good upon the natives. He was content to sink at once to their level, and to lead the purely animal life they led. But when he heard that there was a party of whites on Indented Head, whom the Geelong tribes proposed to murder, he crossed to warn them of their danger. Batman's party clothed him and treated him well, and for a time he acted as interpreter, smoothing over many of the difficulties that arose with the natives, and rendering the formation of the settlement much less difficult than it might have been.

9. Excitement in Tasmania.—The news taken over by Batman caused a commotion in Tasmania. Many settlers crossed in search of the new country, and, before a year had passed, nearly two hundred persons, with more than 15,000 sheep, had landed on the shores of Port Phillip. But they soon spread over a great extent of country—from Geelong to Sunbury. They were in the midst of numerous black tribes, who now, too late, began to perceive the nature of Batman's visit, and commenced to seek revenge. Frequent attacks were made, in one of which a squatter and his servant were killed beside the Werribee. Their bodies lie buried in the Flagstaff Gardens.

10. Governor Bourke.—These were not the only troubles of the settlers; for the Sydney Government declared that all purchases of land from ignorant natives were invalid, and Governor Bourke issued a proclamation, warning the people at Port Phillip against fixing their homes there, as the land did not legally belong to them.

Still new settlers flocked over, and a township began to be formed on the banks of the Yarra. Batman's association found that their claims to the land granted them by the natives would not be allowed; and, after some correspondence on the subject with the Home Government, they had to be content with 28,000 acres, as compensation for the money they had expended.

11. Lonsdale.—Towards the close of 1836 Governor Bourke found himself compelled to recognise the new settlement, and sent Captain Lonsdale to act as a magistrate; thirty soldiers accompanied him to maintain order and protect the settlers. Next year (1837) the Governor himself arrived at Port Phillip, where he found the settlers now numbering 500. He planned out the little town, giving names to its streets, and finally settling that it should be called Melbourne, after Lord Melbourne, who was then the Prime Minister of England.

12. Latrobe.—In 1838 Geelong began to grow into a township, and the settlers spread west as far as Colac. Next year Mr. Latrobe was sent to take charge of the whole district of Port Phillip, under the title of Superintendent, but with almost all the powers of a Governor. The settlers held a public meeting, in an auction-room at Market Square, for the purpose of according a hearty welcome to their new Governor, whose kindliness and upright conduct soon made him a great favourite.

GOVERNOR LATROBE.

A wattle-and-daub building was put up as a police-office, on the site of the Western Markets, where it did duty for some time, until one night it fell; some say because it was undermined by a party of imprisoned natives; but others, because a bull belonging to Mr. Batman had rushed against it. A court-house was erected, and four policemen appointed. A post-office next followed, and, one by one, the various institutions of a civilised community arose in miniature form. Numerous ships began to enter the bay, and a lucrative trade sprang up with Tasmania. In 1838 the first newspaper appeared. It was due to the enterprise of

Fawkner. Every Monday morning sheets containing four pages

COLLINS STREET, MELBOURNE, IN 1840.
(Compare with page 177.)

of writing were distributed to the subscribers, under the title of the *Advertiser*. After nine issues of this kind had been published, a parcel of old refuse type was sent over from Tasmania; and a young man being found in the town who had, in his boyhood, spent a few months in a printing office, he was pressed into the service, and thenceforward the *Advertiser* appeared in a printed form—the pioneer of the press of Victoria. Mr. Batman had fixed his residence not far from the place now occupied by the Spencer Street Railway Station. Here, in the year 1839, he was seized with a violent cold; and, after being carefully nursed by one of his daughters, died without seeing more than the beginning of that settlement he had laboured so hard to found. Mr. Fawkner lived to an advanced age, and saw the city—whose first house he had built—become a vast metropolis.

The year 1839 brought further increase to the population; and before the beginning of 1840 there were 3,000 persons, with 500 houses and 70 shops, in Melbourne. In 1841, within five years of its foundation, it contained 11,000 persons and 1,500 houses.

CHAPTER IX.
SOUTH AUSTRALIA, 1836-1841.

1. Edward Gibbon Wakefield.—In 1829 a small book was published in London which attracted a great deal of attention, not only by reason of its charming style and the liveliness of its manner, but also on account of the complete originality of the ideas it contained. It purported to be a letter written from Sydney, and described the annoyances to be endured by a man of taste and fortune if he emigrated to Australia. He could have no intellectual society; he could not enjoy the pleasures of his library or of his picture gallery; he could hope for none of the delights of easy retirement, seeing that he had to go forth on his land, and with his own hands labour for his daily food. For, said Mr. Wakefield, the author of this little book, you cannot long have free servants in this country; if a free man arrives in the colony, though he may for a short time work for you as a servant, yet he is sure to save a little money, and as land is here so excessively cheap, he soon becomes a landed proprietor. He settles down on his farm, and, though he may have a year or two of heavy toil, yet he is almost certain to become both happy and prosperous. Thus, the colony is an excellent place for a poor man, but it is a wretched abode for a man of means and of culture. Wakefield therefore proposed to found in Australia another colony, which should be better adapted to those who had fortunes sufficient to maintain them and yet desired to emigrate to a new country. His scheme for effecting this purpose was to charge a high price for the land, and so to prevent the poorer people from purchasing it; the money received from the sale of land he proposed to employ in bringing out young men and women, as servants and farm labourers, for the service of the wealthier colonists. Now, said Wakefield, on account of the immense natural resources of these colonies, their splendid soil, their magnificent pasture lands, their vast wealth in minerals, and their widespread forests of valuable timber, which stand ready for the axe, a gentleman possessed of only £20,000 will obtain as large an income from it as could be procured from £100,000 in England; yet he will be able to enjoy his learned and cultured leisure, just as he does at home, because all the work will be done for him by the servants he employs. For three or four years this agreeable fallacy made quite a stir in England: famous authors, distinguished soldiers, learned bishops were deceived by it; noblemen, members of Parliament, bankers and merchants, all combined to applaud this novel and excellent idea of Mr. Wakefield.

South Australian Association.

—In 1831 the first effort was made to give a practical turn to these theories, and the southern shores of Australia were selected as a suitable locality for the proposed colony. A company was formed; but when it applied to the British Government for a charter, which would have conceded the complete sovereignty of the whole southern region of Australia, Lord Goderich, the Secretary of State, replied that it was asking a great deal too much, and abruptly closed the negotiation. Two years later the South Australian Association was formed, and as this company asked for nothing beyond the power to sell waste lands and apply the proceeds to assist immigration, the British Government gave its consent, and an Act was passed by the Imperial Parliament to

SOUTH AUSTRALIA. 69

give the association full power to found a colony. This Act

THE FIRST SETTLEMENT AT ADELAIDE, 1836. (Compare with page 167.)

directed that commissioners should be appointed to frame laws for the colony, to establish courts, and to nominate its officers; land was to be thrown open for sale at not less than twelve shillings an acre, and even this comparatively high price was to be raised, after a short time, to £1 per acre, in order to keep the land in the hands of the wealthy. It was expressly stated that no convict would be allowed to land in the new settlement, which, it was hoped, would become in every respect a model community. The British Government declined to incur any expense in establishing or in maintaining the colony, which was to be purely self-supporting. Eleven commissioners were appointed, of whom Colonel Torrens was chairman in England, and Mr. Fisher the representative in Australia, where he was to take charge of the sale of lands and supervise the affairs of the colony. At the same time, Captain Hindmarsh was appointed Governor, and Colonel Light was sent out to survey the waste lands preparatory to their being offered for sale.

In May, 1835, during the very month in which Batman was wandering for the first time on the banks of the Yarra, these appointments for the foundation of a fourth Australian colony were being published in the English *Government Gazette*. Thus Victoria and South Australia took their widely different origins at almost the same time; but while the first actual settlers landed at Port Phillip towards the end of 1835, the pioneers of South Australia did not reach that colony until the middle of 1836.

3. Adelaide.—The first emigrants to South Australia landed on Kangaroo Island, of which Flinders had given a most attractive account; but though the place was beautifully wooded, and of the most picturesque aspect, it was found to be in many respects unsuitable for the foundation of a city; and when Colonel Light shortly afterwards arrived with his staff of surveyors, he at once decided to remove the settlement to St. Vincent's Gulf. Here, about six miles from the shores of the gulf, he selected a broad plain between the sea and the pleasant hills of the Mount Lofty Range; and on the bank of a small stream, which he called the Torrens, he marked out the lines of the infant city. Queen Adelaide was the wife of the reigning King of England, and, as she was exceedingly popular, the colonists, with enthusiasm, adopted her name for their capital. A harbour was found seven miles distant from the city, and on it a town was established, to which the name Port Adelaide was given.

4. Governor Hindmarsh.—In December, 1836, Governor Hindmarsh landed, and beneath a spreading gum tree near the beach he read his commission to a small audience of emigrants and officials; but when he proceeded to examine what had been done, he was filled with disgust and indignation. The only landing-place for vessels was in the midst of a mangrove swamp at the mouth of a muddy little creek; and all goods would have to be carried six or seven miles inland to the city. To a sailor's eye, it seemed the most reckless folly to make so unusual a choice, and he at once determined to remove the settlement to Encounter Bay; but neither Colonel Light nor Mr. Fisher would permit any change to be made, and a violent quarrel took place. As resident commissioner, Mr. Fisher had powers equal to those of the Governor, and was thus enabled to prolong the contest. Of the settlers, some sided with the Governor; others gave their support to the commissioner, and the colony was quickly divided into two noisy factions.

GOVERNOR HINDMARSH.

After fourteen months of constant wrangling, the English Government interfered. Mr. Fisher was dismissed and Governor Hindmarsh recalled, while the offices of both were conferred on Colonel Gawler, who arrived in the colony during the year 1838.

5. Early Failures.—The Wakefield system could not possibly realise the hopeful anticipations which had been formed of it; for the foundation of a new colony and the reclaiming of the lonely forest wilds are not to be accomplished by merely looking on at the exertions of hired servants. Ladies and gentlemen who had, in England, paid for land they had never seen, were, on their arrival, greatly disgusted at the sight of the toils before them. They had to pull their luggage through the dismal swamp, for there were neither porters nor cabs in waiting; they had to settle down in canvas tents, on a grassy plain, which was called a city, but where a few painted boards here and there, fastened to the trunks of gum trees, were the only indications of streets. Then, when they went out to see their estates, and beheld great stretches of rude and unpromising wilderness—when they considered how many years must pass away before there could possibly arise the terraces and gardens, the orchards and grassy lawns, which make an English country-house delightful—their courage failed them, and, instead of going forth upon the land, they clustered together in Adelaide. Every one wished to settle down in the city, and as it was expected that, with the growth of population, the value of town allotments would rapidly increase, the idea became prevalent that to buy land in the city and keep it for sale in future years would be a profitable investment. But there were so many who entertained the same astute design that, when they all came to put it in practice, there was little gain to any one; and the only result was that Adelaide was turned into a scene of reckless speculation and gambling in land.

6. Governor Gawler.—Meantime poorer emigrants were arriving in expectation of obtaining employment from their wealthier predecessors, who had been able to pay the high price demanded for land. They found that those whom they expected to be their employers had abandoned the idea of going out into the country to cultivate the soil. There was, therefore, nothing for them to do; they had no money with which to speculate in town allotments, they had no land on which to commence farming for themselves, and they were in a wretched plight. Provisions had rapidly increased in price, so that flour rose from £20 to £80 per ton; no food was being produced from the land, and nothing whatever was being done to develop the resources of the colony, whilst the money which the settlers had brought with them was rapidly being spent in importing shiploads of provisions from other countries.

In order to give employment to those of the settlers who were really destitute, Governor Gawler commenced a series of Government works. He constructed a good road between Adelaide and its port. He formed wharves, and reclaimed the unwholesome swamp; he built a Custom House, with warehouses and many other costly buildings, the Government House alone costing £20,000. Now, these were all in themselves very desirable things; but it was difficult to see how they were to be paid for. Colonel Gawler spent nearly the whole of his own private fortune in paying the wages of the unfortunate persons he employed, but that could not long support so great a concourse of people. He persuaded merchants in England to send out provisions and clothing for the famished people; but the only means he had of paying for these goods was by drafts on the British Treasury, which were accepted at first as equivalent to money, for it was believed that, whenever they were presented in London, payment would immediately be made by the British Government. But this was a serious mistake: though the first series of drafts were paid readily enough, yet when the authorities in England found that others, for larger and larger amounts, continued to pour in, they refused to pay, and reminded the colony that, by the terms of its charter, it was to be entirely self-supporting. A series of drafts, to the amount of £69,000, were therefore dishonoured; and the merchants, finding the drafts to be worth no more than so much paper, demanded their money from the Governor; but he had nothing with which to pay, and the colony had to be declared insolvent, having debts to the amount of about £400,000 which it could not meet.

7. The Collapse.—Matters were now in a very gloomy condition. Most of the colonists became anxious to return to England, and therefore sought to sell their land. But when nearly all wished to sell, and scarcely any wished to buy, the price went down to a trifle, and men who had invested fortunes in town allotments, realised no more than enough to pay their passage home. In the meantime the English merchants declined to send out any further supplies, and those who had not the means of leaving Adelaide seemed in great danger of starving. But as land could now be bought very cheaply, many industrious people of the poorer class settled down to clear the country for farming. This was what should have been done at the very beginning; for no colony can be prosperous, or look for anything but bankruptcy, until it commences to produce grain, or wool, or minerals, or some other commodity with which it can purchase from other lands the goods which they produce. The lands of South Australia are admirably adapted for the growth of wheat; and, after a time, success attended the efforts of the farmers, who thus laid the foundations of future prosperity.

Another industry was also added about this time. The young

PROCLAMATION TREE, GLENELG.
(The colony of S. Australia proclaimed a British dependency, 28th December, 1836.)

squatters of New South Wales, attracted by the high prices given for sheep in the early days of Adelaide, had been daring enough, in spite of the blacks and of the toilsome journey, to drive their flocks overland; and the new-comers soon gave quite a wool-growing tone to the community. These "overlanders," as they were called, affected a bandit style of dress; in their scarlet shirts and broad-brimmed hats, their belts filled with pistols, and their horses gaily caparisoned, they caused a sensation in the streets in

Adelaide, which rang all evening with their merriment and dissipation. But as they brought about fifty thousand sheep into the colony during the course of only a year or so, they were of essential benefit to it. Many of them settled down and taught the new arrivals how to manage flocks and prepare the wool, and thus they assisted in raising Adelaide from the state of despondency and distress into which it had sunk.

8. Recall of Governor Gawler.—The British Government eventually decided to lend the colony a sufficient sum of money to pay its debts; but it was resolved to make certain changes. The eleven commissioners were abolished, Captain George Grey, a young officer, was appointed Governor; and one day in May, 1841, he walked into the Government House at Adelaide, presented his commission to Governor Gawler, and at once took the control of affairs into his own hands. This summary mode of dismissing Governor Gawler must now be regarded as somewhat harsh; for he had laboured hard and spent his money freely in trying to benefit the colony, and the mistakes which were made during his administration were not so much due to his incapacity as to the impracticable nature of the theory on which the colony had been founded. In 1841 he sailed for England, deeply regretted by many who had experienced his kindness and generosity in their time of trouble.

CHAPTER X.

NEW SOUTH WALES, 1838-1850.

1. Gipps.—In 1838, when Governor Bourke left Australia to spend the remainder of his life in the retirement of his native county in Ireland, he was succeeded in the government of New South Wales by Sir George Gipps, an officer who had recently gained distinction by his services in settling the affairs of Canada. The new Governor was a man of great ability, generous and well meaning, but of a somewhat arbitrary nature. No Governor has ever laboured more assiduously for the welfare of his people, and yet none has ever been more unpopular than Gipps. During his term of office the colonists were constantly suffering from

troubles, due, in most instances, to themselves, but always attributed to others, and, as a rule, to the Governor. It is true that the English Government, though actuated by a sincere desire to benefit and assist the rising community, often aggravated these troubles by its crude and ill-informed efforts to alleviate them. And as Sir George Gipps considered it his chief duty to obey literally and exactly all the orders sent out by his superiors in England, however much he privately disapproved of them, it was natural that he should receive much of the odium and derision attendant on these injudicious attempts; but, on the whole, the troubles of the colony were due, not so much to any fault of the Governor or to any error of the English Government, as to the imprudence of the colonists themselves.

2. Monetary Crisis.—During twelve years of unalloyed prosperity, so many fortunes had been made that the road to wealth seemed securely opened to all who landed in the colony. Thus it became common for new arrivals to regard themselves, on their first landing, as already men of fortune, and, presuming on their anticipated wealth, they often lived in an expensive and extravagant style, very different from the prudent and abstemious life which can alone secure to the young colonist the success he hopes for. In Sydney the most profuse habits prevailed, and in Melbourne it seemed as if prosperity had turned the heads of the inhabitants. The most expensive liquors were the ordinary beverages of waggoners and shepherds; and, on his visit to Port Phillip in 1843, Governor Gipps found the suburbs of Melbourne thickly strewed with champagne bottles, which seemed to him to tell a tale of extravagance and dissipation.

3. Land Laws.—Whilst many of the younger merchants were thus on their way to ruin, and the great bulk of the community were kept impoverished by their habits, the English Government brought matters to a crisis by its injudicious interference with the land laws. The early years of South Australia, and its period of trouble, have been already described. In 1840 South Australia was on the verge of bankruptcy, and the Wakefield policy of maintaining the land at a high price had not produced the results anticipated. Now, many of the greatest men in England were in favour of the Wakefield theory; and, in particular, the Secretary of State for the Colonies—that is, the member of the British Government whose duty it is to attend to colonial affairs—was a warm supporter of the views of Wakefield; so that when the people of South Australia complained that their scheme could not be successful so long as the other colonies charged so low a price for their land, he sympathised with them in their trouble. "Who," they asked, "will pay one pound an acre for land in South Australia, when, by crossing to Port Phillip, he can obtain land equally good at five shillings an acre?" To prevent the total destruction of South Australia, the Secretary of State ordered the other colonies to charge a higher price for land. New South Wales was to be divided into three districts. (1) The Middle District, round Port Jackson, where land was never to be sold for less than twelve shillings an acre. (2) The Northern District, round Moreton Bay, where the same price was to be charged. (3) The Southern District, round Port Phillip, where the land was of superior quality, and was never to be sold for less than one pound an acre.

A great amount of discontent was caused throughout New South Wales by this order; but South Australia was saved from absolute ruin, and the Secretary of State declined to recall the edict. In vain it was urged that a great part of the land was not worth more than two or three shillings an acre; the answer was that land was worth whatever people were willing to pay for it. For a time it seemed as if this view had been sound, and land was eagerly purchased, even at the advanced prices; in 1840 the amounts received from land sales were three times as great as those received in 1838. But this was mostly the result of speculation, and disastrous effects soon followed; for the prices paid by the purchasers were far above the real value of the land. If a man brought a thousand pounds into the colony and paid it to the Government for a thousand acres of land, he reckoned himself to be still worth a thousand pounds, and the banks would be willing to lend him nearly a thousand pounds on the security of his purchase. But if he endeavoured, after a year or two, to resell it, he would then discover its true value, and find he was in reality possessed of only two or three hundred pounds: every purchaser had found the land to be of less value than he had expected; every one was anxious to sell; and, there being few buyers, most of it was sold at a ruinous price. Men who had borrowed money were unable to pay their debts, and became insolvent. The banks, who had lent them money, were brought to the verge of ruin; and one of the oldest—the Bank of Australia—became bankrupt in 1843, and increased the confusion in monetary affairs. In order to pay their debts, the squatters were now forced to sell their sheep and cattle; but there was scarcely any one willing to buy, and the market being glutted, the prices went down to such an extent that sheep, which two years before had been bought for thirty shillings, were gladly sold for eighteenpence. Indeed, a large flock was sold in Sydney at sixpence per head. Fortunately, it was discovered by Mr. O'Brien, a squatter living at Yass, that about six shillings worth of tallow could be obtained from each sheep by boiling it down; and, if this operation had not been extensively begun by many of the sheep-owners, they would, without doubt, have been completely ruined. So great was the distress that, in 1843, the Governor issued provisions at less than cost price, in order to prevent the starvation of large numbers of the people.

Yet, the Secretary of State in England knew nothing of all this, and in 1843 he raised the price of land still higher, ordering that, throughout all Australia, no land should be sold for less than one pound an acre.

4. Immigration.—It is not to be imagined, however, that the English Government ever took to itself any of this land revenue. Every penny was used for the purpose of bringing immigrants into the colony. Agents in Europe were appointed to select suitable persons, who received what were called bounty orders. Any one who possessed an order of this kind received a free passage to Sydney, all expenses being paid by the Colonial Government with the money received from the sale of land. The Governor had the power of giving these orders to persons in New South Wales, who sent them home to their friends or relatives, or to servants and labourers, whom they wished to bring to the colonies. Now, Governor Gipps imagined that the land would continue to bring in as much revenue every year as it did in 1840, and, in the course of that year and the next, gave bounty orders to the extent of nearly one million pounds. But in 1841 the land revenue fell to about one-twentieth of what it had been in 1840; so that the colony must have become bankrupt had it not been that more than half of those who received bounty orders, hearing of the unsettled state of the colony, never made use of the permission granted. Governor Gipps was blamed by the colonists, and received from the Secretary of State a letter of sharp rebuke.

As for the immigrants who did arrive in New South Wales, their prospects were not bright. For a long time many of them found it impossible to obtain employment. Great numbers landed friendless and penniless in Sydney, and in a few weeks found themselves obliged to sleep in the parks, or in the streets, and, but for the friendly exertions of a benevolent lady, Mrs. Chisholm, who obtained employment at different times for about two thousand of them, their position would, indeed, have been wretched.

Mrs. Chisholm founded a home for defenceless and friendless girls, of whom nearly six hundred were at one time living in Sydney in destitution, having been sent out from home with bounty orders, under the impression that employment was certain whenever they might land at Port Jackson.

Gradually the return of the colonists to habits of prudence and thrift removed the financial distress which had been the primary cause of all these troubles. Land ceased to be bought at the ruinously high rates, and goods returned to their former prices.

5. Separation.—But these were not the only cares which pressed upon the mind of Sir George Gipps. He was entrusted with the management of the eastern half of Australia, a region stretching from Cape York to Wilson's Promontory. There were, it is true, but 150,000 inhabitants in the whole territory. But the people were widely scattered, and there were in reality two distinct settlements—one consisting of 120,000 people round Sydney, the other of 30,000 round Port Phillip. The latter, though small, was vigorous, and inclined to be discontented; it was six hundred miles distant from the capital, and the delays and inconveniences due to this fact caused it no little annoyance.

There was, indeed, a Superintendent in Melbourne, and to him the control of the southern district was chiefly entrusted. But

Mr. Latrobe was undecided and feeble. Though personally a most worthy man, yet, as a ruler, he was much too timid and irresolute. He seldom ventured to take any step on his own responsibility; no matter how urgent the matter was, he always waited for instructions from his superior, the Governor.

Under these circumstances, it was natural that the people of Melbourne should wish for an independent Governor, who would have full power to settle promptly all local affairs. In 1840 they held a meeting in a room at the top of the hill in Bourke Street, to petition for separation from New South Wales. But, next year, the Sydney people held a meeting in the theatre to protest against it. Here, then, was another source of trouble to Gipps; for, from this time, the colony was divided into two parties, eagerly and bitterly disputing on the separation question. Governor Gipps and Mr. Latrobe were not in favour of separation, and, by their opposition, they incurred the deep dislike of the people of Port Phillip. The authorities at home, however, were somewhat inclined to favour the idea, and as Gipps was necessarily the medium of announcing their views to the colonists, and carrying them into force, he became unpopular with the Sydney colonists also. No man has ever occupied a more trying position; and a somewhat overbearing temperament was not at all suited for smoothing away its difficulties.

6. Representative Government.—In 1842 a meeting was held in Sydney to petition for representative government. The British Parliament saw its way clear to concede this privilege; and in July, 1843, the first representatives elected by the people assembled in Sydney. The new Council consisted of thirty-six members, of whom twelve were either officials or persons nominated by the Governor, and the other twenty-four were elective. It was the duty of this body to consult with the Governor, and to see that the legitimate wishes of the people were attended to. Six gentlemen were elected for Port Phillip; but residents of Melbourne found it impossible to leave their business and go to live in Sydney. The people of Port Phillip were therefore forced to elect Sydney gentlemen to take charge of their interests. However, these did their duty excellently. Dr. Lang was especially active in the interests of his constituents, and in the second session of the Council, during the year 1844, he moved that a petition should be presented to the Queen, praying that the Port Phillip district should be separated from New South Wales, and formed into an independent colony. The Port Phillip representatives, together with the now famous Robert Lowe, gave their support to the motion; but there were nineteen votes against it, and this effort was supposed to have been completely baffled. But Dr. Lang drew up a petition of his own, which was signed by all the Port Phillip members and sent to England. Nothing further was heard on the subject for some time, until Sir George Gipps received a letter from Lord Stanley, the Secretary of State, directing him to lay the matter before the Executive Council in Sydney; and stating that, in the opinion of the English Government, the request of Port Phillip was very fair and reasonable. An inquiry was held, the Sydney Council sent to England a report on the subject, and received a reply to the effect that steps would at once be taken to obtain from the Imperial Parliament the required Act.

Colonial Secretary's Office, Sydney.

The people of Port Phillip were overjoyed, and in 1846 gave a grand banquet to Dr. Lang to celebrate the occasion. But they were not destined to quite so speedy a consummation of their desires. The English Government which had given so favourable an ear to their petition was defeated and succeeded by another Government, to whom the whole question was new. Year after year passed away, and the people of Port Phillip began to grow impatient, and to complain loudly of their grievances. First of all, they complained that, although it was a well-recognised principle that the money received by Government for the waste lands of any district should be employed in bringing out emigrants to that district, yet the Sydney Government used much of the money obtained from the sale of land in Port Phillip for the purpose of bringing out new colonists—not to Melbourne or Geelong, but to Sydney itself. And thus, it was said, the people of Sydney were using the money of the Port Phillip district for their own advantage. And, again, the people of Melbourne complained that, although they were allowed to elect six members of the Legislative Council, yet this was merely a mockery, because none of the Port Phillip residents could afford to live in Sydney for five months every year and to neglect their own private business. The former of these accusations seems, so far as we can now determine, to have been unfounded; the latter was undoubtedly a practical grievance, though more or less unavoidable in every system of representation.

7. Earl Grey.—For a year or two the English Government forgot all about the separation question; and, in 1848, the wearied colonists at Port Phillip determined to call attention to their discontent. Accordingly, when the elections for that year approached, they determined not to elect any member, so that the English Government might see of how little use to them their supposed privilege really was. It was agreed that no one should come forward for election, and it seemed likely that there would be no election whatever, when a gentleman named Foster offered himself as a candidate. This placed the non-election party in a dilemma; for if they declined to vote at all, and if Mr. Foster could persuade only two or three of his friends to vote for him, then, since there was no other candidate, he would be legally elected.

Now, at this time, Earl Grey was Secretary of State for the Colonies; and when some one proposed to nominate him for election, in opposition to Mr. Foster, the idea was hailed as a happy one. The non-election party could then vote for Earl Grey, and he would be returned by a large majority. But Earl Grey, being an English nobleman and a member of the British Government, would certainly never go to Sydney to attend a small Colonial Council; so that there would be, in reality, no member elected. But the attention of the Secretary of State would be drawn to the desires of the district. Earl Grey was triumphantly elected, and when the news went home it caused some merriment. He

was jokingly asked in the House of Lords when he would sail for
Sydney. And for several weeks he underwent so much banter
on the subject that his attention was fully aroused to the long-
neglected question. He weighed the matter carefully, and, re-
solving to do the people of Port Phillip full justice, sent out word
that he would at once prepare a Bill for the Imperial Parliament,
in order to obtain the necessary powers. At the same time he
intimated that Queen Victoria would be pleased if the new colony
should adopt her name. Nothing could give the colonists more
satisfaction, and they waited with patience until affairs should
be properly arranged in England.

8. Sir Charles Fitzroy.—All this agitation, however,
had not taken place without much irritation and contention
between the people at Port Phillip and their Governor at Sydney,
from whose authority they wished to free themselves. Sir George
Gipps had much to harass him, and in 1846 he was glad to retire
from his troublesome position. He was succeeded by Sir Charles
Fitzroy, a gentleman in every respect his opposite. By no means
clever, yet good-tempered and amiable, he troubled himself very
little with the affairs of the colony. The Sydney Council managed
everything just as it pleased; Sir Charles was glad to be rid of
the trouble, and the colonists were delighted to have their own
way. As for the separation question, he cared very little whether
Port Phillip was erected into a colony or not.

In 1850 the news arrived that Port Phillip was to be separated
from New South Wales, and in the middle of the next year its
independence was declared. Its Superintendent, Latrobe, was
raised to the dignity of Governor, and the new colony received its
Constitution, conferring on it all the legislative and other powers
which had previously been possessed only by New South Wales.

9. Abolition of Transportation.—It was during
this period that the English Government resolved on sending no
more convicts to Australia. A committee of the Imperial Parliament held an inquiry into the effects of transportation, and
reported that it would be unwise to continue the system. From
1842, therefore, there was practically a cessation of transportation,
although the majority of the squatters were averse to the change.
They found that the convicts, when assigned to them, made good

shepherds and stockmen, and that at cheap rates. They subsequently petitioned for a revival of transportation; but, after some hesitation, the British Government resolved to adhere to their resolution to send no more convicts to Sydney. Van Diemen's Land was still unfortunate; it was to receive, indeed, the full stream of convicts, but from 1842 Australia itself ceased to be the receptacle for the criminals of Great Britain.

CHAPTER XI.

SOUTH AUSTRALIA, 1841-1850.

1. Governor Grey.—The colonists of South Australia had, in 1841, received a sharp but salutary lesson, and we have seen that they profited by it. They had discovered that the land was their only source of wealth, and many, who had sufficient means to purchase farms or stations, went out into the country, determined to endure a year or two of hardship in hopes of prosperity to come. Nor had they very long to wait; in 1844 they were able to export corn to the extent of £40,000, and in that year the colony possessed 355,000 sheep and 22,000 cattle.

The new Governor, Captain George Grey, took every care to assist the colonists in returning to more prudent courses. Many changes were needed; for in 1840, while the colony had a revenue of only £30,000, it had spent at the rate of £171,000 per annum. Such imprudence could lead to nothing but ruin, and the first task of the Governor was to reduce all expenses as far as possible. In the first year the expenditure was cut down to £90,000; in the next, to £68,000; and in 1843, to £34,000.

Instead of employing the poorer labourers on costly and unnecessary public works, he persuaded them to take employment in the country with the farmers and squatters, who were rapidly opening up the interior parts of the colony. He settled many on small farms or stations of their own, but in this he was greatly impeded by the high price of land; for Wakefield's friends in England were not yet convinced that their favourite scheme was defective—they attributed every mishap to the incompetence of Governors Hindmarsh and Gawler. "To lower the price," said they, "will be to ruin the colony;" and lest such a thing should happen, they raised the price of all lands, whether good or bad, to one pound per acre. But many of those who had bought land in the first days of the settlement had been so anxious to part with it during the crisis that they had sold it for much less than it cost them; and thus a great number of the poorer people became possessed of land at very moderate prices. In 1839 there were but 440 acres under cultivation; three years afterwards there were 23,000 acres bearing wheat, and 5,000 acres of other crops. So rich and fertile was the soil that, in 1845, the colonists not only raised enough of corn to supply their own wants, but were able to export about 200,000 bushels at cheap rates to the neighbouring colonies, and even then were left with 150,000 bushels, which they could neither sell nor use. So rapid a development of resources and so sudden an accession of prosperity have probably never occurred in the history of any other country.

2. Mineral Wealth.—Such was the success attendant upon careful industry, exercised with prudence, and under favourable circumstances; but the colony was to owe yet more to accidental good fortune. During the year 1841, a carrier, while driving his team of bullocks over the Mount Lofty Range, had been obliged, by the steepness of the road, to fasten a log to the back of his waggon in order to steady the load and prevent its descending too quickly. As the log dragged roughly behind on the road, it tore great furrows in the soil, and in one of these the carrier noticed a stone which glanced and glittered like a metal. On looking more closely, he saw that there were large quantities of the same substance lying near the surface of the earth in all directions. Having taken some specimens with him, he made inquiries in Adelaide, and learned that the substance he had discovered was galena, a mineral in which sulphur is combined with lead and small quantities of silver. The land on which this valuable ore had been found was soon purchased, and mines opened upon it. At first there was a large profit obtained from the enterprise; and though, in after years, the mines became exhausted, yet they served to call the attention of the colonists to the possibility of discovering more permanent and lucrative sources of mineral wealth.

3. Copper.—At the Kapunda Station, about forty miles

north-west of Adelaide, there lived a squatter named Captain Bagot. One day, during the year 1842, he sent his overseer—Mr. Dutton—to search for a number of sheep which had strayed into the bush. After spending some time in fruitless efforts, Mr. Dutton ascended a small hill in order to have a more extensive view of the country, but still he saw nothing of the lost sheep. On turning to descend, his attention was attracted by a bright green rock jutting from the earth. It seemed to him peculiar, so he broke a small piece off and carried it down to Captain Bagot's house, where he and the captain examined the specimen, and came to the conclusion that it consisted of the mineral malachite, containing copper in combination with water and carbonic dioxide. They let no one know of the discovery, but proceeded to apply for the land in the usual manner, without breathing a word as to their purpose. The section of eighty acres was advertised for a month, and then put up to auction; but as no one was anxious for this barren piece of ground, they had no competitors, and the land fell to them for the price of eighty pounds. As soon as they became possessed of it, they threw off all appearance of mystery, and commenced operations. During the first year the mines yielded £4,000; during the next, £10,000; and for several years they continued to enrich the two proprietors, until each had realised a handsome fortune, when the land was bought by an English company.

4. The Burra Mines.—The discovery of copper at Kapunda caused much excitement in the colony. Every one who possessed land examined it carefully for the trace of any minerals it might contain; and soon it was rumoured that, at a place about one hundred miles north of Adelaide, a shepherd had found exceedingly rich specimens of copper ore. The land on which these were discovered had not yet been sold by the Government, and in great haste a company was formed to purchase it. This company consisted of the merchants, professional men, and officials of Adelaide; but a rival company was immediately started, consisting of shopkeepers and tradesmen, together with the farmers of the country districts. The former always maintained a haughty air, and soon came to be known throughout the colony as the "nobs"; while they, in their turn, fixed on their rivals the nickname of the "snobs". For a week or two the jealousies of

the companies ran high, but they were soon forced to make a
temporary union ; for, according to the land laws of the colony, if
any one wished to buy a piece of land, he had to apply for it and
have it advertised for a month ; it was then put up for auction,
and he who offered the highest price became the purchaser. But
a month was a long time to wait, and it was rumoured that a
number of speculators were on their way from Sydney to offer
a large sum for the land, as soon as it should be put up to
auction. It was, therefore, necessary to take immediate action.
There was another regulation in the land laws, according to
which, if a person applied for 20,000 acres, and paid down
£20,000 in cash, he became at once the proprietor of the land.
The "nobs" determined to avail themselves of this arrangement ;
but when they put their money together, they found they had
not enough to pay so large a sum. They therefore asked the
"snobs" to join them, on the understanding that, after the land
had been purchased, the two companies would make a fair division.
By uniting their funds they raised the required amount, and
proceeded with great exultation to lodge the money. But part of
it was in the form of bills on the Adelaide banks ; and as the
Governor refused to accept anything but cash, the companies
were almost in despair, until a few active members hunted up
their friends in Adelaide, and succeeded in borrowing the number
of sovereigns required to make up the deficiency. The money
was paid into the Treasury, the two companies were the possessors
of the land, and the Sydney speculators arrived a few days too late.

Now came the division of the 20,000 acres. A line was drawn
across the middle ; a coin was tossed up to decide which of the
two should have the first choice, and fortune favoured the
"snobs," who selected the northern half, called by the natives
Burra Burra. To the southern part the "nobs" gave the
name of "Princess Royal". The companies soon began operations ; but though the two districts appeared on the surface to
be of almost equal promise, yet, on being laid open, the Princess
Royal was soon found to be in reality poor, while the Burra Burra
mines provided fortunes for each of the fortunate "snobs".
During the three years after their discovery they yielded copper
to the value of £700,000. Miners were brought from England,

and a town of about 5,000 inhabitants rapidly sprang into existence. The houses of the Cornish miners were of a peculiar kind. A creek runs through the district, with high precipitous banks of solid rock; into the face of these cliffs the miners cut large chambers to serve for dwellings; holes bored through the rock, and emerging upon the surface of the ground above, formed the chimneys, which were capped by small beer barrels instead of chimney-pots. The fronts of the houses were of weatherboard, in which doors were left; and for two miles along each side of the stream these primitive dwellings looked out upon the almost dry bed of the creek, which formed the main street of the village. Here the miners dwelt for years, until the waters rose one night into a foaming flood, which destroyed the houses and swept away several of their inhabitants.

In 1845 Burra Burra was a lonely moor; in 1850 it was bustling with men, and noisy with the sounds of engines, pumps and forges. Acres of land were covered with the company's warehouses and offices, and the handsome residences of its officers; behind these there rose great mounds of blue, green, and dark-red ores of copper, worth enormous sums of money. Along the roads eight hundred teams, each consisting of eight bullocks, passed constantly to and fro, whilst scores of ships were employed in conveying the ore to England. From this great activity the whole community could not but derive the utmost benefit, and for a time South Australia had every prospect of taking the foremost place among the colonies.

5. Governor Robe.—In 1841 Governor Grey had been of the greatest service to the colony in changing the state of its prospects, but he was not permitted to see more than the commencement of its great prosperity; for, in 1845, he was sent to govern New Zealand, where troubles had arisen similar to those which he had helped to cure in South Australia. His place was filled by Colonel Robe, a military gentleman, of what is called the old school, honourable and upright, but inclined to think that everything ought always to be as it has been. He disliked all innovation, and did what he could to prevent it, much to the discontent of the young and thriving colony, which was of necessity the scene of constant and rapid changes. He passed a very troublous time for three years, and in 1848 was heartily glad to be recalled.

6. Governor Young.—The colony was then placed under the care of Sir Henry Young, whose policy was completely the reverse. He sought by every means in his power to encourage the ceaseless activity of the people. His failing was, perhaps, an injudicious zeal for progress. For instance, in his desire to open up the river Murray to navigation, he wasted large sums of money in schemes that proved altogether useless. He made an effort to remove the bar at the mouth of the river, but fresh deposits of sand were constantly being brought down by the current, and lashed up into a new bar by the waves that rolled ceaselessly in from the Southern Ocean. He spent about £20,000 in trying to construct a harbour called Port Elliot, near the entrance to the Murray; but there are now only a few surf-beaten stones to indicate the scene of his fruitless attempt. He offered a bonus of £4,000 to the first person who should ascend the Murray in an iron steamer as far as the river Darling. A gentleman called Cadell made the effort, and succeeded; he obtained the reward, but it was not enough to pay his heavy expenses, and when he endeavoured afterwards to carry on a trade, by transporting wool to the sea in flat-bottomed steamers, he found that the traffic on the river was not sufficiently great to repay his heavy outlay, and in a short time he was almost ruined. The attempt was premature; and though, in our time, the navigation of the Murray is successfully carried on, and is, undoubtedly, of immense advantage not only to South Australia, but also to New South Wales and Victoria, yet, at the time when the first efforts were made, it led to nothing but loss, if not ruin to the pioneers.

CHAPTER XII.

THE DISCOVERY OF GOLD.

1. Importance of the Year 1851.—The year 1851 was in many ways an eventful one to Australia. In that year the colonies received from the Imperial Parliament the amended

Constitutions they had so long expected. Tasmania, South Australia, Port Phillip, and Western Australia were now no longer under the absolute control of Governors sent out by the colonial authorities in England; they could henceforth boast the dignity of being self-governed communities, for, in 1851, they were invested with political powers which had previously been possessed by New South Wales alone. They now had the privilege of electing two-thirds of the members of a Legislative Council which not only had the power of making laws each for its own colony, but also of framing any new constitution for itself according to its own taste and requirements. Each colony kept its Legislative Council for only a year or two until it could discuss and establish a regular system of parliamentary government with two Houses and a Cabinet of responsible Ministers. Again, it was on the 1st of July in the same year that Port Phillip gained its independence; from that date onward its prosperous career must be related under its new title—Victoria.

But the event which made the year 1851 especially memorable in the annals of Australia was the discovery, near Bathurst, of the first of those rich goldfields which, for so long a time, changed the prospects of the colonies. For several years after the date of this occurrence the history of Australia is little more than the story of the feverish search for gold, with its hopes, its labour, its turmoil, and its madness; its scenes of exultation and splendid triumph, and its still more frequent scenes of bitter and gloomy disappointment.

2. Early Rumours of Gold.—For many years there had been rumours that the Blue Mountains were auriferous. It was said that gold had been seen by convicts in the days of Macquarie, and, indeed, still earlier; but to the stories of prisoners, who claimed rewards for alleged discoveries, the authorities in Sydney always listened with extreme suspicion, more especially as no pretended discoverer could ever find more than his first small specimens.

In 1840 a Polish nobleman named Strzelecki, who had been travelling among the ranges round Mount Kosciusko, stated that, from indications he had observed, he was firmly persuaded of the existence of gold in these mountains; but the Governor asked him, as a favour, to make no mention of a theory which might, perhaps, unsettle the colony, and fill the easily excited convicts with hopes which, he feared, would prove delusive. Strzelecki agreed not to publish his belief; but there was another man of science who was not so easily to be silenced. The Rev. W. B. Clarke, a clergyman devoted to geology, exhibited specimens in Sydney, on which he based an opinion that the Blue Mountains would, eventually, be found to possess goldfields of great extent and value. Some of these were taken to London by Strzelecki; and in 1844 a great English scientist, Sir Roderick Murchison, read a paper before the Royal Geographical Society in which he expressed a theory similar to that of Mr. Clarke. In 1846 he again called attention to this subject, and showed that, from the great similarity which existed between the rocks of the Blue Mountains and those of the Urals, there was every probability that the one would be found as rich as the other was known to be in the precious metals. So far as theory could go, the matter had been well discussed before the year 1851, but no one had ventured to spend his time and money in making a practical effort to settle the question.

3. Edward Hargraves.—About that time, however, the rich mines of California attracted a Bathurst settler, named Edward Hargraves, to seek his fortune on the banks of the Sacramento; and though, among the great crowds of struggling and jostling diggers, he met with but little success, yet he learned the methods by which gold is discovered and secured, and laid the foundation for adventures in Australia which were afterwards to bring him both wealth and renown. Whilst he toiled with increasing disappointment on one of these famous goldfields, the scenery around him, and the appearance of the rocks, recalled to his memory a certain secluded valley beyond the Blue Mountains, which he had visited thirteen years before; the notion floated vaguely through his mind that, perhaps, in that silent spot, there might lie great treasures, such as he saw his more fortunate companions from time to time draw forth from the rocks and soil around him. Day after day the image of that winding creek among the hills near Bathurst recurred with increasing vividness to stimulate his imagination and awaken his hopes. At length this feeling impelled him to seek once more the shores of Australia in order to examine the spot which had so often been present to his day-dreams. He lost no time in sailing, and scarcely had he arrived in Sydney ere he set out on horseback to cross the Blue Mountains. On the 11th of February, 1851, he spent the night at a little inn a few miles from the object of his journey, and shortly after dawn he sallied forth on his ride through the forest, carrying with him a spade and a trowel and a little tin dish. In the cool air of the morning the scent of the spreading gum trees braced up his frame as he plunged deeper and deeper among those lonely hollows and wood-clad hills. In an hour or two he reached the well-remembered spot—the dry course of a mountain torrent which, in rainy seasons, finds its way into the Summer-hill Creek. He lost no time in placing a little of the grey-coloured soil into his tin dish, and at once carried it to the nearest pool, where he dipped the whole beneath the water. By moving the dish rapidly, as he had learned to do in California, he washed away the sand and earth; but the particles of gold, which are more than seven and a half times heavier than sand, were not so easily to be carried off. They sank to the corner of the dish, where they lay secure—a few small specks, themselves of little value, yet telling of hidden treasures that lay scattered in all the soil around.

EDWARD HARGRAVES.

A few days were spent in a careful examination of the neighbouring valleys, and when he was absolutely certain that the hopes he had so warmly indulged would not prove empty, he set out for Sydney, taking care, however, to breathe no word of what he thought or of what he had proved. On the 3rd of April he wrote a letter to the Colonial Secretary, in which he stated that, if the Government were willing to give him £500, he would point out localities in New South Wales where gold was abundantly to be found. In reply, the Colonial Secretary announced that no preliminary reward could be given; but that, if he chose first of all to point out the localities, he would afterwards be recompensed in proportion to the results. He accepted these conditions; and Mr. Stutchbury, the Colonial Geologist, was sent to accompany him to the Summerhill Creek. On the 8th of May they set to work, and soon obtained several ounces of grain gold; on the 13th, they discovered a single piece worth £30, and next day Mr. Stutchbury reported to the Government that he had seen enough to convince him that the district was rich in the precious metal. Five days afterwards, the little valley of the Summerhill contained four hundred persons, all stooping over the creek in a row about a mile long, each with a dish in his hand, scarcely ever raising his head, but busily engaged in washing the sand for gold. Lumps were frequently found of value varying from £5 to £200. A week later, there were a thousand persons at work on the creek near the formerly lonely gully.

4. Rush to the Goldfield.—The excitement throughout the colony now became intense: workmen quitted their employment, shepherds deserted their flocks, shopkeepers closed their stores, and a great tide of fortune-seekers pressed onward, day by day, to the west. Most of these had sold everything they possessed, in order to make up a little bundle of necessary articles. Yet there were very many but ill-provided for a lengthened stay; they hurried along the road with the fallacious idea that gold was simply to be shovelled into bags and carted to Sydney. But when they came upon the scene, and saw that in the case of most of them it would only be after weeks and months of severe and constant toil that they could be rich, they grew faint-hearted, lounged for a week or two on the diggings, and then started for home again; so that, for some time, there was a counter-current of grumbling and discontented men passing back to Sydney by the road. These men thought themselves befooled by Hargraves, and it might, perhaps, have cost him his life had he fallen into their hands. On his trip to Sydney he was careful to disguise himself, to avoid their threatened revenge. He received from Government, however, his preliminary reward of £500, and, in after years, New South Wales voted him the sum of £10,000, which was supplemented by a present of £2,381 from Victoria. Other profits also accrued to Hargraves; so that he was, in the end, recompensed for his toil and trouble with a handsome competency.

The gloomy reports of returning diggers checked for a time the flow of people to the west; but in the month of July an aboriginal shepherd on a station near Bathurst burst in upon his master while seated at dinner, his eyes glistening with excitement. He was only able to stammer out: "Oh, massa, white man find little fellow, me find big fellow". When his master drove him in a buggy through the forest, the shepherd pointed to where a hundredweight of gold was sticking out from a rock. It was so heavy that they had to chop it in two with their axes before they could lift it into the buggy. It was afterwards sold for £4,000. So splendid a prize, obtained in so easy a manner, was a temptation too dazzling to be resisted; and the stream of people along the Bathurst road was now tenfold denser than before.

5. Government Regulations.— When the population on the goldfields began to grow numerous, the Government found it necessary to make arrangements for the preservation of law and order. A commissioner was appointed, who was to act as a magistrate; he was to be assisted by a small body of police, and was to take charge of the gold escorts. As the lands on which the gold was being found were the public property of the colony, it was thought to be but just that the community, as a whole, should participate, to some small extent, in the wealth raised from them; and the order was, therefore, issued that diggers should in all cases take out licences before seeking for gold, and should pay for them at the rate of thirty shillings per month.

New diggings were, from time to time, opened up, and fresh crowds of eager men constantly pressed towards them, leaving the towns deserted and the neighbouring colonies greatly reduced in population. For some months the Turon River was the favourite; at one time it had no less than ten thousand men upon its banks. At Ophir, and Braidwood, and Maroo the most industrious and sagacious miners were generally rewarded by the discovery of fine pieces of gold, for which the Californian name of "nuggets" now began to be extensively used.

6. Gold in Victoria.—When Latrobe was sworn in to fill the office of Governor of Victoria on the 16th July, 1851, it appeared probable that he would soon have but a small community to rule over. So great were the numbers of those who were daily packing up their effects and setting off for the goldfields of New South Wales that Victoria seemed likely to sink into a very insignificant place on the list of Australian colonies. In alarm at this prospect, a number of the leading citizens of Melbourne on the 9th of June united to form what was called the Gold Discovery Committee, and offered a reward of £200 to the person who should give the first intimation of a paying goldfield within two hundred miles of Melbourne. Many persons set out, each in hopes of being the fortunate discoverer; and a report having been circulated that signs of gold had been seen on the Plenty Ranges, there were soon no less than two hundred persons scouring those hills, though for a long time without success. The first useful discovery in Victoria seems to have been made on 1st July, by a Californian digger named Esmond, who, like Hargraves, had entered on the search with a practical knowledge of the work. His experience had taught him the general characteristics of a country in which gold is likely to be found, and he selected Clunes as a favourable spot. He found the quartz rock of the district richly sprinkled with gold; and his discovery having been made known, several hundred people were quickly on the scene. Almost on the same day, gold was discovered by a party of six men, at Anderson's Creek, only a few miles up the Yarra from Melbourne. It is thus difficult to determine with certainty whether or not Esmond was in reality the first discoverer; but, at any rate, he received honours and emoluments as such; and in after years the Victorian Parliament presented him with £1,000 for his services.

7. Ballarat.—On the 10th of August the Geelong newspapers announced that deposits of auriferous earth had been discovered at Buninyong, and very soon the sunny slopes of that peaceful and pastoral district were swarming with prospecting parties; the quietly browsing sheep were startled from their favourite solitudes by crowds of men, who hastened with pick and spade to break up the soil in every direction, each eager to outstrip the other in the race for wealth. This region, however, did not realise the expectations that had been formed of it, and many of the diggers began to move northwards, in the direction of Clunes. But at Clunes, also, there had been disappointment, for the gold was mostly embedded in quartz rock, and these early miners were not prepared to extract it; parties from Clunes were therefore moving southwards to Buninyong, and the two currents met on the slopes of the Yarrowee, a streamlet whose banks were afterwards famous as the Ballarat diggings. The first comers began to work at a bend in the creek, which they called Golden Point. Here, for a time, each man could easily earn from £20 to £40 a day, and crowds of people hurried to the scene. Every one selected a piece of ground, which he called his claim, and set to work to dig a hole in it; but when the bottom of the sandy layer was reached, and there seemed to be nothing but pipe-clay below, the claim was supposed to be worked out, and was straightway abandoned. However, a miner named Cavanagh determined to try an experiment, and, having entered one of these deserted claims, he dug through the layer of pipe-clay, when he had the good fortune to come suddenly upon several large deposits of grain gold. He had reached what had been in long past ages the bed of the creek, where, in every little hollow, for century after century, the flowing waters had gently deposited the gold which they had washed out of the rocks in the mountains. In many cases these "pockets," as they were called, were found to contain gold to the value of thousands of pounds, so that very soon all the claims were carried down a few feet further, and with such success that, before a month had passed, Ballarat took rank as the richest goldfield in the world. In October there were ten thousand men at work on the Yarrowee; acre after acre was covered with circular heaps of red and yellow sand, each with its shaft in the middle, in which men were toiling beneath the ground to excavate the soil and pass it to their companions above, who quickly hurried with it to the banks of the creek, where twelve hundred "cradles," rocked by brawny arms, were washing the sand from the gold.

8. Mount Alexander.—In the month of September a party, who had gone about forty miles north-east of Clunes to Mount Alexander, discovered near the present site of Castlemaine a valuable seam of gold-bearing earth. The fame of this place soon spread through all the colony; many left Ballarat to seek it, and crowds of people hastened from Melbourne and Geelong to share in the glittering prizes. In October, eight thousand men had gathered in the district; in November, there were not less than twenty-five thousand diggers at work, and three tons of gold were waiting in the tent of the commissioner to be carried to Melbourne. The road to Mount Alexander was crowded with men of all ranks and conditions, pressing eagerly onward to be in time.

9. Sandhurst.—A few weeks later the glories both of Ballarat and of Mount Alexander were dimmed for a time by the discovery of gold on the Bendigo Creek, which seemed at first to be the richest of all the goldfields. In the course of a few months nearly forty thousand persons were scattered along the banks of the streamlet where the handsome streets of Bendigo now stand.

In the month of May, 1852, there must have been close upon seventy thousand men in the country between Buninyong and Bendigo, all engaged in the same occupation. Melbourne and Geelong were silent and deserted; for all classes were alike infected with the same excitement—lawyers, doctors, clerks, merchants, labourers, mechanics, all were to be found struggling through the miry ruts that served for a highway to Bendigo. The sailors left the ships in the bay with scarcely a man to take care of them; even the very policemen deserted, and the warders in the gaols resigned in a body. The price of labour now became excessive, for no man was willing to stay away from the diggings unless tempted by the offer of four or five times the ordinary wage.

10. Immigration.—Meanwhile the news of these great discoveries had travelled to Europe, so that, after the middle of 1852, ships began to arrive freighted with thousands of men of all nations, who no sooner landed in Melbourne than they started for the diggings. During this year nearly one hundred thousand persons were thus brought into the country, and the population was doubled at a bound. Next year ninety-two thousand fresh arrivals landed, and Victoria thus became the most populous of the colonies. During the two following years it received a further accession of a hundred and fifty thousand; so that, in 1856, it contained four hundred thousand inhabitants, or about five times the number it possessed in 1850. The staple industry was, of course, the mining for gold, of which, in 1852, one hundred and seventy-four tons were raised, valued at £14,000,000. During the next ten years £100,000,000 worth of gold was exported from Victoria.

Some of the nuggets that were found are of historic note. The "Sarah Sands," discovered in 1853, was worth about £6,500. In 1857 the "Blanche Barkly," worth £7,000, was discovered; and the following year produced the "Welcome Nugget," which was sold for £10,500, and was the greatest on record, until, in 1869, the "Welcome Stranger" was dug out, which proved to be slightly larger.

CHAPTER XIII.

VICTORIA, 1851-1855.

1. Effects of Gold Excitement.—For the first few months after the discovery of gold in Victoria, many shrewd persons believed that the colony would be ruined by its seeming good fortune. None of the ordinary industries could be carried on whilst workmen were so scarce and wages so high. But, happily, these expectations proved fallacious; for, in 1852, when the great stream of people from Europe began to flow into the colony, every profession and every trade sprang into new and vigorous life. The vast crowds on the goldfields required to be fed, so the farmers found ample market for their corn, and the squatters for their beef and mutton. The miners required to be clothed, and the tailor and shoemaker must be had, whatever might be the prices they charged. Mechanics and artisans of every class found their labours in demand, and handsomely paid for. The merchants, also, found trade both brisk and lucrative; while the imports in 1850 were worth only three-quarters of a million, those of three years later were worth about twenty times that amount. After this enormous increase in population and business, it was found that there was quite as great an opportunity of gaining riches by remaining quietly engaged in one's own occupation as by joining the restless throng upon the goldfields. The public revenue of the colony was in 1852 six times, and in 1853 twelve times as great as it had been before the discovery of gold; so that, both as individuals and as a nation, the people of Victoria had reason to be satisfied with the change.

2. Convicts Prevention Act.—There existed, however, one drawback; for the attractions of the goldfields had drawn from the neighbouring colonies, and more especially from Tasmania, great numbers of that class of convicts who, having served a part of their time, had been liberated on condition of good behaviour. They crossed over by hundreds, and soon gave rise to a serious difficulty; for, in the confused and unsettled state of the colony, they found only too great an opportunity for the display of their criminal propensities and perverted talents. Being by no means charmed with the toilsome life of the gold-miner, many of them became bushrangers. There were, in 1852, several bands of these lawless ruffians sweeping the country and robbing in all directions. As the gold was being conveyed from the diggings, escorted by bands of armed troopers, the bushrangers lurked upon the road, treacherously shot the troopers, and rifled the chests. On one occasion, their daring rose to such a height that a band of them boarded the ship *Nelson* whilst it lay at anchor in Hobson's Bay, overpowered the crew, and removed gold to the value of £24,000 —remarking, as they handed the boxes over the side of the vessel, that this was the best goldfield they had ever seen.

To prevent any further introduction of these undesirable immigrants, the Legislature, in 1852, passed what was called the "Convicts Prevention Act," declaring that no person who had been convicted, and had not received an absolutely free pardon, should be allowed to enter the colony; and that all persons who came from Tasmania should be required to prove that they were free, before being allowed to land. Any ship captain who brought a convict into the colony was to be fined £100 for the offence.

3. Aspect of Goldfields.—Meanwhile the goldfields were growing apace. The discovery of the Eureka, Gravel Pits, and Canadian Leads made Ballarat once more the favourite; and in 1853 there were about forty thousand diggers at work on the Yarrowee. Hotels began to be built, theatres were erected, and here and there a little church rose among the long line of tents which occupied the slopes above the creek.

4. Scene on the Goldfields.—Below, on the flats, the scene was a busy one. Thousands upon thousands of holes covered the earth, where men emerged and disappeared like ants, each bearing a bag of sand which he either threw on a wheelbarrow or slung over his shoulder, and then carried forward, running nimbly along the thin paths among a multitude of holes, till he reached the little creek where he delivered the sand to one of the men who stood shoulder to shoulder, in long rows, for miles on either bank, all washing the sand and clay into the shallow current, whose waters were turned to a tint of dirty yellow. Such is the scene which presents itself by day; but at sunset a gun is fired from the commissioner's tent and all cease work: then, against the evening sky, ten thousand fires send up their wreaths of thin blue smoke, and the diggers prepare their evening meals. Everything is hushed for a time, except that a dull murmur rises from the little crowds chatting over their pannikins of tea. But, as the darkness draws closer around, the noises begin to assume a merrier tone, and, mingling pleasantly in the evening air, there rise the loud notes of a sailor's song, the merry jingle of a French political chant, or the rich strains of a German chorus.

In some tents the miners sit round boxes or stools, while, by the light of flaming oil-cans, they gamble for match boxes filled with gold-dust; in others they gather to drink the liquors illicitly sold by the "sly grog shops". Many of the diggers betake themselves to the brilliantly-lighted theatres, and make the fragile walls tremble with their rough and hearty roars of applause: everywhere are heard the sounds of laughter and good humour. Then, at midnight, all to bed, except those foolish revellers who have stayed too late at the "grog shop".

At dawn, again, they are all astir; for the day's supply of water must be drawn from the stream ere its limpid current begins to assume the appearance of a clay-stained gutter. Making the allowances proper to the occasion, the community is both orderly and law-abiding, and the digger, in the midst of all his toil, enjoys a very agreeable existence.

5. The Licence Fee.—He had but one grievance to trouble his life, and that was the monthly payment of the licence fee. This tax had been imposed under the erroneous impression that every one who went upon the goldfields must of necessity earn a fortune. For a long time this mistake prevailed, because only the most successful diggers were much heard of. But there was an indistinguishable throng of those who earned much less than a labourer's wage.

The average monthly earnings throughout the colony were not more than eight pounds for each man; and of this sum he had to pay thirty shillings every month for the mere permission to dig. To those who were fortunate this seemed but a trifle; but for those who earned little or nothing there was no resource but to evade payment, and many were the tricks adopted in order to "dodge the commissioners". As there were more than one-fifth of the total number of diggers who systematically paid no fees, it was customary for the police to stop any man they met and demand to see his licence; if he had none, he was at once marched off to the place that served for a gaol, and there chained to a tree.

The police were in the habit of devoting two days a week to what was called "digger hunting"; and as they often experienced much trouble and vexation in doing what was unfortunately their duty, they were sometimes rough and summary in their proceedings. Hence arose a feeling of hostility among the diggers, not only to the police, but to all the officials on the goldfields. The first serious ebullition of the prevailing discontent took place on the Ovens, where a commissioner who had been unnecessarily rough to unlicensed diggers was assaulted and severely injured. But as violence was deprecated by the great body of miners, they held large meetings, in order to agitate in a more constitutional manner for the abolition of the fee. At first they sent a petition to Governor Latrobe, who declined to make any change. It was then hinted that, possibly, they might be driven to use force; and the Governor replied that, if they did, he was determined to do his duty. But in August, 1853, when the agitation was increasing, Latrobe hurriedly reduced the fee to twenty shillings per month. This appeased the miners for a time; but the precipitancy with which the Governor had changed his intention showed too plainly the weakness of the Government, for there was at that time scarcely a soldier in Victoria to repress an insurrection, if one should break out. Among the confused crowds on the goldfields there were numbers of troublesome spirits, many of them foreigners, who were only too happy to foment dissension. Thousands of miners had been disappointed in their hopes of wealth, and, being in a discontented frame of mind, they blamed the Governor for their misfortunes.

In spite of the concession that had been made to them, a spirit of dissatisfaction prevailed throughout all the goldfields; mutterings were heard as of a coming storm, and Latrobe, in alarm, sent to all the neighbouring colonies to ask for troops. As the Ninety-ninth Regiment was lying idle in Hobart Town, it was at once despatched to Melbourne.

6. Governor Hotham.—While matters were in this state, Governor Latrobe retired from office; and in June, 1854, Sir Charles Hotham arrived to fill the position. On his first arrival, he showed that his sympathies were, to a great extent, with the diggers. But he could scarcely be expected to make any important change until he had been a few months in the colony, and had learnt exactly the state of affairs, and, meanwhile, the discontent on the goldfields was daily increasing. The months of September and October, in 1854, were exceedingly dry; the creeks were greatly shrunk in volume, and in many places the diggers could find no water either for drinking or for gold-washing; and their irritation was not at all soothed by the manners of the commissioners and police. Besides this, the Government had thought it necessary to form a camp on the goldfields, so that a large body of soldiers dwelt constantly in the midst of the miners. The soldiers and officers, of course, supported the commissioners, and, like them, soon came to be regarded with the greatest disfavour.

The goldfield population was in this irritable state when a trifling incident kindled revolt.

7. Riot at Ballarat.—A digger named Scobie, late one

evening, knocked at the door of Bentley's Hotel, at Ballarat. Finding the place closed for the night, he tried to force an entrance, and continued his clamour so long that Bentley became angry, and sallied forth to chastise him. A crowd gathered to see the fight, and, in the darkness, Scobie's head was split open with a spade. Whose hand it was that aimed the blow no one could tell; but the diggers universally believed that Bentley was himself the murderer. He was therefore arrested and tried, but acquitted by Mr. Dewes, the magistrate, who was said by the diggers to be secretly his partner in business. A great crowd assembled round the hotel, and a digger, named Kennedy, addressed the multitude, in vigorous Scottish accents, pointing out the spot where their companion's blood had been shed, and asserting that his spirit hovered above and called for revenge. The authorities sent a few police to protect the place, but they were only a handful of men in the midst of a great and seething crowd of over eight thousand powerful diggers. For an hour or two the mob, though indulging in occasional banter, remained harmless. But a mischievous boy having thrown a stone, and broken the lamp in front of the hotel, the police made a movement as if they were about to seize the offender. This roused the diggers to anger, and in less than a minute every pane of glass was broken; the police were roughly jostled and cut by showers of stones; and the doors were broken open. The crowd burst tumultuously into the hotel, and the rooms were soon swarming with men drinking the liquors and searching for Bentley, who, however, had already escaped on a swift horse to the camp. As the noise and disorder increased, a man placed a handful of paper and rags against the wooden walls of the bowling alley, deliberately struck a match, and set fire to the place. The diggers now deserted the hotel and retired to a safe distance, in order to watch the conflagration. Meanwhile a company of soldiers had set out from the camp for the scene of the riot, and on their approach the crowd quietly dispersed; but by this time the hotel was reduced to a heap of smouldering ruins.

8. Conviction of Rioters.—For this outrage three men were apprehended and taken to Melbourne, where they were tried and sentenced to imprisonment. But Bentley was also re-arrested and tried, and as his friend Dewes could on this occasion be of no assistance to him, he was sentenced to three years of hard labour on the roads. Dewes was dismissed from the magistracy, and Sir Charles Hotham did everything in his power to conciliate the diggers. They were not to be thus satisfied, however, and held a stormy meeting at Ballarat, in which they appointed a deputation, consisting of Kennedy, Humffray, and Black, to demand from the Governor the release of the three men condemned for burning Bentley's Hotel. Hotham received them kindly, but declined to accept their message, because, he said, the word "demand" was not a suitable term to use in addressing the representative of Her Majesty. As the diggers were haughty, and refused to alter the phrase, the Governor intimated that, under these circumstances, no reply could be given. The delegates having returned to Ballarat, a great meeting was held, and Kennedy, Humffray, Black, Lalor, and Vern made inflammatory speeches, in which they persuaded the diggers to pass a resolution, declaring they would all burn their licences and pay no more fees.

9. Insurrection at Ballarat.—Skirmishes between the soldiers and diggers now became frequent; and, on the 30th of November, when the last "digger hunt" took place, the police and soldiers were roughly beaten off. The diggers, among their tents, set up a flagstaff, and hoisted a banner of blue, with four silver stars in the corner. Then the leaders knelt beneath it, and, having sworn to defend one another to the death, proceeded to enrol the miners and form them into squads ready for drilling. Meantime the military camp was being rapidly fortified with trusses of hay, bags of corn, and loads of firewood. The soldiers were in hourly expectation of an attack, and for four successive nights they slept fully accoutred, and with their loaded muskets beside them. All night long lights were seen to move busily backwards and forwards among the diggers' tents, and the solid tread of great bodies of men could be heard amid the darkness. Lalor was marshalling his forces on the slopes of Ballarat, and drilling them to use such arms as they possessed—whether rifles, or pistols, or merely spikes fastened at the ends of poles.

10. The Eureka Stockade.—Sir Charles Hotham now sent up the remaining eight hundred soldiers of the Ninety-ninth

Regiment, under Sir Robert Nickle, and to these he added all the marines from the men-of-war and nearly all the police of the colony. They were several days on the march, and only arrived when the disturbance was over. The diggers had formed an entrenchment, called the Eureka Stockade, and had enclosed about an acre of ground with a high slab fence. In the midst of this stronghold they proclaimed the "Republic of Victoria"; and here they were able to carry on their drilling unmolested, under the command of the two leaders—Vern, a German, and Peter Lalor, the son of an Irish gentleman. They sent out parties in every direction to gather all the arms and ammunition they could obtain, and made extensive preparations for an assault; but, imagining that the soldiers would never dream of attacking them until the arrival of Sir Robert Nickle, they kept guard but carelessly. Captain Thomas—who commanded the troops in the camp—determined to finish the affair by a sudden attack; and, on Saturday night, whilst the diggers were amusing themselves in fancied security, he was carefully making his preparations. On Sunday morning, just after daybreak, when the stockade contained only two hundred men, Captain Thomas led his troops quietly forth, and succeeded in approaching within three hundred yards of the stockade without being observed. The alarm was then given within; the insurgents rushed to their posts, and poured a heavy volley upon the advancing soldiers, of whom about twelve fell. The attacking party wavered a moment, but again became steady, and fired with so calm and correct an aim, that, whenever a digger showed himself, even for a moment, he was shot. Peter Lalor rose on a sand heap within the stockade to direct his men, but immediately fell, pierced in the shoulder by a musket ball. After the firing had lasted for twenty minutes there was a lull; and the insurgents could hear the order "Charge!" ring out clearly. Then there was an ominous rushing sound—the soldiers were for a moment seen above the palisades, and immediately the conflict became hand-to-hand. The diggers took refuge in the empty claims, where some were bayoneted and others captured, whilst the victors set fire to the tents, and soon afterwards retired with 125 prisoners. A number of half-burnt palisades, which had fallen on Lalor, concealed him from view; and, after the departure of the soldiers, he crawled forth, and escaped to the ranges, where a doctor was found, who amputated his arm. The Government subsequently offered a reward of £500 for his capture; but his friends proved true, and preserved him till the trouble was all past.

The number of those who had been wounded was never exactly known, but it was found that twenty-six of the insurgents had died during the fight, or shortly afterwards; and in the evening the soldiers returned and buried such of the dead bodies as were still lying within the stockade. On the following day, four soldiers who had been killed in the engagement were buried with military honours. Many of the wounded died during the course of the following month, and in particular the colony had to lament the loss of Captain Wise, of the Fortieth Regiment, who had received his death wound in the conflict.

11. Trial of the Rioters.—When the news of the struggle and its issue was brought to Melbourne, the sympathies of the people were powerfully roused in favour of the diggers. A meeting, attended by about five thousand persons, was held near Prince's Bridge, and a motion, proposed by Mr. David Blair, in favour of the diggers, was carried almost unanimously. Similar meetings were held at Geelong and Sandhurst, so that there could be no doubt as to the general feeling against the Government; and when, at the beginning of 1855, thirteen of the prisoners were brought up for trial in Melbourne, and each in his turn was acquitted, crowds of people, both within and without the courts, greeted them, one after another, with hearty cheers as they stepped out into the open air, once more free men.

12. Improvements on the Goldfields.—The commission appointed by Sir Charles Hotham commenced its labours shortly after the conclusion of the riot, and in its report the fact was clearly demonstrated that the miners had suffered certain grievances. Acting upon the advice of this commission, the Legislative Council abolished the monthly fee, and authorised the issue of "Miners' Rights," giving to the holders, on payment of one pound each per annum, permission to dig for gold in any part of the colony. New members were to be elected to the Council, in order to watch over the interests of the miners, two to represent

Sandhurst, two for Ballarat, two for Castlemaine, and one each for the Ovens and the Avoca Diggings. Any man who held a "Miner's Right" was thereby qualified to vote in the elections for the Council.

These were very just and desirable reforms, and the Government added to the general satisfaction by appointing the most prominent of the diggers to be justices of the peace on the goldfields. Thus the colony very rapidly returned to its former state of peaceful progress, and the goldfields were soon distinguished for their orderly and industrious appearance.

CHAPTER XIV.

NEW SOUTH WALES, 1851-1860.

1. Effects of Gold Discovery.—For some years after 1851 the colony of New South Wales passed through a severe ordeal. The separation of Port Phillip had reduced her population by one-fourth and decreased her wealth by fully a third; the discoveries of gold at Ballarat and Bendigo had deprived her of many of her most desirable colonists. But the resources of the colony were too vast to allow of more than a merely temporary check, and, after a year or two, her progress was steady and marked. The gloomy anticipations with which the gold discoveries had been regarded by the squatters and employers of labour were by no means realised; for though men were for a time scarce, and wages exceedingly high, yet, when the real nature of a gold-digger's life and the meagreness of the average earnings became apparent, the great majority of the miners returned to their ordinary employments and the colony resumed its former career of steady progress, though with this difference, that the population was greater, and business consequently brisker than it had ever been before.

Fortune, however, had given to Victoria so great an impetus in 1851, that the firm prosperity of New South Wales was completely lost sight of in the brilliant success of its younger neighbour. The yield of gold in New South Wales was never great as compared with that of Victoria; for, with the exception of 1852, no year produced more than two million pounds worth. But the older colony learnt more and more to utilise its immense area in the growth of wool, an industry which yielded greater and more permanent wealth than has ever been gained from gold mining.

2. Governor Denison.—Governor Fitzroy, who had been appointed in 1847, remained eight years in office, and thus was present during the events which made so great a change in the prospects of the colonies. In 1855 he returned to England, and his place was taken by Sir William Denison, who had previously been Governor of Tasmania. In 1854 great excitement had been caused in Sydney by the outbreak of the Crimean War, and the people, in their fear lest they might suddenly receive an unwelcome visit from Russian cruisers, hastened to complete a system of fortifications for the harbour. The new Governor, who had in youth been trained as an officer of the Royal Engineers in England, took a warm interest in the operations. He built a small fortress on an islet in the middle of the harbour, and placed batteries of guns at suitable spots along the shores. The advance of the science of warfare in recent times has left these little fortifications but sorry defences against modern ironclads; but they have since been replaced by some of those improvements in defence which have accompanied the invention of new methods of attack.

3. Constitutional Changes.—The Constitutions which had been framed for the colonies by the Imperial Parliament in 1850 were not expected to be more than temporary. The British Government had wisely determined to allow each of the colonies to frame for itself the Constitution which it deemed most suitable to its requirements, and had instructed the Legislative Councils which were elected in 1851 to report as to the wishes of their respective colonies. In Sydney the Council entrusted the framing of the new Constitution to a committee, which decided to adopt the English system of government by two Houses—the one to represent the people as a whole, the other to watch over the interests of those who, by their superior wealth, might be supposed to have more than an ordinary stake in the welfare of the country. It was very quickly arranged that the popular House should consist of not less than fifty-four members, to be elected by men who paid a small rental, or possessed property of a certain annual value. But with regard to the nature of the Upper House, it was much more difficult to come to a decision. Wentworth proposed that the Queen should establish a colonial peerage to form a small House of Lords, holding their seats by hereditary right ; but this idea raised so great an outcry that he made haste to abandon it. Several of the committee were in favour of the scheme, afterwards adopted in Victoria, of making the Upper House elective, while limiting the choice of members to those who possessed at least £5,000 worth of real property. After much discussion, however, it was decided to give to the Governor the power of nominating the members of this chamber, which was to consist of not less than twenty-one persons.

The Legislative Council adopted this scheme, and sent it to England for the assent of the Queen ; they also requested that their Constitution might be still further assimilated to that of Great Britain by the introduction of responsible government, so that the Ministers who controlled the affairs of the colony should be no longer officials appointed or dismissed by the Governor and Secretary of State, but should, in future, be chosen by the Parliament to advise the Governor on all matters of public interest, and should be liable to dismissal from office so soon as the Parliament lost confidence in their ability or prudence. The British Government at once gave its assent to this Constitution, which was accordingly inaugurated in 1856 ; and from that date the political management of New South Wales has been an imitation of that of the British Empire. In 1858 two small modifications were introduced : the Lower House was increased in numbers to sixty-eight members, and the privilege of voting for it was extended to every male person over twenty-one years of age who had dwelt not less than six months in the colony.

4. Floods and Droughts.—From the very commencement of its existence, New South Wales has been subject to the two extremes of heavy floods and dreary periods of drought. The mountains are so near to the coast that the rivers have but short courses, and the descent is so steep that, during rainy seasons, the rush of waters deluges the plains near the sea, causing floods of fatal suddenness. At the same time, the waters are carried off so rapidly that there are no supplies of moisture left to serve for those seasons in which but little rain falls. The districts along the banks of the Hunter, Hawkesbury, and Shoalhaven Rivers have been especially liable to destructive inundations; and, from time to time, the people of Sydney have been obliged to send up lifeboats for the purpose of releasing the unfortunate settlers from the roofs and chimneys of their houses, where they have been forced to seek refuge from the rising waters. The Murrumbidgee also used occasionally to spread out into a great sea, carrying off houses and crops, cattle, and, oftentimes, the people themselves. In 1852 a flood of this description completely destroyed the town of Gundagai, and no less than eighty persons perished, either from drowning or from being exposed to the storm as they clung to the branches of trees.

5. The Dunbar.—A great gloom was cast over the colony in 1857 by the loss of a fine ship within seven miles of the centre of Sydney. The *Dunbar* sailed from Plymouth in that year with about a hundred and twenty people on board, many of them well-known colonists who had visited England, and were now on their way homewards. As the vessel approached the coast, a heavy gale came down from the north-east, and, ere they could reach the entrance to Port Jackson, night had closed around them. In the deep and stormy gloom they beat to and fro for some time, but at length the captain thought it safer to make for Sydney Heads than to toss about on so wild a sea. He brought the vessel close in to the shore in order to search for the entrance, and when against the stormy sky he perceived a break in the black cliffs he steered for the opening. This, however, was not the entrance, but only a hollow in the cliffs, called by the Sydney people the "Gap". The vessel was standing straight in for the rocks, when a mass of boiling surf was observed in the place where they thought the opening was, and ere she could be put about she crashed violently upon the foot of a cliff that frowned ninety feet above; there was a shriek, and then the surf rolled back the fragments and the drowning men. At daybreak the word was given that a ship had been wrecked at the Gap, and during the day thousands of people poured forth from Sydney to view the scene of the disaster. On the following morning it was discovered that there was a solitary survivor, who, having been washed into a hollow in the face of the rock, lay concealed in his place of refuge throughout that dreadful night and all the succeeding day. A young man was found who volunteered to let himself down by a rope and rescue the half-dead seaman.

To prevent the repetition of so sad an occurrence, lighthouses were erected for the guidance of ship captains entering the harbour.

In 1852 the people of Sydney had the satisfaction of inaugurating the first Australian University—a structure whose noble front, magnificent halls, and splendid appointments for the furtherance of science will always do credit to the liberality and high aspirations of the colony. In 1857 the "Australian Museum" was opened, and formed the nucleus of the present excellent collection of specimens. During this period several newspapers sprang into existence, railways began to stretch out from the metropolis, and lines of telegraph united Sydney with the leading cities of the other colonies. In August, 1853, the first mail steamer from England, named the *Chusan*, arrived in Port Jackson, and helped to make the settlers of Australia feel less exiled, as they now could have regular news of their friends and of European events little more than two months old.

CHAPTER XV.

WEST AUSTRALIA, 1829-1890.

1. King George's Sound.—In 1825, when Sir Ralph Darling was appointed Governor of New South Wales, his commission was supposed to extend over all that part of Australia which lies between the 139th meridian and the eastern coast. Not that the whole of this country, or even the twentieth part of it, was occupied by settlers—the region was merely claimed as British territory. But the remainder of Australia, comprising about two-thirds of the continent, had not, as yet, been annexed by any European nation; and when, in 1826, a rumour prevailed that the French were about to occupy that region, the Sydney people were alarmed lest so great a territory should thus be lost for ever to the British Empire; they, therefore, in that year, sent a detachment of soldiers to take formal possession of the country and to found a settlement at King George's Sound. From this early effort, however, no practical result ensued; and, during the few years of its existence, the place continued to be nothing more than a small military station.

2. Swan River.—But, in 1827, an English captain, named Stirling, after having sailed along the western coast, gave a most favourable account of a large river he had seen on his voyage. He was not the first discoverer of this river, which, as early as 1697, had been visited by a Dutch navigator, named Vlaming, who was sailing in quest of a man-of-war supposed to have been wrecked on these shores. Vlaming had seen this stream, and, astonished by the wonderful sight of thousands of jet black swans on its surface, had given to it the name of Swan River. But it had remained unthought of till Captain Stirling, by his report, awakened a warm and hopeful interest in this district.

Shortly afterwards the British Government resolved to found a colony on the banks of this river, and Captain Fremantle arrived as the pioneer of the intended settlement. When he landed on the shore, he found that a nearer view of the country was far from realising the expectations formed by those who had viewed it merely from the open sea. He began to have forebodings, but it was now too late—the ships, containing eight hundred of the first settlers, were already close at hand; and, in the course of a week or two, after narrowly escaping shipwreck on the reefs along the shore, they landed Captain Stirling, the first Governor, with his little band, on the wilderness of Garden Island. Here, in this temporary abode, the colonists remained for several months— sheltering themselves in fragile tents, or in brushwood huts, from the rough blasts and the rains that beat in from the winter storms of the Indian Ocean. Exploring parties set out from time to time to examine the adjoining mainland; but, however fair it seemed from a distance, they found it to be merely a sandy region, covered with dense and scrubby thickets. The only port was at a place called Fremantle, where there was but little shelter from the storms of the open ocean; and the only place suitable for a town was several miles up the Swan River, where the waters expand into broad but shallow lagoons. Here the colonists determined to build their city, to which they gave the name of Perth. But the site was not favourable to enterprise; an impassable bar stretched across the mouth of the river, which was, therefore, inaccessible to vessels. The goods of the colonists had to be landed on an exposed beach at Fremantle, and then carried overland through miles of sand and scrub.

In 1830 about a thousand new immigrants arrived; and towards the end of this year the colonists succeeded in settling down in their new homes at Perth.

3. Land Grants.—Most of these immigrants were attracted to Western Australia by the prospect of obtaining large estates; they knew how valuable land was in the well-settled countries of Europe, and, when they heard of square miles in Australia to be had for a few pounds, they were captivated by the notion of so easily becoming great landed proprietors. But the value of land depends upon surrounding circumstances, and ten acres in England may be worth more than a whole wilderness in West Australia. At that time foolish notions were in every quarter prevalent as to what could be done by means of land. The British Government thought it possible to make the colony self-supporting by paying for everything with grants which cost it nothing, but which would be readily accepted by others as payment. Thus the Governor, instead of his yearly salary, was to receive a hundred thousand acres, and all the officials were to be paid in the same manner. The land was distributed in great quantities to people who had no intention of using it, but who expected that, by the progress of colonisation, it would increase enormously in value, and might then be sold for splendid prices.

To induce immigrants to bring with them useful property, the Government offered a bonus of twenty acres for every three pounds worth of goods imported; and the colonists—quite unconscious of the future that lay before them—carried out great numbers of costly, though often unsuitable, articles, by means of which the desired grants were obtained. It was found difficult to convey this property to the town, and much of it was left to rot on the shore, where carriages, pianos, and articles of rich furniture lay half-buried in sand and exposed to the alternations of sun and rain.

114 HISTORY OF AUSTRALIA AND NEW ZEALAND.

PERTH, WESTERN AUSTRALIA, IN 1838.

Splendid horses and cattle of the finest breed had been brought out, but they wandered useless in the bush. For, till

Perth, 1890.

the country was surveyed, nothing could be done in the way of agriculture; and, even after the surveys were completed, owing to a regulation that those whose grants exceeded a square mile should be allowed the first choice, all the sections nearest to the town were obtained by officials and wealthy speculators, who had no intention of using them. Many of these persons held a district almost as large as an English county, and, therefore, the lands remaining for selection by farmers and small purchasers were generally far in the interior. The sections were pointed out on the maps, but the places themselves had never been trodden by a white man's foot, and were held by tribes of hostile savages. Some, indeed, tried to settle upon these distant regions, but they were lonely and isolated, and many of them perished, either from disease and hunger, or by the spears of the natives. Yet there were very few who made any attempt at agriculture, and the costly ploughs and implements that had been imported lay rusting on the beach. The horses and cattle died off, the sheep that had been introduced at great expense were almost all killed through feeding on a poisonous plant, which grew in patches over the country; and the men themselves were forced to loiter at Perth, consuming their provisions and chafing at their ruinous inaction.

4. Mr. Peel.—There was one gentleman who had spent fifty thousand pounds in bringing with him to the colony everything that could be required for farming and sheep-breeding on a magnificent scale. He brought with him three hundred labourers; but the land was by no means so fertile as he had imagined, and he had scarcely commenced his farming operations when he found that his only escape from ruin was to enter, single-handed, on the self-dependent life of the ordinary settler.

5. Gloomy Prospects.—Matters grew worse and worse, and those of the disappointed colonists who had sufficient prudence to start before their means were all exhausted either returned to Europe or sought the other colonies, where several achieved success—notably the brothers Henty, who settled at Launceston and established at Portland Bay the whaling station already mentioned. The gloomy reports of those who reached England prevented any further accession of immigrants, and in 1835 it was rumoured, though erroneously, that the British Government intended to abandon the place.

In the following year (1836) the colony of South Australia was founded; and a great extent of territory previously marked as belonging to West Australia was assigned to the new settlement. These two colonies, during their early years, experienced trials and difficulties of the same kind; but while South Australia, in a short time, emerged to a career of brilliant prosperity through sturdy determination to make the land productive, West Australia for forty years never enjoyed more than a transitory gleam of success.

6. Introduction of Convicts.—This little improvement consisted of a message received from Earl Grey in 1848 asking the settlers if they were willing to accept convicts in their midst. The other colonies had refused them, but it was thought not unlikely that West Australia might be glad to get them. Opinions were divided as to the reply which ought to be given: while some were averse to the idea, others believed that the money sent out by the British Government to maintain the convicts and soldiers would originate a trade which might give to the colony new life and fresh prospects. These arguments prevailed, and in 1849 the first shipload of convicts arrived. From time to time new gangs were received, and the place began to be much more populous than before. The shopkeepers in Perth became rich, and the farmer squatters of the surrounding districts found a ready market for their produce. Yet this success was only partial; and there was nothing which might be said to constitute general prosperity. In the little town of Fremantle, the few and scattered houses had still a rural aspect, and the streets echoed to the sound of no commercial bustle. In Perth the main street was still a grassy walk, shaded by avenues of trees, and even in the business quarter the houses stood each in the midst of its spacious garden.

7. Evils of Convictism.—West Australia had now to suffer the consequences of having become a penal settlement. Many of the convicts, on being liberated, took up their abode in the colony; but their dispositions were seldom either amiable or virtuous, and from the vices of these men the whole population began to lose character in the eyes of other countries. A large number of the prisoners were no sooner liberated than they set off for the goldfields in the eastern colonies, which thus began to share in the evils of convictism. These colonies were not inclined to suffer long in this manner; and, to defend themselves, they refused admission to any person who came from West Australia, unless he could show that he had never been a convict. Thus the colony at Swan River was branded, and held to be contaminated; no free immigrants sought its shores, and many of its best inhabitants departed.

This stigma continued to rest on West Australia until the year 1868, when the transportation of criminals from Great Britain altogether ceased, and the colony no longer received its periodical supply of convicts. Since that time it has, in a great measure, retrieved its character; it is now doing what it can to attract free immigrants, and offers large tracts of pastoral land at low rentals, while the farming classes are attracted by free selection at only ten shillings an acre, with ten years in which to pay it. It has joined Perth to Albany by a good railway, and several branch railways have been constructed, as well as a large number of telegraph lines; and at Albany, the town on King George's Sound, it has established a coaling depôt for the mail steamers on their way to Adelaide, Melbourne, and Sydney. But West Australia is still what it was called twenty years ago, "the giant skeleton of a colony," consisting of about forty thousand people, scattered over a hundred thousand square miles of territory, behind which stretches a vast region of unexplored wilderness. There is every indication, however, that its progress in the near future will be rapid. Up to 1870 it formed what was called a Crown colony: the people had no voice in their own government; their affairs were managed for them by the officers of the English Government. At that date, however, when transportation was abolished, the colony was promoted to the partial management of its own affairs, and the people began periodically to elect a Legislative Council. In 1890 it was still further promoted, being raised to the full dignity of an independent colony, having, like the other colonies of Australia, a Parliament of two Houses, with power to make and unmake its own laws as it pleases. Perth is now rapidly increasing, and the colony is on the eve of its palmy days.

CHAPTER XVI.

QUEENSLAND, 1823-1890.

1. Moreton Bay.—When Captain Cook, in 1770, sailed into the wide opening of Moreton Bay, several of his friends on board observed the sea to be paler than usual, and formed the opinion that, if a careful search were made along the shores, it would be found that a large river fell into the sea somewhere in the neighbourhood. Cook attached so little weight to this idea that he did not stay to make any examination; and when, about twenty years later, Captain Flinders surveyed the same bay, he saw no trace of a river, though he made special search for one.

But the reports of both these travellers were subsequently found to be erroneous; for, in 1823, when Governor Brisbane sent the discoverer Oxley, in the *Mermaid*, to select a place for a new convict station in the northern district of New South Wales, Moreton Bay was found to receive the waters of a large and important river. His success was, at least in part, due to accident. Among the blacks, on the shores of the bay, was a naked man, who was seen to be white. This man was taken on board. He had sailed in an open boat from Sydney, with three others, about a year before, but had been driven by gales out to sea and far to the north. They had landed and had been well received by the blacks. The rest had started to walk along the shore to Sydney, but one man, named Pamphlett, had remained with the natives; and it was he who now was rescued by Oxley, to whom he gave the information that, when roving inland with the tribe among whom he was living, he had seen a fine river of fresh water. Under the guidance of Pamphlett, Oxley left his little vessel in the bay, and with a boat entered upon the broad current of the stream. Before sunset he had ascended about twenty miles, and had been delighted by the richness of the scenery and the magnificence of the timber. On the following day he proceeded thirty miles farther up, and throughout the whole distance found the stream to be broad and of sufficient depth to be navigable for vessels of considerable size. Oxley was justly proud of his discovery, and wished to penetrate still farther into the forests that lay beyond; but his boat's crew had been so exhausted by their long row under a burning sun that he could go no farther, and found it necessary to turn and glide with the current down to his vessel, which he reached late on the fourth night. To the stream he had thus discovered he gave the name of the Brisbane River.

2. Convict Station.—On his return he recommended this district as a suitable position for the new convict station, and during the following year (1824) he was sent to form the settlement. With a small party, consisting of convicts and their guards, he landed at Redcliff, now known as Humpy Bong, a peninsula which juts out into Moreton Bay a few miles above the mouth of the Brisbane. Here the settlement remained for a few months, but afterwards it was moved twenty miles up the river to that pleasant bend which is now occupied by the city of Brisbane. Here, under Captain Logan, the first permanent commandant of the settlement, large stone barracks for the soldiers were erected, and lines of gaols and other buildings for the convicts. And in these for twelve or fourteen years the lonely community dwelt—about a thousand twice-convicted prisoners, and a party of soldiers and officials to keep them in order. No free person was allowed to approach within fifty miles of the settlement, unless with special permission, which was very sparingly granted. The place was a convict settlement of the harshest type; and stern were the measures of that relentless commandant, Captain Logan, who flogged and hanged the unfortunate people under his charge until he became hated with a deadly hatred. He was an active explorer, and did much to open up the interior country, till at length, on a trip in which he was accompanied only by some convicts, they glutted their vengeance by spearing him and battering his head with a native tomahawk.

3. The Squatters.—For thirteen years the settlement was not affected by anything that went on in that outside world from which it was so completely excluded. But in 1840 the onward progress of squatting enterprise brought free men with sheep and cattle close to Moreton Bay. That fine district, discovered by Allan Cunningham in 1827, and called by him the Liverpool Plains, had almost immediately attracted squatters, who by degrees filled up the whole of the available land, and those who were either new-comers, or who found their flocks increasing too fast for the size of their runs, were forced to move outward, and, as a rule, northward. It was about the year 1840 that the pioneers entered that fine tableland district called by Allan Cunningham, in 1829, the Darling Downs, and when the year 1844 was ended there were at least forty squatters over the Queensland borders, with nearly 200,000 sheep and 60,000 cattle, and with many hundreds of shepherds and stockmen to attend them.

4. A Free Settlement.—Whilst the squatters were gathering all round, a change took place at Brisbane itself. We have seen that about 1840 the English Government had resolved to discontinue transportation, except to Van Diemen's Land. The word, therefore, went forth that Brisbane was no longer to be a place of exile for criminals. It was to be the home of free men and the capital of a new district. In 1841 Governor Sir George Gipps arrived from Sydney, and laid out the plan of what is now a handsome city. Blocks of land were offered for sale to free settlers, and eagerly bought. The Governor also laid out a little town, now called Ipswich, farther inland. Meanwhile the township of Drayton, and that which is now much larger, Toowoomba, began to gather round two wayside inns established for the convenience of travellers. Captain Wickham was sent up to assume the position of Superintendent of Moreton Bay, which thus became practically a new colony, just as Port Phillip was in the south, though both were then regarded as only districts of New South Wales.

5. The Natives.—In these early years the squatters of the district were scattered, at wide intervals, throughout a great extent of country, and, being in the midst of native tribes who were not only numerous but of a peculiarly hostile disposition, they often found themselves in a very precarious situation. The blacks swarmed on the runs, killing the sheep, and stealing the property of the squatters, who had many annoyances to suffer and injuries to guard against. But their retaliation oftentimes exhibited a ferocity and inhumanity almost incredible in civilised men.

The Government troopers showed little compunction in destroying scores of natives, and, strange to say, the most inhuman atrocities were committed by blacks, who were employed to act as troopers. On one occasion, after the murder of a white man by two blacks, a band of troopers, in the dead of night, stealthily surrounded the tribe to which the murderers belonged, whilst it was holding a corrobboree, and, at a given signal, fired a volley into the midst of the dancing crowd—a blind and ruthless revenge, from which, however, the two murderers escaped. On another occasion the shepherds and hutkeepers out on a lonely plain had begun to grow afraid of the troublesome tribes in the neighbourhood, and cunningly made them a present of flour, in which white arsenic had been mixed. Half a tribe might then have been seen writhing and howling in the agony of this frightful poison till death relieved them. On such occasions the black tribes took a terrible revenge when they could, and so the hatred of black for white and white for black became stronger and deadlier.

BOOMERANGS, OR KYLIES.

6. Separation.—In less than five years after the removal of convicts the district began to agitate for separation from New South Wales; and, in 1851, a petition was sent to the Queen, urging the right of Moreton Bay to receive the same concession as had, in that year, been made to Port Phillip. On this occasion their request was not granted, but, on being renewed about three years later, it met with a very favourable reception; and, in the following year, an Act was passed by the Imperial Parliament giving to the British Government power to constitute the new colony. Again, as in the case of Port Phillip, delays occurred; and, in 1856, a change of Ministry caused the matter to be almost forgotten. It was not until the year 1859 that the territory to the north of the twenty-ninth parallel of latitude was proclaimed a separate colony, under the title of QUEENSLAND.

In the December of that year Sir George F. Bowen, the first

PARLIAMENT HOUSE, BRISBANE.

Governor, arrived; and the little town of Brisbane, with its 7,000 inhabitants, was raised to the dignity of being a capital, the seat of government of a territory containing more than 670,000 square miles, though inhabited by only 25,000 persons. A few months later Queensland received its Constitution, which differed but little from that of New South Wales. There were established two Houses of Legislature, one consisting of members nominated by the Governor, and the other elected by the people.

7. Gold.—In 1858 it was reported that gold had been discovered far to the north, on the banks of the Fitzroy River, and in a short time many vessels arrived in Keppel Bay, their holds and decks crowded with men, who eagerly landed and hastened to

Canoona, a place about sixty or seventy miles up the river. Ere long there were about fifteen thousand diggers on the scene; but it was soon discovered that the gold was confined to a very small area, and by no means plentiful; and those who had spent all their money in getting to the place were in a wretched plight. A large population had been hurriedly gathered in an isolated region, without provisions, or the possibility of obtaining them; their expectations of the goldfield had been disappointed, and for some time the Fitzroy River was one great scene of misery and starvation till the Governments of New South Wales and Victoria sent vessels to convey the unfortunate diggers away from the place. Some, however, in the extremity of the famine, had selected portions of the fertile land on the banks of the river, and had begun to cultivate them as farms. They were pleased with the district, and, having settled down on their land, founded what is now the thriving city of Rockhampton.

A great amount of success, however, attended a subsequent effort in 1867. The Government of Queensland offered rewards, varying from two hundred to a thousand pounds, for the discovery of paying goldfields. The result was that during the course of the next two or three years many districts were opened up to the miner. Towards the end of 1867 a man named Nash, who had been wandering in an idle way over the country, found an auriferous region of great extent at Gympie, about 130 miles from Brisbane. He concealed his discovery for a time, and set to work to collect as much of the gold as possible, before attracting others to the spot. In the course of a day or two he gathered several hundred pounds worth of gold, being, however, often disturbed in his operations by the approach of travellers on the adjacent road, when he had to crouch among the bushes, until the footsteps died away and he could again pursue his solitary task. After some time it seemed impossible to avoid discovery; and lest any one should forestall him in making known the district, he entered Maryborough, not far away, announced his discovery, and received the reward. A rush took place to the Gympie, which was found to be exceedingly rich, and it was not long before a nugget worth about four thousand pounds was met with close to the surface.

Far to the north, on the Palmer River, a tributary of the

Mitchell, there have been discovered rich goldfields, where, in spite of the great heat and dangers from the blacks, there are crowds of diggers at work. Many thousands of Chinamen have settled down in the district, and to these the natives seem to have a special antipathy, as they spear them on every possible occasion.

But all the stories which Australia offers of gold-digging romance are eclipsed by that of the Mount Morgan Mine. Near Rockhampton, and in the midst of that very district to which the diggers had rushed in 1858, but in which they had starved through being unable to find gold, a young squatter bought from the Government of Queensland a selection of 640 acres. It was on a rocky hill, so barren that he considered it useless, and was glad to sell it for £640 to three brothers of the name of Morgan. These gentlemen were lucky enough to find out that the dirty grey rocks of which the hill was composed were very richly mixed with gold, so that twenty or thirty pounds worth of gold could be got by crushing and washing every cart-load of rock. They immediately set to work, and before long showed that they were the possessors of the richest gold mine in the world. A year or two later the hill was sold at a price equivalent to eight millions of pounds, and it is now reckoned that it contains gold to the value of at least double that sum. What a strange adventure for the man who owned it and reckoned it worth almost nothing!

8. Cotton.—Throughout most of the colony the climate is either tropical or semi-tropical, and it is therefore, in its more fertile parts, well suited to the growth of cotton and sugar. About the year 1861 the cultivation of the cotton plant was commenced on a small scale; but, although the plantations were found to thrive, yet the high rate of wages which prevailed in Queensland, and the low price of cotton in Europe, caused the first attempts to be very unprofitable.

Matters were changed, however, in 1863, for then a great civil war was raging in America; and as the people of the Southern States were prevented, by the long chain of blockading vessels stationed by the Northern States along their coasts, from sending their cotton to Europe, there was a great scarcity of cotton in England, and its price rose to be exceedingly high. This was a favourable opportunity for Queensland. The plantations were, of course, still as expensive as ever, but the handsome prices obtained for the cotton not only covered this great expense, but also left considerable profits. The cultivation of the sugar cane was introduced in 1865, and, after a few years had passed away, great fields of waving cane were to be seen in various parts of the country, growing ripe and juicy beneath the tropical sun.

9. Polynesian Labour.—The prices of cotton and sugar remained high for some years; but when the American Civil War was over they fell to their former rates, and the planters of Queensland found it necessary to obtain some cheaper substitute for their white labourers. At first it was proposed to bring over Hindoos from India, but nothing came of this idea; and afterwards, when Chinese were introduced, they were not

VICTORIA BRIDGE, BRISBANE.

found to give the satisfaction expected. But it happened that one of the planters, named Robert Towns, was the owner of a number of ships which traded to the South Sea Islands, and having persuaded a few of the islanders to cross to Queensland, he employed them on his sugar plantation. He took some little trouble in teaching them the work he wished them to do, and found that they soon became expert at it. As the remuneration they required was very small, they served admirably to supply the necessary cheap labour.

The practice of employing these South Sea Islanders, or "Kanakas," as they were called, soon became general, and parts of Queensland had all the appearance of the American plantations, where crowds of dusky figures, decked in the brightest of colours, plied their labours with laughter and with song, among the tall cane brakes or the bursting pods of cotton. The "Kanakas" generally worked for a year or two in the colony, then, having received a bundle of goods—consisting of cloth, knives, hatchets, beads, and so forth, to the value of about £10—they were again conveyed to their palm-clad islands. A system of this kind was apt to give rise to abuses, and it was found that a few of the more unscrupulous planters, not content with the ordinary profits, stooped to the shameful meanness of cheating the poor islander out of his hard-earned reward. They hurried him on board a vessel, and sent after him a parcel containing a few shillings worth of property; then, when he reached his home, he found that all his toil and his years of absence from his friends had procured him only so much trash.

Happily, this was not of very frequent occurrence; but there was another abuse both common and glaring. As the plantations in Queensland increased, they required more labourers than were willing to leave their homes in the South Sea Islands; and, as the captains of vessels were paid by the planters a certain sum of money for every "Kanaka" they brought over, there was a strong temptation to carry off the natives by force, when, by other means, a sufficient number could not be obtained. There were frequent conflicts between the crews of labour vessels and the inhabitants of the islands. The white men burnt the native villages, and carried off crowds of men and women; while, in revenge, the islanders often surprised a vessel and massacred its crew; and in such cases the innocent suffered for the guilty. The sailors often had the baseness to disguise themselves as missionaries, in order the more easily to effect their purpose; and when the true missionaries, suspecting nothing, approached the natives on their errand of good will, they were speared or clubbed to death by the unfortunate islanders. But, as a rule, the "Kanakas" were themselves the sufferers; the English vessels pursued their frail canoes, ran them down, and sank them; then, while struggling in the sea, the men were seized and thrust into the hold, and the hatches were fastened down. When in this dastardly manner a sufficient number had been gathered together, and the dark interior of the ship was filled with a steaming mass of human beings densely huddled together, the captains set sail for Queensland, where they landed those of their living cargoes who had escaped the deadly pestilence which filth and confinement always engendered in such cases.

10. Polynesian Labourers' Act.—These were the deeds of a few ruthless and disreputable seamen; but the people of Queensland, as a whole, had no sympathy with such barbarities, and in 1868 a law was passed to regulate the labour traffic. It enacted that no South Sea Islanders were to be brought into the colony unless the captain of the vessel could show a document, signed by a missionary or British consul, stating that they had left the islands of their own free will; Government agents were to accompany every vessel, in order to see that the "Kanakas" were well treated on the voyage; and, on leaving the colony, no labourer was to receive less than six pounds worth of goods for every year he had worked.

These regulations were of great use, but they were often evaded; for, by giving a present to the king of an island, the sailors could bribe him to force his people to express their willingness before the missionary. The trembling men were brought forward, and, under the fear of their chief's revenge, declared their perfect readiness to sail. Sometimes the Government agents on board the vessels were bribed not to report the misdeeds of the sailors; and in the case of the *Jason*, on which the agent was too honest to be so bribed, he was chained below by the captain, on the pretence that he was mad. When the ship arrived in Queensland, the unfortunate man was found in a most miserable state of filth and starvation. For this offence the captain was arrested, tried, and imprisoned. Whatever regulations may be made, a traffic of this sort will occasionally have its dark and ugly features, yet it may be truly enough said that while the "Kanakas" have been of great service to Queensland, the colony has also been of service to them. The islanders are generally glad to be taken; they have better food and easier lives on the plantations than they have in their homes; they gather a trunkful of property such as passes for great wealth in the islands, and when they are sent home, after two years' absence, to their palms and coral shores, it is in full costume, generally in excellent spirits, and always more or less civilised. Sometimes, poor fellows, they are stripped and plundered by their naked relatives, but at any rate they help, by what they have learnt, to improve the style of life in those native groves, so sunny but so full of superstition and barbarous rites.

11. Present State of the Colony.—In 1868 Sir George Bowen was sent to govern New Zealand, and Governor Blackall took charge of affairs in Queensland. He was a man of fine talents, and amiable character, and was greatly respected by the colonists; but he died not long after his arrival, and was succeeded by the Marquis of Normanby, who, in his turn, was succeeded, in 1874, by Mr. Cairns. Sir Arthur Kennedy, in 1877, Sir Anthony Musgrave, in 1883, Sir Arthur Hunter Palmer, in 1888, and General Sir H. Wylie Norman bring the list of Governors to the present year (1894).

Queensland possesses magnificent resources, which have only recently been made known, and are now in process of development. Her exports of gold exceed two million pounds a year; she produces large quantities of tin, copper, silver, and other minerals. The wool clipped from her sheep exceeds one million four hundred thousand pounds in annual value; and her total exports, including cotton, sugar, and other tropical productions, amount to about six million pounds per annum. The population is now about half a million, and immigrants continue to arrive at the rate of about sixteen thousand a year. Though the youngest of the Australian colonies, Queensland now ranks fourth on the list, and appears to have a most promising future before her. Her cotton industry has almost vanished, and her sugar plantations have passed through troublous times, but there seem to be good hopes for them in the future. However, it will be in the raising of sheep and of cattle, as well as in gold-mining, that the colony will have to look for her most permanent resources. She has now nearly twenty million sheep and six million cattle, and sends wool, tallow, hides, and frozen meat to England, while she supplies prime bullocks for the Melbourne Market.

12. The Aborigines.—Australian history practically begins with the arrival of the white man, for before that time, though tribe fought with tribe and there were many doings of

GOVERNMENT HOUSE, BRISBANE.

savage men, there is nothing that could be told as a general story. Each tribe of from twenty to a couple of hundred dusky forms wandered over the land, seeking animals to hunt and fresh water to drink. They were very thinly spread, not more than one person to ten square miles, yet every little tribe was at deadly feud with its neighbour.

The tribe wandered over the grassy and park-like lands, the men stalking ahead with spears and boomerang in hand; the women trudging behind loaded with babies, and utensils. At evening they camp and the men put up frail break-winds, consisting of a few branches and leafy tufts; behind this on the sheltered side a few leaves made a bed. Meantime the fire was lit close by, and soon a dozen little columns of blue smoke curl up among the trees. The opossum, or duck, or wallaby is soon cooked or half-cooked; the men devour as much as they want and pass on the remains to the women and children. A frog or two and a lizard, or a few grubs taken out of decayed timber, or perhaps a few roots that have been dug up on the march by the women, form a sort of dessert. After dusk there is the sound of chatter round the fires; then all retire to rest, with the glowing embers of the fires to give them warmth. At daybreak all are awake. If there is food at hand they may stay in the same camp for weeks together, but if not they journey on.

Each man had as many wives as he could obtain. He did not support them, but they supported him, and when children became too numerous he lessened his family by killing off a few. More than half the children were thus destroyed. Their enjoyments consisted of games with a kind of ball, and mock-fights, but especially in a wild dance they called the corrobboree. They were in general good-humoured when things went pleasantly; but a man would spear his wife through the leg or dash his child's brains out readily enough when things were not to his taste, and nobody would think any the worse of him for it.

CHAPTER XVII.

EXPLORATIONS IN THE INTERIOR, 1840-1860.

1. Progress of Exploration.—The coasts of Australia had all been examined before the year 1815. From that date those who wished to make fresh discoveries were obliged to penetrate into the interior; and we have already seen that, previous to the year 1836, explorers were busy in opening up the south-east portion of the continent. Oxley had made known the northern districts of New South Wales, and Allan Cunningham the southern part of what is now the colony of Queensland. Hume and Hovell, Sturt and Mitchell, had traversed the southern districts of New South Wales and the territory now occupied by Victoria. Following closely in the footsteps of these intrepid discoverers, the squatters had entered all these districts, and, wherever the land was suitable, had settled down with their flocks; so that, ere long, all that corner of Australia which would be cut off by drawing a straight line from Brisbane to Adelaide was fully surveyed. But there still remained to be explored about seven-eighths of the continent; and from this date onward there was an unbroken succession of adventurous travellers, who entered the vast central territory for the purpose of making known its nature and capacities. But the manner of conducting an expedition was now very different from what it had been. Previous explorers had been provided with parties of convicts, and had traversed lands for the greater part grassy and well watered. These expeditions had their dangers, arising chiefly from the hostility of the blacks; and Allan Cunningham, his brother Richard, with many others, sacrificed their lives in their ardour for discovery. But subsequent travellers had to encounter, in addition, the pangs of hunger and thirst in that dry and desolate country which occupies so great a portion of Central Australia.

2. Eyre.—The first on this roll of gallant discoverers was Edward John Eyre, who, in 1840, offered to conduct an expedition to the interior. He himself provided about half the money required, the South Australian Government—which was then in difficulties—gave a hundred pounds, and a number of Eyre's personal friends made up the remainder. With five Europeans, three natives, and thirteen horses, and with forty sheep to serve as food on the way, he set out from Adelaide and travelled to the head of Spencer's Gulf, where a small vessel lay waiting to supply them with provisions sufficient for three months. Having traversed forty or fifty miles of desert land, he turned to the west, and came in sight of what he called Lake Torrens. It was now dried up, so that in place of a sheet of water twenty miles broad, he saw only a dreary region covered with glittering salt. When he entered upon it the thin crust of salt broke, and a thick black mud oozed up. The party plunged onward for about six miles, the mud becoming always deeper and deeper, till at length it half covered the saddles of their horses. He was then forced to turn back, and to seek a passage round this lake of mud; but, having followed its shores for many miles, there seemed to be so little prospect of reaching the end of the obstacle, that he turned his course again, from west to north. After travelling about two hundred miles through a very desolate country, he was once more arrested by coming upon a similar sheet of salt-encrusted mud, which he called Lake Eyre. Again there appeared no hope of either crossing the lake or going round it; no water was to be found, and his supplies were fast failing, so that he was forced to hasten back a long distance to the nearest stream. Setting out once more, he twice attempted to penetrate westward into the interior, but, on each occasion, the salt lakes barred his progress, and as a last effort he urged his failing party towards the north-east. Here the country was the most barren and desolate that can be imagined. It was not always so, but after a period of drought, when the grass is burnt to the roots and not a drop of fresh water to be seen in a hundred miles, it has all the appearance of a desert. His supplies of water ran short, and frequently the explorers were on the point of perishing. When they approached the Frome River—a creek which flows northwards into Lake Eyre—they were inexpressibly delighted to view from afar the winding current; but its waters were found to be as salt as the ocean. After a long and dreary journey, Eyre ascended a hill, in order to see if there was any hope of finding better country; but the view was only a great and barren level, stretching far away to the horizon on every side. He had now no water, and his only course was to turn back; so, leaving this place—which he called Mount Hopeless—he retraced his steps to the head of Spencer's Gulf.

3. Australian Bight.—Here he changed the object of his journey, and made efforts to go along the shores of the Great Australian Bight, in order to reach West Australia. Three times he rounded Streaky Bay; but in that bare and desert land the want of water was an insuperable obstacle, and each time he was forced to retreat to less desolate country. Governor Gawler now sent word to him to return to Adelaide, as it seemed madness to make further efforts; but Eyre replied that to go back without having accomplished anything would be a disgrace he could never endure. Seeing that his only chance of reaching West Australia was to push rapidly forward with a simple and light equipment, he sent back the whole of his party except Mr. Baxter, his black servant Wylie, and the other two natives; and taking with him a few horses, carrying a supply of water and provisions for several weeks, he set out to follow the coast along the Great Australian Bight. His party had to scramble along the tops of rough cliffs which everywhere frowned from three hundred to six hundred feet above the sea; and if they left the coast to travel inland they had to traverse great stretches of moving sands, which filled their eyes and ears, covered them when asleep, and, when they sat at meals, made their food unpleasant. But they suffered most from want of water; for often they were obliged to walk day after day beneath a broiling sun when all their water was gone, and not a drop to be seen on the burning soil beneath them. On one occasion, after they had thus travelled 110 miles, the horses fell down from exhaustion, and could not be induced to move. Eyre and a native hastened forward; but, though they wandered for more than eighteen miles, they saw no sign of water, and when darkness came on they lay down, with lips parched and burning, and tossed in feverish slumber till morning. At early dawn they perceived a ridge of sandhills not far away, and making for them they found a number of little wells—places where the natives had dug into the sand for six or eight feet, and so had reached fresh water. Here Eyre and his black companion drank a delicious draught, and hastened back with the precious beverage to revive the horses. The whole party was then able to go forward; and there, around these little waterholes, Eyre halted for a week to refresh his men and animals before attempting another stretch of similar country. They saw some natives, who told them that there was plenty of water farther on, and when Eyre set out again he carried very little with him, so as not to overburden the horses. But after sixty miles of the desert had been traversed without meeting any place in which water was to be found, he became alarmed, and sent back Mr. Baxter with the horses to bring up a better supply, whilst he himself remained to take charge of the baggage. When Baxter returned they all set forward again, and reached a sandy beach, where they had great difficulty in preventing the horses from drinking the sea-water, which would certainly have made them mad. As it was, two of them lay down to die, and part of the provisions had to be abandoned. Baxter now grew despondent, and wished to return; but Eyre was determined not yet to give up. Onward they toiled through the dreary wilderness, and two more horses fell exhausted; 126 miles from the last halting-place, and still no signs of water. Still onward, and the horses continued to drop by the way, Baxter constantly entreating Eyre to return. It was only after a journey of 160 miles that they came to a place where, by digging, they could obtain fresh water in very small quantities. They were now forced to eke out their failing provisions by eating horseflesh. Baxter was altogether disheartened; and, if to return had not been as dangerous as to go forward, Eyre would himself have abandoned the attempt. The three natives, however, were still as light-hearted and merry as ever; whilst the food lasted they were always full of frolic and laughter.

4. Death of Baxter.—Each evening Eyre formed a little camp, loaded the muskets, and laid them down ready for use in case of an attack by the blacks; the horses were hobbled, and set free to gather the little vegetation they could find. But this forced Eyre and Baxter to keep watch by turns, lest they should stray so far as to be lost. One evening when Eyre had taken the first watch, the horses, in their search for grass, had wandered about a quarter of a mile from the camp. He had followed them, and was sitting on a stone beneath the moonlight, musing on his gloomy prospects, when he was startled by a flash and a report. Hastening to the camp, he was met by Wylie, who was speechless with terror, and could only wring his hands and cry: "Oh, massa". When he entered, he saw Baxter lying on his face, whilst the baggage was broken open, and scattered in all directions. He raised the wounded man in his arms, but only in time to support him as his head fell back in death. Then placing the body on the ground, and looking around him, he perceived that two of his natives had plundered the provisions, shot Mr. Baxter as he rose to remonstrate with them, and had then escaped. The moon became obscured, and in the deep gloom, beside the dead body of his friend, Eyre passed a fearful night, peering into the darkness lest the miscreants might be lurking near to shoot him also. He says, in his diary: "Ages can never efface the horrors of that single night, nor would the wealth of the world ever tempt me to go through a similar one". The slowly-spreading dawn revealed the bleeding corpse, the plundered bags, and the crouching form of Wylie, who was still faithful. The ground at this place consisted of a great hard sheet of rock, and there was no chance of digging a grave; so Eyre could only wrap the body in a blanket, leave it lying on the surface, and thus take farewell of his friend's remains.

5. Arrival at King George's Sound.—Then he and Wylie set out together on their mournful journey. They had very little water, and seven days elapsed before they reached a place where more was to be obtained. At intervals they could see the murderers stealthily following their footsteps, and Eyre was afraid to lie down lest his sleep should prove to have no awaking; and thus, with parching thirst by day, and hours of watchfulness by night, he slowly made his way towards King George's Sound. After a time the country became better; he saw and shot two kangaroos, and once more approached the coast. His surprise was great on seeing two boats some distance out at sea. He shouted and fired his rifle, without attracting the attention of the crews. But, on rounding a small cape, he found the vessel to which these boats belonged. It was a French whaling ship; and the two men, having been taken on board, were hospitably entertained for eleven days. Captain Rossiter gave them new clothes and abundance of food; and when they were thoroughly refreshed, they landed to pursue their journey. The country was not now so inhospitable; and three weeks afterwards they stood on the brow of a hill overlooking the little town of Albany, at King George's Sound. Here they sat down to rest; but the people, hearing who they were, came out to escort them triumphantly into the town, where they were received with the utmost kindness. They remained for eleven days, and then set sail for Adelaide, which they reached after an absence of one year and twenty-six days.

This expedition was, unfortunately, through so barren a country that it had but little practical effect beyond the additions it made to our geography; but the perseverance and skill with which it was conducted are worthy of all honour, and Eyre is to be remembered as the first explorer who braved the dangers of the Australian desert.

6. Sturt.—Two years after the return of Eyre, Captain Sturt, the famous discoverer of the Darling and Murray, wrote to Lord Stanley offering to conduct an expedition into the heart of Australia. His offer was accepted; and in May, 1844, a well-equipped party of sixteen persons was ready to start from the banks of the Darling River. Places which Sturt had explored sixteen years before, when they were a deep and unknown solitude, were now covered with flocks and cattle; and he could use, as the starting-place of this expedition, the farthest point he had reached in that of 1828. Mr. Poole went with him as surveyor, Mr. Browne as surgeon, and the draughtsman was Mr. J. M'Douall Stuart, who, in this expedition, received a splendid training for his own great discoveries of subsequent years. Following the Darling, they reached Laidley's Ponds, passed near Lake Cawndilla, and then struck northward for the interior. The country was very bare—one dead level of cheerless desert; and when they reached a few hills which they called Stanley Range, now better known as Barrier Range, Sturt, who ascended to one of the summits, could see nothing hopeful in the prospect. How little did he dream that the hills beneath him were full of silver, and that one day a populous city of miners should occupy the waterless plain in front of him! In this region he had to be very careful how he advanced, for he had with him eleven horses, thirty bullocks, and two hundred sheep, and water for so great a multitude could with difficulty be procured. He had always to ride forward and find a creek or pond of sufficient size, as the next place of encampment, before allowing the expedition to move on; and, as water was often very difficult to find, his progress was but slow. Fortunately for the party, it was the winter season, and a few of the little creeks had a moderate supply of water. But after they had reached a chain of hills, which Sturt called the Grey Range, the warm season was already upon them. The summer of 1844 was one of the most intense on record; and in these vast interior plains of sand, under the fiery glare of the sun, the earth seemed to burn like plates of metal: it split the hoofs of the horses; it scorched the shoes and the feet of the men; it dried up the water from the creeks and pools, and left all the country parched and full of cracks. Sturt spent a time of great anxiety, for the streams around were rapidly disappearing; and, when all the water had been dried up, the prospects of his party would, indeed, be gloomy. His relief was therefore great when Mr. Poole found a creek in a rocky basin, whose waters seemed to have a perennial flow. Sturt moved forward, and formed his depôt beside the stream; and here he was forced to remain for six weeks. For it appeared as though he had entered a trap; the country before him was absolutely without water, so that he could not advance; while the creeks behind him were now only dry courses, and it was hopeless to think of returning. He made many attempts to escape, and struck out into the country in all directions. In one of his efforts, if he had gone only thirty miles farther, he would have found the fine stream of Cooper's Creek, in which there was sufficient water for the party; but hunger and thirst forced him to return to the depôt. He followed down the creek on which they were encamped, but found that, after a course of twenty-nine miles, it lost itself in the sand.

Meantime the travellers passed a summer such as few men have ever experienced. The heat was sometimes as high as 130 deg. in the shade, and in the sun it was altogether intolerable. They were unable to write, as the ink dried at once on their pens; their combs split; their nails became brittle and readily broke, and if they touched a piece of metal it blistered their fingers. In their extremity they dug an underground room, deep enough to be beyond the dreadful furnace-glow above. Here they spent many a long day, as month after month passed without a shower of rain. Sometimes they watched the clouds gather, and they could hear the distant roll of thunder, but there fell not a drop to refresh the dry and dusty desert. The party began to grow thin and weak; Mr. Poole became ill with scurvy, and from day to day he sank rapidly. At length, when winter was again approaching, a gentle shower moistened the plain; and, as the only chance of saving the life of Poole, half of the party was sent to carry him quickly back to the Darling. They had been gone only a few hours when a messenger rode back with the news that he was already dead. The mournful cavalcade returned, bearing his remains, and a grave was dug in the wilderness. A tree close by, on which his initials were cut, formed the only memorial of the hapless explorer.

7. Journey to the Centre.—Shortly afterwards there came a succession of wet days, and, as there was now an abundance of water, the whole party once more set off; having travelled north-west for sixty-one miles farther, they formed a new depôt, and made excursions to explore the country in the neighbourhood. M'Douall Stuart crossed over to Lake Torrens; while Sturt, with Dr. Browne and three men, pushing to the north, discovered the Strzelecki Creek, a stream which flows through very agreeable country. But as they proceeded farther to the north their troubles began again; they came upon a region covered with hill after hill of fiery red sand, amid which lay lagoons of salt and bitter water. They toiled over this weary country in hopes that a change for the better might soon appear; but when they reached the last hill, they had the mortification to see a great plain, barren, monotonous and dreary, stretching with a purple glare as far as the eye could reach on every side. This plain was called by Sturt the "Stony Desert," for, on descending, he found it covered with innumerable pieces of quartz and sandstone, among which the horses wearily stumbled. Sturt wished to penetrate as far as the tropic of Capricorn; but summer was again at hand, their water was failing, and they could find neither stream nor pool. When the madness of any farther advance became apparent, Sturt, with his head buried in his hands, sat for an hour in bitter disappointment. After toiling so far, and reaching within 150 miles of his destination, to be turned back for the want of a little water was a misfortune very hard to bear, and, but for his companions, he would have still gone forward and perished. As they hastened back their water was exhausted, and they were often in danger of being buried by moving hills of sand; but at length they reached the depôt, having traversed 800 miles during the eight weeks of their absence.

It was not long before Sturt started again, taking with him M'Douall Stuart as his companion. On this trip he suffered the same hardships, but had the satisfaction of discovering a magnificent stream, which he called Cooper's Creek. On crossing this creek he again entered the Stony Desert, and was once more compelled reluctantly to retrace his steps. When he reached the depôt he was utterly worn out. He lay in bed for a long time, tenderly nursed by his companions; and, when the whole party set out on its return to the settled districts, he had to be lifted in and out of the dray in which he was carried. As they neared their homes his sight began to fail. The glare of the burning sands had destroyed his eyes, and he passed the remainder of his days in darkness. His reports of the arid country gave rise to the opinion that the whole interior of Australia was a desert; but this was afterwards found to be far from correct.

8. Leichardt.—Allan Cunningham's discoveries extended over the northern parts of New South Wales and the southern districts of Queensland. But all the north-eastern parts of the continent were left unexplored until 1844, when an intrepid young German botanist, named Ludwig Leichardt, made known this rich and fertile country. With five men he started from Sydney, and, passing through splendid forests and magnificent pasture lands, he made his way to the Gulf of Carpentaria, discovering and following up many large rivers—the Fitzroy, with its tributaries—the Dawson, the Isaacs and the Mackenzie; the Burdekin, with several of its branches; then the Mitchell; and, lastly, the Gilbert. He also crossed the Flinders and Albert, without knowing that, a short time previously, these rivers had been discovered and named by Captain Stokes, who was exploring the coasts in a British war-ship. Having rounded the gulf, he discovered the Roper, and followed the Alligator River down to Van Diemen's Gulf, where a vessel was waiting to receive his party. On his return to Sydney the utmost enthusiasm prevailed; for Leichardt had made known a wide stretch of most valuable country. The people of Sydney raised a subscription of £1,500, and the Government rewarded his services with £1,000. Leichardt was of too ardent a nature to remain content with what he had already done; and, in 1847, he again set out to make further explorations in the north of Queensland. On this occasion, however, he was not so successful. He had taken with him great flocks of sheep and goats, and they impeded his progress so much that, after wandering over the Fitzroy Downs for about seven months, he was forced to return. In 1848 he organised a third expedition, to cross the whole country from east to west. He proposed to start from Moreton Bay, and to take two years in traversing the centre of the continent, so as to reach the Swan River settlement. He set out with a large party, and soon reached the Cogoon River, a tributary of the Condamine. From this point he sent to a friend in Sydney a letter, in which he described himself as in good spirits, and full of hope that the expedition would be a success. He then started into the wilderness, and was lost for ever from men's view. For many years parties were, from time to time, sent out to rescue the missing explorers, if perchance they might still be wandering with the blacks in the interior; but no traces of the lost company have ever been brought to light.

9. Mitchell.—Whilst Leichardt was absent on his first journey, Sir Thomas Mitchell—the discoverer of the Glenelg—had prepared an expedition for the exploration of Queensland. Having waited till the return of Leichardt, in order not to go over the same ground, he set out towards the north, and, after discovering the Culgoa and Warrego—two important tributaries of the Darling—he turned to the west. He travelled over a great extent of level country, and then came upon a river which somewhat puzzled him. He followed the current for 150 miles, and it seemed to flow steadily towards the heart of the continent. He thought that its waters must eventually find their way to the sea, and would, therefore, after a time, flow north to the Indian Ocean. If that were the case, the river—which the natives called the Barcoo—must be the largest stream on the northern coast, and he concluded that it was identical with the Victoria, whose mouth had been discovered about nine years before by Captain Stokes. He, therefore, provisionally gave it the name of the Victoria River.

10. Kennedy.—On the return of Mitchell, the further prosecution of exploration in these districts was left to his assistant-surveyor—Edmund Kennedy—who, having been sent to trace the course of the supposed Victoria River, followed its banks for 150 miles below the place where Mitchell had left it. He was then forced to return through want of provisions; but he had gone far enough, however, to show that this stream was only the higher part of Cooper's Creek, discovered not long before by Captain Sturt. This river has a course of about 1,200 miles; and it is, therefore, the largest of Central Australia. But its waters spread out into the broad marshes of Lake Eyre, and are there lost by evaporation.

In 1848 Kennedy was sent to explore Cape York Peninsula. He was landed with a party of twelve men at Rockingham Bay, and, striking inland to the north-west, travelled towards Cape York, where a small schooner was to wait for him. The difficulties met by the explorers were immense; for, in these tropical regions, dense jungles of prickly shrubs impeded their course and lacerated their flesh, while vast swamps often made their journey tedious and unexpectedly long. Thinking there was no necessity for all to endure these hardships, he left eight of his companions at Weymouth Bay, intending to call for them on his way back in the schooner. He was courageously pushing through the jungle towards the north with three men and his black servant Jackey, when one of the party accidentally received a severe gunshot wound, which made it impossible for him to proceed. Kennedy was now only a few miles distant from Cape York; and, leaving the wounded man under the care of the two remaining whites, he started—accompanied by Jackey—to reach the cape and obtain assistance from the schooner. They had not gone far, and were on the banks of the Escape River, when they perceived that their steps were being closely followed by a tribe of natives, whose swarthy bodies, from time to time, appeared among the trees. Kennedy now proceeded warily, keeping watch all around; but a spear, urged by an unseen hand from among the leaves, suddenly pierced his body from behind, and he fell. The blacks rushed forward, but Jackey fired, and at the report they hastily fled. Jackey held up his master's head for a short time, weeping bitterly. Kennedy knew he was dying, and he gave his faithful servant instructions as to the papers he was to carry, and the course he must follow. Not long after this he breathed his last, and Jackey, with his tomahawk, dug a shallow grave for him in the forest. He spread his coat and shirt in the hollow, laid the body tenderly upon them, and covered it with leaves and branches. Then, packing up the journals, he plunged into the creek, along which he walked, with only his head above the surface, until he neared the shore. Hastily making for the north, he reached the cape, where he was taken on board the schooner. This expedition was one of the most disastrous of the inland explorations. The wounded man, and the two who had been left with him, were never afterwards heard of—in all probability they were slaughtered by the natives; whilst the party of eight, who had been left at Weymouth Bay, after constant struggles with the natives, had been reduced, by starvation and disease, to only two ere the expected relief arrived.

11. Gregory.—In 1856 A. C. Gregory went in search of Leichardt, and, thinking he might possibly have reached the north-west coast, took a small party to Cambridge Gulf. Travelling along the banks of the Victoria River, he crossed a low range of hills and discovered a stream, to which he gave the name of "Sturt Creek". By following this, he was led into a region covered with long ridges of glaring red sand, resembling those which had baffled Captain Sturt, except that in this desert there grew the scattered blades of the spinifex grass, which cut like daggers into the hoofs of the horses. The creek was lost in marshes and salt lakes, and Gregory was forced to retrace his steps till he reached the great bend in the Victoria River; then, striking to the east, he skirted the Gulf of Carpentaria about fifty miles from the shore; and, after a long journey, arrived at Moreton Bay, but without any news regarding Leichardt and his party. His expedition, however, had explored a great extent of country, and had mapped out the courses of two large rivers—the Victoria and the Roper.

CHAPTER XVIII.

DISCOVERIES IN THE INTERIOR, 1860-1886.

1. Burke and Wills.—In the year 1860 a merchant of Melbourne offered £1,000 for the furtherance of discovery in Australia; the Royal Society of Victoria undertook to organise an expedition for the purpose of crossing the continent, and collected subscriptions to the amount of £3,400; the Victorian Government voted £6,000, and spent an additional sum of £3,000 in bringing twenty-six camels from Arabia. Under an energetic committee of the Royal Society, the most complete arrangements were made. Robert O'Hara Burke was chosen as leader; Landells was second in command, with special charge of the camels, for which three Hindoo drivers were also provided; W. J. Wills, an accomplished young astronomer, was sent to take charge of the costly instruments and make all the scientific observations. There were two other scientific men and eleven subordinates, with twenty-eight horses to assist in transporting the baggage. On the 20th August, 1860, the long train of laden camels and horses set out from the Royal Park of Melbourne, Burke heading the procession on a little grey horse. The mayor made a short speech, wishing him God-speed; the explorers shook hands with their friends, and, amid the ringing cheers of thousands of spectators, the long and picturesque line moved forward.

ROBERT O'HARA BURKE.

The journey, as far as the Murrumbidgee, lay through settled country, and was without incident; but, on the banks of that river, quarrelling began among the party, and Burke dismissed the foreman; Landells then resigned, and Wills was promoted to be second in command. Burke committed a great error in his choice of a man to take charge of the camels in place of Landells. On a sheep station he met with a man named Wright, who made himself very agreeable; the two were soon great friends, and Burke, whose generosity was unchecked by any prudence, gave to this utterly unqualified person an important charge in the expedition.

On leaving the Murrumbidgee they ascended the Darling, till they reached Menindie—the place from which Sturt had set out sixteen years before. Here Burke left Wright with half the expedition, intending himself to push on rapidly, and to be followed up more leisurely by Wright.

Burke and Wills, with six men and half the camels and horses,

DISCOVERIES IN THE INTERIOR.

set off through a very miserable country—not altogether barren, but covered with a kind of pea, which poisoned the horses. A rapid journey brought them to the banks of Cooper's Creek, where they found fine pastures and plenty of water. Here they formed a depôt and lived for some time, waiting for Wright, who, however, did not appear. The horses and camels, by this rest, improved greatly in condition, and the party were in capital quarters. But Burke grew tired of waiting, and, as he was now near the centre of Australia, he determined to make a bold dash across to the Gulf of Carpentaria. He left one of his men, called Brahe, and three assistants, with six camels and twelve horses, giving them instructions to remain for three months; and if within that time he did not return, they might consider him lost, and would then be at liberty to return to Menindie. On the 16th December Burke and Wills, along with two men, named King and Gray, started on their perilous journey, taking with them six camels and one horse, which carried provisions to last for three months.

WILLIAM JOHN WILLS.

2. Rapid Journey to Gulf of Carpentaria.—

They followed the broad current of Cooper's Creek for some distance, and then struck off to the north, till they reached a stream, which they called Eyre Creek. From this they obtained abundant supplies of water, and, therefore, kept along its banks till it turned to the eastward; then abandoning it, they marched due north, keeping along the 140th meridian, through forests of boxwood, alternating with plains well watered and richly covered with grass. Six weeks after leaving Cooper's Creek they came upon a fine stream, flowing north, to which they gave the name "Cloncurry," and, by following its course, they found that it entered a large river, on whose banks they were delighted to perceive the most luxuriant vegetation and frequent clusters of palm trees. They felt certain that its waters flowed into the Gulf of Carpentaria, and therefore, by keeping close to it, they had nothing to fear. But they had brought only three months' provisions with them; more than half of that time had now elapsed, and they were still 150 miles from the sea. Burke now lost no time, but hurried on so fast that, one after another, the camels sank exhausted; and, when they had all succumbed, Burke and Wills took their only horse to carry a small quantity of provisions, and, leaving Gray and King behind, set out by themselves on foot. They had to cross several patches of swampy ground; and the horse, becoming inextricably bogged, was unable to go farther. But still Burke and Wills hurried on by themselves till they reached a narrow inlet on the Gulf of Carpentaria, and found that the river they had been following was the Flinders, whose mouth had been discovered by Captain Stokes in 1842. They were very anxious to view the open sea; but this would have required another couple of days, and their provisions were already exhausted; they were, therefore, obliged to hasten back as quickly as possible. The pangs of hunger overtook them before they could reach the place where King and Gray had remained with the provisions. Burke killed a snake, and ate a part of it, but he felt very ill immediately after; and when, at length, they reached the provisions, he was not able to go forward so quickly as it was necessary to do, if they wished to be safe. However, they recovered the horse and camels, which had been greatly refreshed by their rest; and, by taking easy stages, they managed to move south towards home. But their hurried journey to the north, in which they had traversed, beneath a tropical sun, about 140 miles every week, had told severely on their constitutions; Gray became ill, and it was now necessary to be so careful with the provisions that he had little chance of regaining his lost strength. One evening, after they had come to a halt, he was found sitting behind a tree, eating a little mixture he had made for himself of flour and water. Burke said he was stealing the provisions, fell upon him, and gave him a severe thrashing. He seems after this never to have rallied; whilst the party moved forward he was slowly sinking. Towards the end of March their provisions began to fail; they killed a camel, dried its flesh, and then went forward. At the beginning of April this was gone, and they killed their horse. Gray now lay down, saying he could not go on; Burke said he was "shamming," and left him. However, the gentler counsel of Wills prevailed; they returned and brought him forward. But he could only go a little farther; the poor fellow breathed his last a day or two after, and was buried in the wilderness. Burke now regretted his harshness, all the more as he himself was quickly sinking. All three, indeed, were utterly worn out; they were thin and haggard, and so weak that they tottered rather than walked along. The last few miles were very, very weary; but, at last, on the 21st of April, they came in sight of the depôt, four months and a half after leaving it. Great was their alarm on seeing no sign of people about the place; and, as they staggered forward to the spot at sunset, their hearts sank within them when they saw a notice, stating that Brahe had left that very morning. He would be then only seven hours' march away. The three men looked at one another in blank dismay; but they were so worn out that they could not possibly move forward with any hope of overtaking the fresh camels of Brahe's party. On looking round, however, they saw the word "dig" cut on a neighbouring tree; and, when they turned up the soil, they found a small supply of provisions.

Brahe had remained a month and a half longer than he had been told to wait; and as his own provisions were fast diminishing, and there seemed, as yet, to be no signs of Wright with the remainder of the expedition, he thought it unsafe to delay his return any longer. This man Wright was the cause of all the disasters that ensued. Instead of following closely on Burke, he had loitered at Menindie for no less than three months and one week, amusing himself with his friends; and, when he did set out, he took things so leisurely that Brahe was half-way back to the Darling before they met.

3. Sufferings.—On the evening when they entered the depôt, Burke, Wills, and King made a hearty supper; then, for a couple of days, they stretched their stiff and weary limbs at rest. But inaction was dangerous, for, even with the greatest expedition, their provisions would only serve to take them safely to the Darling. They now began to deliberate as to their future course.

Burke wished to go to Adelaide, because, at Mount Hopeless—where Eyre had been forced to turn back in 1840—there was now a large sheep station, and he thought it could not be more than 150 miles away. Wills was strongly averse to this proposal. "It is true," he said, "Menindie is 350 miles away, but then we know the road, and are sure of water all the way." But Burke was not to be persuaded, and they set out for Mount Hopeless. Following Cooper's Creek for many miles, they entered a region of frightful barrenness. Here, as one of the camels became too weak to go farther, they were forced to kill it and to dry its flesh. Still they followed the creek, till at last it spread itself into marshy thickets and was lost; they then made a halt, and found they had scarcely any provisions left, while their clothes were rotten and falling to pieces. Their only chance was to reach Mount Hopeless speedily; they shot their last camel, and, whilst Burke and King were drying its flesh, Wills struck out to find Mount Hopeless; but no one knew which way to look for it, and Wills, after laboriously traversing the dry and barren wastes in all directions, came back unsuccessful. A short rest was taken, and then the whole party turned southward, determined this time to reach the mount. But they were too weak to travel fast; day after day over these dreary plains, and still no sign of a hill; till at length, when they were within fifty miles of Mount Hopeless, they gave in. Had they only gone but a little farther, they would have seen the summit of the mountain rising upon the horizon; but just at this point they lost hope and turned to go back. After a weary journey, they once more reached the fresh water and the grassy banks of Cooper's Creek, but now with provisions for only a day or two. They sat down to consider their position, and Burke said he had heard that the natives of Cooper's Creek lived chiefly on the seed of a plant which they called nardoo; so that, if they could only find a native tribe, they might, perhaps, learn to find sufficient subsistence from the soil around them. Accordingly, Burke and King set out to seek a native encampment; and, having found one, they were kindly received by the blacks, who very willingly showed them how to gather the little black seeds from a kind of grass which grows close to the ground.

With this information they returned to Wills; and, as the nardoo seed was abundant, they began at once to gather it; but they found that, through want of skill, they could scarcely obtain enough for two meals a day by working from morning till night; and, when evening came, they had to clean, roast, and grind it; and, besides this, whatever it might have been to the blacks, to them it was by no means nutritious—it made them sick, and gave them no strength.

Whilst they were thus dwelling on the lower part of Cooper's Creek, several miles away from the depôt, Brahe had returned to find them and bring them relief. On his way home he had met with Wright leisurely coming up, and had hastened back with him to the depôt; but when they reached it they saw no signs of Burke and Wills, although the unfortunate explorers had been there only a few days before. Brahe, therefore, concluded that they were dead, and once more set out for home. Meanwhile Burke thought it possible that a relief party might in this way have reached the creek, and Wills volunteered to go to the depôt to see if any one was there. He set out by himself, and after journeying three or four days reached the place; but only to find it still and deserted. He examined it carefully, but could see no trace of its having been recently visited; there could be no advantage in remaining, and he turned back to share the doom of his companions. He now began to endure fearful pangs from hunger. One evening he entered an encampment that had just been abandoned by the natives, and around the fire there were some fish bones, which he greedily picked. Next day he saw two small fish floating dead upon a pool, and they made a delicious feast; but, in spite of these stray morsels, he was rapidly sinking from hunger, when suddenly he was met by a native tribe. The black men were exceedingly kind; one carried his bundle for him, another supported his feeble frame, and gently they led the gaunt and emaciated white man to their camp. They made him sit down and gave him a little food. Whilst he was eating he saw a great quantity of fish on the fire. For a few minutes he wondered if all these could possibly be for him, till at length they were cooked and the plentiful repast was placed before him. The natives then gathered round and clapped their hands with delight when they saw him eat heartily. He stayed with them for four days, and then set out to bring his friends to enjoy likewise this simple hospitality. It took him some days to reach the place where he had left them; but when they heard his good news they lost no time in seeking their native benefactors. Yet, on account of their weakness, they travelled very slowly, and when they reached the encampment it was deserted. They had no idea whither the natives had gone. They struggled a short distance farther; their feebleness overcame them, and they were forced to sink down in despair. All day they toiled hard to prepare nardoo seed; but their small strength could not provide enough to support them. Once or twice they shot a crow, but such slight repasts served only to prolong their sufferings. Wills, throughout all his journeyings, had kept a diary, but now the entries became very short; in the struggle for life there was no time for such duties, and the grim fight with starvation required all their strength.

At this time Wills records that he cannot understand why his legs are so weak; he has bathed them in the stream, but finds them no better, and he can hardly crawl out of the hut. His next entry is, that unless relief comes shortly he cannot last more than a fortnight. After this his mind seems to have begun to wander; he makes frequent and unusual blunders in his diary. The last words he wrote were that he was waiting, like Mr. Micawber, for something to turn up, and that, though starving on nardoo seed was by no means unpleasant, yet he would prefer to have a little fat and sugar mixed with it.

4. Death of Burke and Wills.—Burke now thought that their only chance was to find the blacks, and proposed that he and King should set out for that purpose. They were very loath to leave Wills, but, under the circumstances, no other course was possible. They laid him softly within the hut, and placed at his head enough of nardoo to last him for eight days. Wills asked Burke to take his watch, and a letter he had written for his father; the two men pressed his hands, smoothed his couch tenderly for the last time, and set out. There, in the utter silence of the wilderness, the dying man lay for a day or two: no ear heard his last sigh, but his end was as gentle as his life had been free from reproach.

Burke and King walked out on their desperate errand. On the first day they traversed a fair distance; but, on the second, they had not proceeded two miles when Burke lay down, saying he could go no farther. King entreated him to make another effort, and so he dragged himself to a little clump of bushes, where he stretched his limbs very wearily. An hour or two afterwards he was stiff and unable to move. He asked King to take his watch and pocket-book, and, if possible, to give them to his friends in Melbourne; then he begged of him not to depart till he was quite dead: he knew he should not live long, and he should like some one to be near him to the last. He spoke with difficulty, but directed King not to bury him, but to let him lie above the ground, with a pistol in his right hand. They passed a weary and lonesome night; and in the morning, at eight o'clock, Burke's restless life was ended. King wandered for some time forlorn, but, by good fortune, he stumbled upon an abandoned encampment, where, by neglect, the blacks had left a bag of nardoo, sufficient to last him a fortnight; and, with this, he hastened back to the hut where Wills had been laid. All he could do now, however, was to dig a grave for his body in the sand, and, having performed that last sad duty, he set out once more on his search, and found a tribe, differing from that which he had already seen. They were very kind, but not anxious to keep him, until, having shot some birds and cured their chief of a malady, he was found to be of some use, and soon became a great favourite with them. They made a trip to the body of Burke, but, respecting his last wishes, they did not seek to bury it, and merely covered it gently with a layer of leafy boughs.

5. Relief Parties.—When Wright and Brahe returned to Victoria with the news that, though it was more than five months since Burke and Wills had left Cooper's Creek, there were no signs of them at the depôt, all the colonies showed their solicitude by organising parties to go to the relief of the explorers, if, perchance, they should be still alive. Victoria was the first in the field, and the Royal Society equipped a small party, under Mr. A. W. Howitt, to examine the banks of Cooper's Creek. Queensland offered five hundred pounds to assist in the search, and with this sum an expedition was sent to examine the Gulf of

Carpentaria. Landsborough, its leader, was conveyed in the Victoria steamer to the gulf, and followed the Albert almost to its source, in hopes that Burke and Wills might be dwelling with the natives on that stream. Walker was sent to cross from Rockhampton to the Gulf of Carpentaria; he succeeded in reaching the Flinders River, where Burke and Wills had been; but, of course, he saw nothing of them. M'Kinlay was sent by South Australia to advance in the direction of Lake Torrens and reach Cooper's Creek. These various expeditions were all eager in prosecuting the search, but it was to Mr. Howitt's party that success fell. In following the course of Cooper's Creek downward from the depôt he saw the tracks of camels, and by these he was led to the district in which Burke and Wills had died.

Several natives, whom he met, brought him to the place where, beneath a native hut, King was sitting, pale, haggard, and wasted to a shadow. He was so weak that it was with difficulty Howitt could catch the feeble whispers that fell from his lips; but a day or two of European food served slightly to restore his strength. Howitt then proceeded to the spot where the body of Wills was lying partly buried, and, after reading over it a short service, he interred it decently. Then he sought the thicket where the bones of Burke lay with the rusted pistol beside them, and, having wrapped a union jack around them, he dug a grave for them hard by.

Three days later the blacks were summoned, and their eyes brightened at the sight of knives, tomahawks, necklaces, looking-glasses, and so forth, which were bestowed upon them in return for their kindness to King. Gay pieces of ribbon were fastened round the black heads of the children, and the whole tribe moved away rejoicing in the possession of fifty pounds of sugar, which had been divided among them.

When Howitt and King returned, and the sad story of the expedition was related, the Victorian Government sent a party to bring the remains of Burke and Wills to Melbourne, where they received the melancholy honours of a public funeral amid the general mourning of the whole colony. In after years, a statue was raised to perpetuate their heroism and testify to the esteem with which the nation regarded their memory.

6. M'Douall Stuart.—Burke and Wills were the first who ever crossed the Australian Continent; but, for several years before they set out, another traveller had, with wonderful perseverance, repeatedly attempted this feat. John M'Douall Stuart had served as draughtsman in Sturt's expedition to the Stony Desert, and he had been well trained in that school of adversity and sufferings. He was employed, in 1859, by a number of squatters, who wished him to explore for them new lands in South Australia, and having found a passage between Lake Eyre and Lake Torrens, he discovered, beyond the deserts which had so much disheartened Eyre, a broad district of fine pastoral land.

Next year the South Australian Government offered £2,000 as a reward to the first person who should succeed in crossing Australia from south to north; and Stuart set out from Adelaide to attempt the exploit. With only two men he travelled to the north, towards Van Diemen's Gulf, and penetrated much farther than Sturt had done in 1844. Indeed, he was only 400 miles from the other side of Australia, when the hostility of the blacks forced him to return: he succeeded, however, in planting a flag in the centre of the continent, at a place called by him Central Mount Stuart. Next year he was again in the field, and following exactly the same course, approached very near to Van Diemen's Gulf; being no more than 250 miles distant from its shores, when want of provisions forced him once more to return. The report of this expedition was sent to Burke and Wills, just before they set out from Cooper's Creek on their fatal trip to the Gulf of Carpentaria.

It was not until the following year, 1862, that Stuart succeeded in his purpose. He had the perseverance to start a third time, and follow his former route; and on this occasion he was successful in reaching Van Diemen's Gulf, and returned safely, after having endured many sufferings and hardships.

His triumphal entry into Adelaide took place on the very day when Howitt's mournful party entered that city, bearing the remains of Burke and Wills, on their way to Melbourne. Stuart then learnt that these brave explorers had anticipated him in crossing the continent, for they had reached the Gulf of Carpentaria in February, 1861; whilst he did not arrive at Van

Diemen's Gulf until July, 1862. However, Stuart had shown so great a courage, and had been twice before so near the completion of his task, that every one was pleased when the South Australian Government gave him the well-merited reward.

7. Warburton.—In a subsequent chapter it will be told how a line of telegraph was, in 1872, constructed along the track followed by Stuart ; and as the stations connected with this line are numerous, it is now an easy matter to cross the continent from south to north. But in recent years a desire has arisen among the adventurous to journey overland from east to west. Warburton, in 1873, made a successful trip of this kind. With his son, two men, and two Afghans to act as drivers of his seventeen camels, he started from Alice Springs, a station on the telegraph line close to the tropic of Capricorn.

The country immediately round Alice Springs was very beautiful, but a journey of only a few days served to bring the expedition into a dry and barren plain, so desolate that Warburton declared it could never be traversed without the assistance of camels. After travelling about four hundred miles, he reached those formidable ridges of fiery red sand in which the waters of Sturt's Creek are lost, and where A. C. Gregory was in 1856 compelled to turn back. In traversing this district, the party suffered many hardships; only two out of seventeen camels survived, and the men were themselves frequently on the verge of destruction. It was only by exercising the greatest care and prudence that Warburton succeeded in bringing his party to the Oakover River, on the north-west coast, and when he arrived once more in Adelaide it was found that he had completely lost the sight of one eye.

8. Giles and Forrest.—Towards the close of the same year, 1873, a young Victorian named Giles started on a similar trip, intending to cross from the middle of the telegraph line to West Australia. He held his course courageously to the west, but the country was of such appalling barrenness that, after penetrating half-way to the western coast, he was forced to abandon the attempt and return. But when three years afterwards he renewed his efforts, he succeeded, after suffering much and making long marches without water. He had more than one encounter with the natives, but he had the satisfaction of crossing from the telegraph line to the West Australian coast, through country never before traversed by the foot of civilised man. In 1874 this region was successfully crossed by Forrest, a Government surveyor of West Australia, who started from Geraldton, to the south of Shark Bay, and, after a journey of twelve hundred miles almost due east, succeeded in reaching the telegraph line. His entry into Adelaide was like a triumphal march, so great were the crowds that went out to escort him to the city. Forrest was then a young man, but a most skilful and sagacious traveller. Lightly equipped, and accompanied by only one or two companions, he has on several occasions performed long journeys through the most formidable country with a celerity and success that are indeed surprising.

His brother, Alexander Forrest, and a long list of bold and skilful bushmen, have succeeded in traversing the continent in every direction. It is not all desert. They have found fine tracts of land in the course of their journeys. Indeed, more than half of the recently explored regions are suitable for sheep and cattle, but there are other great districts which are miserable and forbidding. However, thanks to the heroic men whose names have been mentioned, and to such others as the Jardine Brothers, Ernest Favene, Gosse, and the Baron von Mueller, almost the whole of Australia is now explored. Only a small part of South Australia and the central part of West Australia remain unknown. We all of us owe a great debt of gratitude to the men who endured so much to make known to the world the capabilities of our continent.

CHAPTER XIX.

TASMANIA, 1837-1890.

1. Governor Franklin.—Sir John Franklin, the great Arctic explorer, arrived in 1837 to assume the Governorship of Tasmania. He had been a midshipman under Flinders, during the survey of the Australian coasts, and for many years had been engaged in the British Navy in the cause of science. He now expected to enjoy, as Governor of a small colony, that ease and retirement which he had so laboriously earned. But his hopes were doomed to disappointment. Although his bluff and hearty manner secured to him the good-will of the people, yet censures on his administration were both frequent and severe; for during his rule commenced that astonishing decline of the colony which continued, with scarcely any interruption, for nearly thirty years.

2. Flood of Convicts.—After the cessation of trans-

SIR JOHN FRANKLIN.

portation to New South Wales, in 1840, hopes were entertained that Tasmania would likewise cease to be a penal settlement; and, under this impression, great numbers of immigrants arrived in the colony. But, ere long, it became known that Tasmania was not only to continue, as before, a receptacle for British felons, but was, in fact, to be made the *only* convict settlement, and was destined to receive the full stream of criminals, that had formerly been distributed over several colonies. The result was immediately disastrous to the free settlers, for convict labour could be obtained at very little cost, and wages therefore fell to a rate so miserable that free labourers, not being able to earn enough for the support of their families, were forced to leave the island. Thus, in 1844, whilst the arrival of energetic and hard-working immigrants was adding greatly to the prosperity of the other colonies, Tasmania was losing its free population, and was sinking more and more into the degraded position of a mere convict station.

Lord Stanley, the British Colonial Secretary, in 1842, proposed a new plan for the treatment of convicts, according to which they were to pass through various stages, from a condition of absolute confinement to one of comparative freedom; and, again, instead of being all collected into one town, it was arranged that they should be scattered throughout the colony in small gangs. By this system it was intended that the prisoners should pass through several periods of probation before they were set at liberty; and it was, therefore, called the Probation Scheme. The great objection to it was that the men could scarcely be superintended with due precaution when they were scattered in so many separate groups, and many of them escaped, either to the bush or to the adjacent colonies.

3. Franklin's Difficulties.—The feelings of personal respect with which the people of Van Diemen's Land regarded Sir John Franklin were greatly increased by the amiable and high-spirited character of his wife. Lady Franklin possessed, in her own right, a large private fortune, which she employed in the most generous and kindly manner; her counsel and her wealth were ever ready to promote prosperity and alleviate sufferings. And yet, in spite of all this personal esteem, the experience of the new Governor among the colonists was far from being agreeable.

Before the arrival of Sir John Franklin, two nephews of Governor Arthur had been raised to very high positions. One of them, Mr. Montagu, was the Chief Secretary. During his uncle's government he had contrived to appropriate to himself so great a share of power that Franklin, on assuming office, was forced to occupy quite a secondary position. By some of the colonists the Governor was blamed for permitting the arbitrary acts of the Chief Secretary; while, on the other hand, he was bitterly denounced as an intermeddler by the numerous friends of the ambitious Montagu, who, himself, lost no opportunity of bringing the Governor's authority into contempt. At length Montagu went so far as to write him a letter containing—amid biting sarcasm and mock courtesy—a statement equivalent to a charge of falsehood. In consequence of this he was dismissed; but Sir John Franklin, who considered Montagu to be a man of ability, magnanimously gave him a letter to Lord Stanley, recommending him for employment in some other important position. This letter, being conveyed to Lord Stanley, was adduced by Montagu as a confession from the Governor of the superior ability and special fitness of the Chief Secretary for his post. Lord Stanley ordered his salary to be paid from the date of his dismissal; and Franklin, shortly after this insult to his authority, suddenly found himself superseded by Sir Eardley Wilmot, without having received the previous notice which, as a matter of courtesy, he might have expected. In 1843 he returned to England, followed by the regrets of nearly all the Tasmanians.

Two years afterwards he sailed with the ships *Erebus* and *Terror* to search for a passage into the Pacific Ocean through the Arctic regions of North America. He entered the ice-bound regions of the north, and for many years no intelligence regarding his fate could be obtained. Lady Franklin prosecuted the search with a wife's devotion, long after others had given up hope; and, at last, the discovery of some papers and ruined huts proved that the whole party had perished in those frozen wastes.

4. Governor Wilmot.—Sir Eardley Wilmot had gained distinction as a debater in the British Parliament. Like Governors Bligh and Gipps, in New South Wales, Wilmot found that to govern at the same time a convict population and a colony of free settlers was a most ungrateful task. A large proportion of the convicts, after being liberated, renewed their former courses: police had to be employed to watch them, judges and courts appointed to try them, gaols built to receive them, and provisions supplied to maintain them. If a prisoner was arrested and again convicted for a crime committed in Tasmania, then the colony was obliged to bear all the expense of supporting him, and amid so large a population of criminals these expenses became intolerably burdensome. It is true that colonists had to some extent a compensating advantage in receiving, free of charge, a plentiful supply of convict labour for their public works. But when Lord Stanley ordered that they should in future pay for all such labour received, they loudly complained of their grievances. "Was it not enough," they asked, "to send out the felons of Great Britain to become Tasmanian bushrangers, without forcing the free settlers to feed and clothe them throughout their lives, after the completion of their original sentences?" To all such remonstrances Lord Stanley's answer was that Tasmania had always been a convict colony; and that the free settlers had no right to expect that their interests would be specially consulted in the management of its affairs. Sir Eardley Wilmot found it impossible to obtain the large sums required for the maintenance of the necessary police and gaols, and he proposed to the Legislative Council to borrow money for this purpose. Those of the Council who were Government officials were afraid to vote in opposition to the wishes of the Governor, who, therefore, had a majority at his command. But the other members, six in number, denounced the proposed scheme as injurious to the colony; and when they found that the Governor was determined to carry it out, they all resigned their seats. For this action they were honoured with the title of the "Patriotic Six".

About this time Mr. Gladstone succeeded Lord Stanley in England as the Secretary of State for the Colonies; and as he had shortly afterwards to complain that, in reporting on these and other important matters, Sir Eardley had sent home vague statements for the purpose of deceiving the Imperial authorities, the Governor was recalled. But he was destined never to leave the scene of his troubles; for, two or three months after his recall, he became ill and died in the colony.

5. Denison and the Transportation Question.

—On the arrival of the next Governor, Sir William Denison, in 1847, the Queen reinstated the "Patriotic Six"; and the colonists, encouraged by this concession, vigorously set to work to obtain their two great desires—namely, government by elective parliaments, and the abolition of transportation. It was found that, between the years 1846 and 1850, more than 25,000 convicts had been brought into Tasmania; free immigration had ceased, and the number of convicts in the colony was nearly double the number of free men. In all parts of the world, if it became known that a man had come from Tasmania, he was looked upon with the utmost distrust and suspicion, and was shunned as contaminated. On behalf of the colonists, a gentleman named M'Lachlan went to London for the purpose of laying before Mr. Gladstone the grievances under which they suffered; at the same time, within the colony, Mr. Pitcairn strenuously exerted himself to prepare petitions against transportation, and to forward them to the Imperial authorities. These representations were favourably entertained, and, in a short time, Sir W. Denison received orders to inquire whether it was the unanimous desire of the people of Tasmania that transportation should cease entirely. The question was put to all the magistrates of the colony, who submitted it to the people in public meetings. The discussion was warm, and party feeling ran high. There were some who had been benefited by the trade and the English subsidies which convicts brought to the colony, and there were others who desired, at all hazards, to retain the cheap labour of the liberated convicts. These exerted themselves to maintain the system of transportation; but the great body of the people were determined on its abolition, and the answer returned by every meeting expressed the same unhesitating sentiment—Transportation ought to be abolished entirely. Accordingly, it was not long before the Tasmanians were informed by the Governor that transportation should, in a short time, be discontinued. But Earl Grey was now preparing another scheme for the treatment of convicts: they were to be kept for a time in English prisons; after they had served a part of their sentence, if they had been well conducted, the British Government would take them out to the colonies and land them there as free men, so as to give them a chance of starting an honourable career in a new country. It was a scheme of kind intention for the reformation of criminals that were not utterly bad, while the English Government would keep all the worst prisoners at home under lock and key. But the colonies had no desire to receive even the better half of the prisoners. They were afraid that cunning criminals would sham a great deal of reformation in order to be set free, and would then revert to their former ways whenever they were let loose in the colonies. But Earl Grey was resolved to give the criminal a fair chance. Ships filled with convicts were sent out to the various colonies, but the prisoners were not allowed to land. In 1849 the *Randolph* appeared at Port Phillip Heads; but the people of Melbourne forbade the captain to enter. He paid no attention to the order, and sailed up the bay to Williamstown. But when he was preparing to land the convicts, he perceived among the colonists signs of resistance so stern and resolute that he was glad to take the advice of Mr. Latrobe and sail for Sydney. But in Sydney also the arrival of the convicts was viewed with the most intense disgust. The inhabitants held a meeting on the Circular Quay, in which they protested very vigorously against the renewal of transportation to New South Wales. West Australia alone accepted its share of the convicts; and we have seen how the reputation of that colony suffered in consequence.

6. The Anti-Transportation League.—The vigorous protest of the other colonies had procured their immunity from this evil in its direct form; but many of the "ticket-of-leave men" found their way to Victoria and New South Wales, which were, therefore, all the more inclined to assist Tasmania in likewise throwing off the burden. A grand Anti-Transportation League was formed in 1851; and the inhabitants of all the colonies banded themselves together to induce the Home Government to emancipate Tasmania. Immediately after this, the discovery of gold greatly assisted the efforts of the league, because the British Government perceived that prisoners could never be confined in Tasmania, when, by escaping from the colony, and mixing with the crowds on the goldfields, they might not only escape notice but also make their fortunes; and there was now reason to suppose that banishment to Australia would be rather sought than shunned by the thieves and criminals of England.

7. End of Transportation.—In 1850 Tasmania, like the other colonies, received its Legislative Council; and when the people proceeded to elect *their* share of the members, no candidate had the slightest hope of success who was not an adherent of the

Anti-Transportation League. After this new and unmistakable expression of opinion, the English authorities no longer hesitated, and the new Secretary of State, the Duke of Newcastle, directed that, from the year 1853, transportation to Tasmania should cease.

Up to this time the island had been called Van Diemen's Land. But the name was now so intimately associated with ideas of crime and villainy, that it was gladly abandoned by the colonists, who adopted, from the name of its discoverer, the present title of the colony.

Sir Henry Young, formerly Governor of South Australia, was appointed to Tasmania in 1855, and held office till 1861. During this period responsible government was introduced. When the Legislative Council undertook the task of drawing up the new Constitution, it was arranged that the nominee element, which had now become extremely distasteful, should be entirely abolished, and that both of the legislative bodies should be elected by the people.

After Sir Henry Young, the next three Governors were Colonel Browne, Mr. Du Cane, and Mr. Weld—all men of ability, and very popular among the Tasmanians. After the initiation of responsible government in 1856, various reforms were introduced. By a very liberal Land Act of 1863, inducements were offered to industrious men to become farmers in the colony. For the purpose of opening up the country by means of railways, great facilities were given to companies who undertook to construct lines through the country districts; and active search was made for gold and other metals. But, in spite of these reforms, the population was steadily decreasing, owing to the attractions of the gold-producing colonies. No great amount of land was occupied for farming purposes, and even the squatters on the island were contented with smaller runs than those in the other colonies. They reared stock on the English system, and their domains were sheep-farms rather than stations. Indeed, the whole of Tasmania wore rather the quiet aspect of rural England than the bustling appearance of an Australian colony. But the efforts to throw off the taint of convictism were crowned with marked success; and, from being a gaol for the worst of criminals, Tasmania has become one of the most moral and respectable of the colonies.

Of late years Tasmania has made great advances. Her population has risen to about 150,000, and her resources have been enormously increased by the rapid development of her mineral enterprise. Tin mines of great value are now widely spread over the west of the island, and gold mines of promising appearance are giving employment to many persons who formerly could find little to do. There is room for a very great further development of the resources of Tasmania; but the colony is now on the right track, and her future is certain to be prosperous.

The Tasmanian natives were of a different type from those of Australia, having more of the negro in them. They were even ruder and

QUEEN TRUGANINA, THE LAST OF THE TASMANIANS.

less advanced in their habits, although not without qualities of simplicity and good-humour that were attractive. When white men first landed in their island there were about 7,000 of them roving through the forest and living upon opossums. But by the year 1869 all were gone but a man and three women. In that year, the man died, and one by one the women disappeared, till at last with the death of Truganina in 1877 the race became extinct.

CHAPTER XX.

SOUTH AUSTRALIA, 1850-1890.

1. Temporary Decline.—In 1851 the prosperity of South Australia was somewhat dimmed by the discovery of gold in Victoria; for, before the middle of the following year, the colony was deserted by a very large proportion of its male inhabitants. The copper mines were with difficulty worked, for want of men; the fields were uncultivated, the sheep untended, and the colony experienced a short period of rapid decline. However, the results obtained on the goldfields by most of these fortune-seekers were hardly to be compared with the steady yield of the fertile cornfields and rich copper mines of South Australia; and the majority of those who had thus abandoned the colony returned in a short time to their families and their former employments.

Governor Young adroitly turned the discovery of gold to the advantage of his own colony by establishing an escort between Bendigo and Adelaide; and, as this was remarkably well equipped, many of the diggers sent their gold by this route rather than to Melbourne, thus giving to South Australia some of the advantages of a gold-producing country. The crowds of people rushing to the goldfields had carried with them nearly all the coins of the colony; and the banks, although they had plenty of rough gold, were yet unable, from scarcity of coined money, to meet the demands upon them. In this emergency, Sir Henry Young took the extreme and somewhat illegal step of instituting a new currency, consisting of gold cast into small bars or ingots; and, although afterwards mildly censured by the Home Government for exceeding his powers, yet he could justly assert that this measure had saved the colony from serious commercial disaster.

But South Australia was still more benefited by the great market opened for its flour and wheat among the vast crowds on the goldfields; and, when the first period of excitement was over, it was found that the colony was, at any rate, not a loser by the success of its neighbours.

2. The Real Property Act.—In 1858 South Australia took the lead in a reform which is now being adopted by nearly all the civilised nations of the world. According to English law, each time an estate was transferred from one person to another, a deed had to be made out for the purpose; and if changes in its ownership had been frequent, it would be held by the last purchaser in virtue of a long series of documents. Now, if any one wished to buy a piece of land, he was obliged for safety to examine all the preceding deeds in order to be quite certain that they were valid; even then, if he bought the land, and another person, for any reason whatever, laid claim to it, the owner had to prove the validity of each of a long series of documents, going back, perhaps, for centuries. A flaw in any one of these would give rise to a contest which could be settled only after a very tedious investigation; and thus arose the long and ruinous Chancery suits which were the disgrace of English law. When a man's title to his estate was disputed, it often happened that he had to spend a fortune and waste half a lifetime in protracted litigation before all the antecedent deeds could be proved correct.

Mr. R. Torrens had his attention drawn to this very unsatisfactory state of things by the ruin of one of his relatives in a Chancery suit. He thought long and carefully over a scheme to prevent the occurrence of such injustice, and drafted a bill for a new method of transferring property. He proposed to lay this before the South Australian Parliament, but his friends discouraged him by declaring it was impossible to make so sweeping a change; and the lawyers actively opposed any innovation. But Torrens brought forward the bill; its simplicity and justice commended themselves to the people and to the House of Assembly, and it was carried by a large majority. According to the new scheme, all transferences of land were to be registered in a public office called the Lands Titles Office, the purchaser's name was to be recorded, and a certificate of title given to him; after this his right to the property was indisputable. If his possession was challenged, he had simply to go to the Lands Titles Office and produce his certificate to the officer in charge, who could turn to the register and at once decide the question of ownership. After this, no dispute was possible. If he sold his land, his name was cancelled in the public register, and the buyer's name was inserted instead, when he became the undisputed owner. Mr. Torrens was appointed to be registrar of the office, and soon made the new system a great success; it was adopted one after another in all the colonies of Australia, and must become eventually the law of all progressive nations.

3. The Northern Territory.—In 1864 the Northern

Territory was added to the dominion of South Australia, and from Adelaide an expedition was despatched by sea to the shores of Van Diemen's Gulf, in order to form a new settlement. After many difficulties, caused chiefly by the disputes between the first Government Resident, or Superintendent, and the officers under him, a branch colony was successfully founded at Port Darwin, opposite to Melville Island. This settlement has become a prosperous one: all the fruits and grains of tropical countries flourish and thrive to perfection; gold has been discovered; and it is asserted that there exist in the neighbourhood rich mines of other metals, which will, in the future, yield great wealth, while the stations that are now being formed are peculiarly favourable to the rearing of cattle and of horses. Yet the number of people who settle there continues small on account of the very hot climate; Palmerston, the capital, is as yet a town of only a few hundred inhabitants, and all the really hard work of the district is done by Chinese.

4. Overland Telegraph.—In a previous chapter it has been described how M'Douall Stuart, after two unsuccessful efforts, managed to cross the continent from Adelaide to Van Diemen's Gulf. Along the route which he then took, the people of South Australia resolved to construct a telegraph line. A gentleman named Charles Todd had frequently urged the desirability of such a line, and in 1869 his representations led to the formation of the British Australian Telegraph Company, which engaged to lay a submarine cable from Singapore to Van Diemen's Gulf, whilst the South Australian Government pledged itself to connect Port Darwin with Adelaide by an overland line, and undertook to have the work finished by the 1st of January, 1872. Mr. Todd was appointed superintendent, and divided the whole length into three sections, reserving the central portion for his own immediate direction, and entrusting the sections at the two ends to contractors. It was a daring undertaking for so young a colony. For thirteen hundred miles the line would have to be carried through country which never before had been traversed by any white men but Stuart's party. Great tracts of this land were utterly destitute of trees, and all the posts required for the line had to be carted through rocky deserts and over treacherous sand-hills. Todd had, with wonderful skill and energy, completed his difficult portion of the task, and the part nearest to Adelaide had also been finished before the time agreed upon; but it fared differently with those who had undertaken to construct the northern section. Their horses died, their provisions failed, and the whole attempt proved a miserable collapse. The Government sent a party to the north, in order to make a fresh effort. Wells were dug, at intervals, along the route, and great teams of

KING WILLIAM STREET, ADELAIDE.

bullocks were employed to carry the necessary provisions and materials to the stations; and yet, in spite of every precaution, the result was a failure. Meanwhile the cable had been laid, and the first message sent from Port Darwin to England announced that the overland telegraph was not nearly finished. The 1st of January, 1872, being now close at hand, Mr. Todd was hastily sent to complete the work. But the time agreed upon had expired before he had even made a commencement, and the company threatened to sue the South Australian Government for damages, on account of the losses sustained by its failure to perform its share of the contract. For the next eight months the work was energetically carried forward; Mr. Todd rode all along the line to see that its construction was satisfactory throughout. He was at Central Mount Stuart in the month of August, when the two ends of the wire were joined, and the first telegraphic message flashed across the Australian Continent. But, meantime, a flaw had occurred in the submarine cable, and it was not until October that communication was established with England. On the second day of that month, the Lord Mayor of London, standing at one end of the line, sent his hearty congratulations through twelve thousand five hundred miles of wire to the Mayor of Adelaide, who conversed with him at the other extremity. The whole work was undertaken and accomplished within two years; and already not only South Australia, but all the colonies, are reaping the greatest benefits from this enterprising effort. Another undertaking of a similar character has been completed by the efforts of both South and West Australia; along the barren coast on which Eyre so nearly perished there stretches a long line of posts, which carries a telegraph wire from Perth to Adelaide.

A period of depression began in South Australia after 1882. For a time everything was against the colony. Long droughts killed its sheep and ruined its crops; while the copper mines were found to be worked out. But fortune began to smile again after a few years of dull times, and when in 1887 an exhibition was held in Adelaide to commemorate the jubilee of the colony, it was also the commemoration of the return of brighter prospects. In the growth of wheat and fruits as well as in the making of wine South Australia has great openings for future prosperity.

CHAPTER XXI.

NEW SOUTH WALES, 1860-1890.

1. The Land Act.—Sir John Young became Governor of New South Wales in 1861. He was a man of great talent; but, at this stage of the colony's history, the ability of the Governor made very little difference in the general progress of affairs.

NEW SOUTH WALES. 169

GEORGE STREET, SYDNEY.

The political power was now chiefly in the hands of responsible
Ministers, and without their advice the Governor could do

nothing. The Ministry of the period—headed by Charles Cowper and John Robertson—prepared a bill to alter the regulations for the sale of land, and to give to the poor man an opportunity of obtaining a small farm on easy terms. Any person who declared his readiness to live on his land, and to cultivate it, was to be allowed to select a portion, not exceeding a certain size, in any part of the colony which he thought most convenient. The land was not to be given gratuitously; but, although the selector was to pay for it at the rate of one pound per acre, yet he was not expected to give more than a quarter of the price on taking possession. Three years afterwards he had the option of either paying at once for the remaining three-quarters, or, if this were beyond his means, of continuing to hold the land at a yearly rental of one shilling an acre. This was an excellent scheme for the poorer class of farmers; but it was not looked upon with favour by the squatters, whose runs were only rented from the State, and were, therefore, liable, under this new Act, to be invaded by selectors, who would pick out all the more fertile portions, break up the runs in an awkward manner, and cause many annoyances.

Hence, though the Legislative Assembly passed the bill, the Upper House, whose members were mostly squatters, very promptly rejected it; and upon this there arose a struggle, the Ministry being determined to carry the bill, and the Council quite as resolute never to pass it. Acting on the advice of his Ministers, Sir John Young entreated the Upper House to give way; but it was deaf to all persuasions, and the Ministers determined to coerce it by adopting extreme measures. Its members had been nominated by a previous Governor for a period of five years, as a preliminary trial before the nominations for life; the term of their appointment was now drawing to a close, and Sir John Young, by waiting some little time, might easily have appointed a new Council of his own way of thinking. But the Ministers were impatient to have their measure passed, and, instead of waiting, they advised the Governor to nominate twenty-one new members of Council, who, being all supporters of the bill, would give them a majority in the Upper House; so that, on the very last night of its existence, it would be obliged to pass the measure and make it law. But when the opponents of the bill saw the trick which was being played upon them, they rose from their seats and resigned in a body. The President himself vacated his chair; and as no business could then be carried on, the Land Bill was delayed until the Council came to an end, and the Ministers thus found themselves outwitted. They were able, somewhat later, to effect their purpose; but this little episode in responsible government caused considerable stir at the time, and Sir John subsequently received a rebuke from the Colonial Secretary for his share in it.

2. Prince Alfred.—In 1868 Lord Belmore became Governor of New South Wales, and during his term of office all the colonies passed through a period of excitement on the occasion of a visit from the Queen's second son, Prince Alfred. He was the first of the Royal Family who had ever visited Australia, and the people gave to him a hearty and enthusiastic reception. As he entered the cities flower-decked arches spanned the streets; crowds of people gathered by day to welcome him, and at night the houses and public buildings were brilliantly illuminated in his honour. But during the height of the festivities at Sydney a circumstance occurred which cast a gloom over the whole of Australia. The Prince had accepted an invitation to a picnic at Clontarf, and was walking quietly on the sands to view the various sports of the holiday-makers, when a young man named O'Farrell rushed forward and discharged a pistol at him. The ball entered his back, and he fell dangerously wounded. For a day or two his life trembled in the balance, and the colonists awaited the result with the greatest excitement, until it was made known that the crisis was past. No reason was alleged for the crime except a blind dislike to the Royal Family; and O'Farrell was subsequently tried and executed.

3. Railway Construction.—New South Wales has three main lines of railway with many branches. One starts from Sydney, and passes through Goulburn to Albury on its way to Melbourne; one goes north to Newcastle, then through the New England district, and so to Brisbane; and the third runs from Sydney over the Blue Mountains to Bathurst, and away to Bourke, on the Darling River. Those rugged heights, which so long

172   HISTORY OF AUSTRALIA AND NEW ZEALAND.

The Lithgow Zigzag, the Blue Mountains.

opposed the westward progress of the early colonists, have proved no insuperable barrier to the engineer; and the locomotive now slowly puffs up the steep inclines and drags its long line of heavily-laden trucks where Macquarie's road, with so much trouble, was carried in 1815. The first difficulty which had to be encountered was at a long valley named Knapsack Gully. Here the rails had to be laid on a great viaduct, where the trains run above the tops of the tallest trees. The engineers had next to undertake the formidable task of conducting the line up a steep and rocky incline, seven hundred feet in height. This was effected by cutting a "zigzag" in the rock; the trains run first to the left, rising upon a slight incline; then, reversing, they go to the right, still mounting slightly upwards; then, again, to the left; and so on till the summit is reached. By these means the short distance is rendered long, but the abrupt steepness of the hill is reduced to a gentle inclination. The trains afterwards run along the top of the ridge, gradually rising, till, at the highest point, they are three thousand five hundred feet above the level of the Sydney station. The passengers look down from the mountain tops on the forest-clad valleys far below; they speed along vast embankments or dash through passages cut in the solid rock, whose sides tower above them to the height of an ordinary steeple. In some places long tunnels were bored, so that the trains now enter a hill at one side and emerge from the other.

One of these tunnels was thought to be unsafe; the immense mass of rock above it seemed likely to crush downwards upon the passage, and the engineers thought that their best course would be to remove the hill from above it. Three and a half tons of gunpowder were placed at intervals in the tunnel, and connected by wires with a galvanic battery placed a long distance off. The operation of firing the mine was made a public occasion, and Lady Belmore agreed to go up to the mountains and perform the ceremony of removing the hill. When all was ready, she touched the knob which brought the two ends of the wire together. A dull and rumbling sound was heard, the solid rock heaved slowly upward, and then settled back to its place, broken in a thousand pieces, and covered with rolling clouds of dust and smoke. All that the workmen had then to do was to carry away the immense pile of stone, and the course was clear for laying the rails.

When the line reached the other side of the Blue Mountains there were great difficulties in the descent, and here the engineers had to lay out zigzags of greater extent than the former. By these the trains now descend easily and safely from the tops of the mountains down into the Lithgow Valley far below.

By the southern railway to Albury, crowds of people are daily whirled in a few hours to places which, forty years ago, were reached by Sturt, and Hume, and Mitchell, only after weeks of patient toil, through unknown lands that were far removed from civilisation.

4. Sydney Exhibition.—

So on every hand the colony made progress. Her railways expanded in scores of branches; her telegraph lines stretched out their arms in every direction; her sheep increased so that now there are nearly sixty millions of them; her wheat and maize extended to more than half a million of acres; her orangeries and vineyards and orchards, her mines of coal and tin, and her varied and extensive manufactures, make her people, now numbering a million, one of the most prosperous on the face of the earth. Her pride was pardonable when, in 1879, she held an international exhibition to compare her industries side by side with those of other lands, so as to show how much she had done and to discover how much

THE TOWN HALL, SYDNEY.

she had yet to learn. A frail, but wonderfully pretty building rapidly arose on the brow of the hill between Sydney Cove and Farm Cove; and that place, the scene of so much squalor and misery a hundred years before, became gay with all that decorative art could do, and busy with daily throngs of gratified visitors. The place had a most distinguished appearance; seen from the harbour, its dome and fluttering flags rose up from among the luxuriant foliage of the Botanic Gardens, as if boldly to proclaim that New South Wales had completed the period of her infancy and was prepared to take her place among the nations as one grown to full and comely proportions. When the building had served its purpose, the people were too fond and too proud of it to dismantle and destroy it, but unfortunately it was not long after swept away by an accidental fire.

In 1885, the colony was stirred by a great wave of enthusiasm when it was known that its Government had sent to England the offer of a regiment of soldiers to fight in the Soudan side by side with British troops. The offer was accepted, and some seven or eight hundred soldiers, well equipped and full of high hopes, sailed for Africa. The war was too soon over for them to have any chance of displaying what an Australian force may be like upon a battle-field. There were many persons who held that the whole expedition was a mistake. But it had one good effect; for it showed that, for the present at least, the Australian colonies are proud of their mother-country; that their eyes are fondly turned to her, to follow all her destinies in that great career which she has to accomplish as the leading nation of the earth; and that if ever she needed their help, assistance would flow spontaneously from the fulness of loving hearts. The idea of this expedition and its execution belonged principally to C. B. Dalley. But the great leader of New South Wales during the last quarter of a century, and the most zealous worker for its welfare and prosperity, has been the veteran statesman Sir Henry Parkes.

CHAPTER XXII.

VICTORIA, 1855-1890.

1. Responsible Government.—In 1855, when each of the colonies was engaged in framing for itself its own form of government, Victoria, like all the others, chose the English system of two Houses of Legislature. At first it was resolved that the Lower House, called the Legislative Assembly, should consist of only sixty members; but by subsequent additions, the number has been increased to eighty-six: in 1857 the right of voting was conferred upon every man who had resided a sufficient length of time in the colony. With regard to the Upper House Victoria found the same difficulty as had been experienced in New South Wales; but, instead of introducing the system of nomination by the Government, it decided that its Legislative Council should be elected by the people. In order, however, that this body might not be identical in form and opinion with the Lower House, it was arranged that no one should be eligible for election to it who did not possess at least five thousand pounds worth of real property, and that the privilege of voting should be confined to the wealthier part of the community.

Along with this new Constitution responsible government was introduced; and Mr. Haines, being sent for by the Governor, formed the first Ministry. Before the close of the year, the first contest under the new system took place. Mr. Nicholson, a member of the Assembly, moved that the voting for elections should in future be carried on in secret, by means of the ballot-box, so that every man might be able to give his opinion undeterred by any external pressure, such as the fear of displeasing his employer or of disobliging a friend. The Government of Mr. Haines refused its assent to this proposal, which was, nevertheless, carried by the Assembly. Now, the system of responsible government required that, in such a case, Mr. Haines and his fellow-Ministers, being averse to such a law and declining to carry it out, should resign and leave the government to those who were willing and able to inaugurate the newly-appointed system. Accordingly they gave in their resignations, and the Governor asked Mr. Nicholson to form a new Ministry; but, though many members had voted for his proposal, they were not prepared to follow him as their leader. He could obtain very few associates, and was thus unable to form a Ministry; so that there appeared some likelihood of a total failure of responsible government before it had been six months in existence. In the midst

VICTORIA. 177

COLLINS STREET, MELBOURNE.

of this crisis Sir Charles Hotham was taken ill. He had been present at a prolonged ceremony—the opening of the first gasworks in Melbourne—and a cold south wind had given him a dangerous chill. He lay for a day or two in great danger; but the crisis seemed past, and he had begun to recover, when news was brought to him of Mr. Nicholson's failure. He lay brooding over these difficulties, which pressed so much upon his mind that he was unable to rally, and on the last day of the year 1855 he died. This was a great shock to the colonists, who had learnt highly to respect him. The vacant position was for a year assumed by Major-General Macarthur, who invited Mr. Haines and his Ministry to return. They did so, and the course of responsible government began again from the beginning. At the end of 1856 another Governor—Sir Henry Barkly—arrived; and during the seven years of his stay the new system worked smoothly enough, the only peculiarity being the rapid changes in the Government. Some of the Ministries lasted only six weeks, and very few protracted their existence to a year.

2. The Deadlock.—Sir Henry Barkly left the colony in 1863, and his place was immediately filled by Sir Charles Darling, nephew of Sir Ralph Darling, who, forty years before, had been Governor of New South Wales. Sir Charles was destined to troublous times; for he had not been long in the colony ere a most vexatious hitch took place in the working of constitutional government. It arose out of a struggle with regard to what is called "Protection to Native Industry".

The colony was filled with vigorous and enterprising men, who had come to it for the purpose of digging for gold. For four or five years gold digging had been on the average a fairly remunerative occupation. But when all the surface gold had been gathered, and it became necessary to dig shafts many hundreds of feet into the earth, and even then in many cases only to get quartz, from which the gold had to be extracted by crushing and careful washing, then the ordinary worker, who had no command of capital, had to take employment with the wealthier people, who could afford to sink shafts and wait for years before the gold appeared. These men, therefore, had to take small wages for toiling at a most laborious occupation. But most of them had learnt trades of some sort in Europe; and the idea sprang up that if the colony prevented boots from coming into it from outside there would be plenty of work for the bootmakers; if it stopped the importation of engines there would no longer be any reason why engineers should work like navvies at the bottom of gold mines—they would be wanted to make the engines of the colony. After a long agitation, therefore, James M'Culloch, the Premier of the colony, in 1864 brought a bill into the Victorian Legislative Assembly according to which taxes were to be placed on all goods coming into the colony if they were of a sort that might be made within the colony. M'Culloch proposed to make this change because it was ardently desired by the working men of the colony, and these could by their votes control the action of the Legislative Assembly. But the Upper House, called the Legislative Council, composed of wealthy men, who had been elected by the wealthier part of the community, thought, after careful decision, that any such plan would ruin the commerce of the colony without much benefiting its industries. They therefore rejected the proposed bill.

M'Culloch tried to persuade them to pass it, but they were obstinate. He then resorted to a trick which is in itself objectionable, but which is perhaps excusable when the great body of the people wish a certain thing and a small body like the Legislative Council are resolved to thwart them. It is part of our constitutional law that all bills dealing with money matters must be prepared in the Lower House; the Upper House can then accept them or reject them as they stand, but is not allowed to alter them.

Now, once a year Parliament has to pass a bill called the Appropriation Act, by which authority is given to the Government to spend the public money in the various ways that Parliament directs. In 1865 M'Culloch put the whole of the Protective Tariff Bill into the Appropriation Act as if it were a part of that Act, though really it had nothing to do with it. The Legislative Assembly passed the Appropriation Act with this insertion. The Legislative Council now found itself in a most unlucky position. If it passed the Appropriation Act it would also pass the Protective Tariff Bill, which it detested. But if it rejected the Appropriation Act, then the Government would have no authority to pay away any money, and so all the officers of the State, the civil servants and the policemen, the teachers, the gaolers, the surveyors and the tide-waiters, would all have to go on for a year without any salaries. There was no middle course open, for the Council could not alter the Appropriation Act and then pass it.

Whether was it to pass the Act and make the protective tariff the law of the land; or reject it, and run the risk of making a number of innocent people starve? It chose the latter alternative, and threw out the bill. The whole country became immensely excited, and seemed like one debating club, where men argued warmly either for or against the Council.

Matters were becoming serious, when the Ministry discovered an ingenious device for obtaining money. According to British law, if a man is unable to obtain from the Government what it owes him, he sues for it in the Supreme Court; and then, if this Court decides in his favour, it orders the money to be paid, quite independently of any Appropriation Act, out of the sums that may be lying in the Treasury. In their emergency, the Ministry applied to the banks for a loan of money; five of them refused, but the sixth agreed to lend forty thousand pounds. With this the Government servants were paid, and then the bank demanded its money from the Government; but the Government had no authority from Parliament to pay any money, and could not legally pay it. The bank then brought its action at law. The Supreme Court gave its order, and the money was paid to the bank out of the Treasury. Thus a means had been discovered of obtaining all the money that was required without asking the consent of Parliament. Throughout the year 1865 the salaries of officers were obtained in this way; but in 1866 the Upper House, seeing that it was being beaten, offered to hold a conference. Each House made concessions to the other, the Tariff Bill was passed, with some alterations, the Appropriation Bill was then agreed to in the ordinary way, and the "Deadlock" came to an end.

3. The Darling Grant.—But, in its train, other troubles followed; for the English authorities were displeased with Sir Charles Darling for allowing the Government to act as it did. They showed how he might have prevented it, and, to mark their dissatisfaction, they recalled him in 1866. He bitterly complained of this harsh treatment; and the Assembly, regarding him as, in some measure, a martyr to the cause of the people, determined to recompense him for his loss of salary. In the Appropriation Act of 1867 they therefore passed a grant of £20,000 to Lady Darling, intending it for the use of her husband. The Upper House owed no debt of gratitude to Sir Charles, and, accordingly, it once more threw out the Appropriation Bill. Again there was the same bitter dispute, and again the public creditors were obliged to sue for their money in the Supreme Court. In a short time four thousand five hundred such pretended actions were laid, the Government making no defence, and the order being given in each case that the money should be paid.

In 1866 the new Governor—Viscount Canterbury—arrived; but the struggle was still continued, till, in 1868, Sir Charles Darling informed M'Culloch that Lady Darling would decline to receive the money, as he was receiving instead five thousand pounds as arrears of salary and a lucrative position in England. The Upper House then passed the Appropriation Bill, and the contest came to an end.

4. Payment of Members.—But they had other things to quarrel about. The working men of the colony thought that they never would get fair treatment in regard to the laws until working men were themselves in Parliament. But that could not be, so long as they had to leave their trades and spend their time in making laws while getting nothing for it. Hence they were resolved on having all members of Parliament paid, and they elected persons to the Lower House who were in favour of that principle. But the better-off people sent persons into the Upper House who were against it. Thus for twenty years a struggle took place, but in the end the working men carried their point; and it was settled that every member of Parliament should receive three hundred pounds a year. The two Houses also quarrelled about the manner in which the land was to be sold; the Lower House being anxious to put it into the hands of industrious people who were likely to work on it as farmers, even though they could pay very little for it; the Upper House preferring that it should be sold to the people who offered the most money for it. On this and other questions in dispute the Lower House gained the victory.

5. Exhibitions.—It was not till the year 1880 that all these contentions were set at rest, but from that time the colony passed into a period of peace, during which it made the most astonishing progress in all directions. That progress was indicated in a most decided way by the exhibitions held in the colony. It had from time to time in previous years held inter-colonial exhibitions at which all the colonies had met in friendly

THE TOWN HALL, MELBOURNE.

competition. But in 1880, and again in 1888, Victoria invited all the world to exhibit their products at her show. A magnificent building was erected in one of the parks of Melbourne, and behind it were placed acres of temporary wooden erections, and the whole was filled with twenty acres of exhibits. A similar show, held in 1888, was much larger, and helped, by its fine collection of pictures, its grand displays of machinery, its educational courts, its fine orchestral music, and so on, in a hundred ways to stimulate and develop the minds of the people.

During recent years Victoria has been very busy in social

legislation. While enjoying peace under the direction of a coalition Government with Mr. Duncan Gillies and Mr. Alfred Deakin at its head, the colony has tried experiments in regulating the liquor traffic; in closing shops at an early hour; in irrigating the waterless plains of the north-west, and in educating farmers and others into the most approved methods of managing their

THE PORT OF MELBOURNE.

businesses. What is to be the eventual result no one can as yet very definitely prophesy. But the eyes of many thoughtful persons throughout the world are at present turned to Victoria to see how those schemes are working which have been so zealously undertaken for the good of the people.

Up till 1890 the progress of the colony was astonishing. Its central half forms a network of railways. Its agriculture and its trades have doubled themselves every few years; and though a period of restless activity and progress was in 1890 followed by a time of severe depression, the community, like all the other Australian colonies, has great times of prosperity in store for it.

CHAPTER XXIII.

THE TIMES OF THE MAORIS.

1. The Maoris.—So far as we know, the original inhabitants of New Zealand were a dark-skinned race called Maoris, a people lithe and handsome of body, though generally plain of features: open, frank and happy in youth, grave and often melancholy in their older years.

They numbered forty thousand in the North Island, where the warmth of the climate suited them, but in the South Island there were only two thousand. They were divided into tribes, who fought fiercely with one another; cooked and ate the bodies of the slain, and carried off the vanquished to be slaves. They dwelt in houses sometimes neatly built of wooden slabs, more often of upright poles with broad grass leaves woven between them. The roofs were of grass, plaited and thatched.

To these abodes the entrances were only some two or three feet high, and after crawling through, the visitor who entered at night would see the master of the house, his wives, his children, his slaves, indeed all his household, to the number of twenty or thirty, lying on mats in rows down either side, with their heads to the walls and their feet to the centre, leaving a path down the middle. In these rooms they slept, with a fire burning all night, till, what with the smoke and the breaths of so many people, the place was stifling. The roofs were only four feet higher than the ground outside, but, then, inside, the earth was hollowed a foot or two to make the floor so that a man could just stand upright.

These houses were gathered in little villages, often pleasantly situated beside a stream, or on the sea-shore; but sometimes for defence they were placed on a hill and surrounded by high fences with ditches and earthen walls so as to make a great stronghold of the kind they called a "pah". The trenches were sometimes twenty or thirty feet deep; but generally the pah was built so that a rapid river or high precipices would defend two or three sides of it, while only the sides not so guarded by nature were secured by ditches and a double row of palisades. Within these enclosures stages were erected behind the palisades so that the fighting men could hurl stones and spears and defy an attacking party.

A MAORI DWELLING.

2. Maori Customs.—Round their villages and pahs they dug up the soil and planted the sweet potato, and the taro, which is the root of a kind of arum lily; they also grew the gourd called calabash, from whose hard rind they made pots and bowls and dishes. When the crops of sweet potato and taro were over they went out into the forest and gathered the roots of certain sorts of ferns, which they dried and kept for their winter food. They netted fish and eels; they caught sharks with hook and line and dried their flesh in the sun. To enjoy these meals in comfort they had a broad verandah round their houses which formed an open and generally pleasant dining-room, where they gathered in family circles bound by much affection for one another. The girls especially were sweet and pretty; their mild manners, their soft and musical voices, the long lashes of their drooping eyes, with the gloss of their olive-tinted skins made them perfect types of dusky beauty. Grown a little older they were by no means so attractive, and then when married they deeply scored their faces by the process of tattooing.

The men had their faces, hips, and thighs tattooed, that is, all carved in wavy lines which were arranged in intricate patterns. The women tattooed only their lips, chins, and eyelids, but often smeared their faces with red ochre, and soaked their hair with oil. Men and women wore round the waist a kilt of beautifully woven flax, and over the shoulders a mat of the same material. They were expert sailors, and built themselves large canoes which thirty or forty men would drive forward, keeping time with their paddles. Their large war canoes were sixty and seventy feet long, and would carry 100 men.

Thus they were by no means uncivilised, but their condition was in some respects most barbarous. In person they were dirty, and in manners proud and arrogant. They were easily offended, and never forgave what they considered as an injury or insult. This readiness to take offence and to avenge themselves caused the neighbouring tribes to be for ever at war. They fought with great bravery, slaughtered each other fiercely, and ate the bodies. Sometimes they killed their captives or slaves in order to hold a cannibal feast.

According to their own traditions they had not been always in these islands. Their ancestors came from afar, and each tribe had its own legendary account. But they all agreed that they came from an island away to the north in the Pacific, which they called Hawaiki, and there is little doubt but that some hundreds of years ago their forefathers must in truth have emigrated from some of the South Sea Islands. Whether they found natives on the islands and killed them all, we cannot now discover. There are no traces of any earlier people, but the Maoris in their traditions say that people were found on the islands and slain and eaten by the invaders.

One tribe declared that long ago in far-off Hawaiki a chief hated another, but was too weak to do him harm. He fitted out a canoe for a long voyage, and suddenly murdered the son of his enemy. He then escaped on board the canoe with his followers and sailed away for ever from his home. This legend declared how after many adventures he at length reached New Zealand. Another legend relates that in Hawaiki the people were fighting, and a tribe being beaten was forced to leave the island. Sorrowfully it embarked in two canoes and sailed away out upon the tossing ocean, till, directed by the voice of their god sounding from the depths below them, they landed on the shores of New Zealand.

How many centuries they lived and multiplied there it is impossible to say, as they had no means of writing and recording their history.

3. Tasman.—The earliest we know of them for certain is in the journal of Tasman, who writes under the date of 13th December, 1642, that he had that day seen shores never before beheld by white men. He was then holding eastward after his visit to Tasmania, and the shore he saw was the mountainous land in the North Island. He rounded what we now call Cape Farewell, and anchored in a fine bay, whose green and pleasant shores were backed by high snow-capped mountains. Several canoes came off from the beach filled by Maoris, who lay about a stone's throw distant and sounded their war trumpets. The Dutch replied by a flourish of their horns. For several days the Maoris would come no nearer, but on the sixth they paddled out with seven canoes and surrounded both vessels. Tasman noticed that they were crowding in a somewhat threatening manner round one of his ships, the *Heemskirk*, and he sent a small boat with seven men to warn the captain to be on his guard. When the Maoris saw these seven men without weapons sailing past their canoes they fell on them, instantly killed three and began to drag away their bodies; no doubt to be eaten. The other four Dutchmen, by diving and swimming, escaped and reached the ship half dead with fright. Then with shouts the whole line of Maori canoes advanced **to attack the ships; but a broadside**

startled them. They were stupefied for a moment at the flash and roar of the cannon and the crash of the wood-work of their canoes; then they turned and fled, carrying with them, however, one of the bodies. Tasman sailed down into Cook Strait, which he very naturally took to be a bay, the weather being too thick for him to see the passage to the south-east. He then returned and coasted northwards to the extreme point of New Zealand, which he called Cape Maria Van Diemen, probably after the wife of that Governor of Batavia who had sent out the expedition. Tasman called the lands he had thus discovered "New Zealand," after that province of Holland which is called Zealand, or the Sea-land. The bay in which he had anchored was called Murderers' or Massacre Bay.

4. Captain Cook.—For more than a hundred years New Zealand had no white men as visitors. It was in 1769 that Captain Cook, on his way home from Tahiti, steering to the south-west in the hope of discovering new lands, saw the distant hills of New Zealand. Two days later he landed on the east coast of the North Island, a little north of Hawke Bay. There lay the little ship the *Endeavour* at anchor, with its bulging sides afloat on a quiet bay, in front a fertile but steeply sloping shore with a pah on the crown of a hill, and a few neat little houses by the side of a rapid stream. In the evening Cook, Banks, and other gentlemen took the pinnace and rowed up the streamlet. They landed, leaving some boys in charge of the boat, and advanced towards a crowd of Maoris, making friendly signs as they approached. The Maoris ran away, but some of them seeing their chance made a dash at the boys in the boat and tried to kill them. The boys pushed off, and dropped down the stream; the Maoris chased them, determined on mischief. Four of them being very murderous, the coxswain fired a musket over their heads. They were startled, but continued to strike at the boys with wooden spears. Seeing the danger the coxswain levelled his musket and shot one of the Maoris dead on the spot. The others fled, and Cook, hearing the report of the gun, hurried back and at once returned to the ship.

Over and over again Cook did everything he could devise to secure the friendship of these people; but they always seemed to have only one desire, and that was to kill and eat the white visitors. One day five canoes came out to chase the *Endeavour* as she was sailing along the coast. Another time nine canoes densely filled with men sailed after her, paddling with all their might to board the vessel. In these and many other cases cannon had to be fired over their heads to frighten them before they would desist from their attempt to capture the ship. At one bay, the Maoris made friends and went on board the *Endeavour* to sell provisions, but when all was going forward peaceably they suddenly seized a boy and pulled him into their canoe. They were paddling away with him when some musket shots frightened them, and in the confusion the boy dived and swam back.

Cook sailed completely round the North Island, charting the shores with great care, often landing, sometimes finding tribes who made friends, more often finding tribes whose insolence or treachery led to the necessity of firing upon them with small shot. If he had only known the customs of these people he would have understood that to be friendly with one tribe meant that the next tribe would murder and eat them for revenge. He then sailed round the South Island, landing less frequently, however, till at length he took his leave of New Zealand at what he called Cape Farewell, and sailed away to Australia. He had been nearly six months exploring the coasts of these islands, and that in a very small vessel. During this time he had left pigs and goats, fowls and geese to increase in the forests, where they soon multiplied, especially the pigs. Potatoes and turnips were left with many tribes, who quickly learnt how to grow them, so that after ten or twelve years had passed away these vegetables became the chief food of all the Maoris.

5. French Visitors.—Whilst Cook was sailing round the North Island, a French vessel anchored in a bay of that island in search of fresh water. The Ngapuhi tribe received them with pleasure and gave them all the assistance in their power, but some of them stole a boat. The captain, named De Surville, then seized one of the chiefs and put him in irons. The boat not being given up, he burnt a village and sailed to South America, the chief dying on the road.

Three years later in 1772 came another Frenchman, Marion du Fresne, with two ships; this time for the express purpose of making discoveries. He sailed up the west coast, rounded the North Cape and anchored in the Bay of Islands. He landed and made friends with the Ngapuhi tribe and took his sick sailors ashore. The Maoris brought him plenty of fish, and Du Fresne made them presents in return. For a month the most pleasant relations continued, the Maoris often sleeping on board and the French officers spending the night in the Maori houses. One day Captain Marion went ashore with sixteen others to enjoy some fishing. At night they did not return. Captain Crozet, who was second in command, thought they had chosen to sleep ashore, but the next day he sent a boat with twelve men to find where they were. These men were scattering carelessly through the woods when suddenly a dense crowd of Maoris, who had concealed themselves, attacked and killed all the Frenchmen but one. He who escaped was hidden behind some bushes, and he saw his comrades brained one after another; then he saw the fierce savages cut their bodies in pieces, and carry them away in baskets to be eaten. When the Maoris were gone he crept along the shore and swam to the ship, which he reached half dead with terror. Crozet landed sixty men, and the natives gathered for a fight; but the Frenchmen merely fired volley after volley into a solid mass of Maori warriors, who, stupefied at the flash and roar, were simply slaughtered as they stood. Crozet burnt both the Maori villages and sailed away. In later times the Maoris explained that the French had desecrated their religious places by taking the carved ornaments out of them for firewood.

6. Cook's Later Visits.—In his second voyage Cook twice visited New Zealand in 1773 and 1774. He had two vessels, one of them under the command of Captain Furneaux. While this latter vessel was waiting in Queen Charlotte Sound, a bay opening out of Cook Strait, Captain Furneaux sent a boat with nine men who were to go on shore and gather green stuff for food. A crowd of Maoris surrounded them, and one offered to sell a stone hatchet to a sailor, who took it; but to tease the native, in silly sailor fashion, this sailor would neither give anything for it nor hand it back. The Maori in a rage seized some bread and fish which the sailors were spreading for their lunch. The sailors closed to prevent their touching the victuals; a confused struggle took place, during which the English fired and killed two natives, but before they could load again they were all knocked on the head with the green-stone axes of the Maoris. An officer sent ashore later on with a strong force found several baskets of human limbs, and in one of them a head which he recognised as that of a sailor belonging to the party. The officer

MILFORD SOUND, SOUTH ISLAND, NEW ZEALAND.

attacked some hundreds of the Maoris as they were seated at their cannibal feast, and drove them away from the half-gnawed bones.

Cook again touched at New Zealand in the course of his third voyage, and this time succeeded in maintaining friendly relations with the Maoris during a short visit. But when the story of Cook's voyage was published in later years the people of Europe conceived a deep horror of these fierce man-eating savages.

7. The Whalers.—For ten or twelve years New Zealand was not visited by white men, but the foundation of a town at

Sydney, in 1788, brought ships out much more often into these waters, and before long it was found that the seas round New Zealand were well stocked with whales. Vessels came out to carry on the profitable business of catching them and taking their oil to Europe. For fresh water and for fuel for their stoves they called at the shores of New Zealand, chiefly at Queen Charlotte Sound, at Dusky Bay on the west coast of South Island, but especially at the Bay of Islands near the extreme north of North Island. There they not only got fresh water but bought fish and pork and potatoes from the friendly tribes of natives, paying for them with knives and blankets; and although quarrels sometimes occurred and deaths took place on both sides, the whalers continued more and more to frequent these places. Sometimes the sailors, attracted by the good looks of the Maori girls, took them as wives and lived in New Zealand. These men generally acted as sealers. They caught the seals that abounded on some parts of the coast, and gathered their skins until the ships called back, when the captain would give them tobacco and rum, guns and powder in exchange for their seal-skins. These the sealers generally shared with the Maoris, who therefore began to find out that it was good to have a white man to be dwelling near them: he brought ships to trade, and the ships brought articles that the Maoris began to value.

8. Maoris visit Sydney.— In 1793, Governor Hunter at Sydney directed that the convicts at Norfolk Island should be set to weave the fine flax that grew wild in that island. They tried, but could make no cloth so fine and soft as that made by the Maoris out of very much the same sort of plant. A ship was sent to try and persuade some Maoris to come over and teach the art. The captain of the ship, being lazy or impatient, did not trouble to persuade; he seized two Maoris and carried them off. They were kept for six months at Norfolk Island, but Captain King treated them very well, and sent them back with ten sows, two boars, a supply of maize-seed and other good things to pay them for their time. When King became Governor of New South Wales he sent further presents over to Te Pehi, chief of the tribe to which these young men belonged, and hence Te Pehi longed to see the sender of these things. He and his four sons ventured to go in an

English vessel to Sydney, where they were astonished at all they saw. On his return Te Pehi induced a sailor named George Bruce, who had been kind to him when he was sick on board ship, to settle in the tribe; the young Englishman married Te Pehi's most charming daughter, and was tattooed and became the first of the Pakeha Maoris, or white men who lived in Maori fashion. Pleased by Te Pehi's account of what he had seen, other Maoris took occasional trips to Sydney, working their passages in whaling ships.

9. Friendly Relations.—Meanwhile English vessels more and more frequently visited New Zealand for pork and flax and kauri pine, or else to catch seals, or merely to take a rest after a long whaling trip. The Bay of Islands became the chief anchorage for that purpose, and thither the Maoris gathered to profit by the trade. Some of the more adventurous, when they found that the English did them no harm, shipped as sailors for a voyage on board the whalers; but though they made good seamen they were sometimes sulky and revengeful, and rarely continued at it more than two or three years.

In 1805 a Maori went with an English surgeon all the way to England, and returned with the most astounding tales of London and English wonders. During the next four or five years several other Maoris went to England, while, on the other hand, a few very respectable white men began to settle down in New Zealand. They were far superior to the rough sailors and liberated convicts of Sydney, who so far had been the most frequent visitors, so that mutual good-will seemed to be established, as the Maoris found that there was much they could gain by the visits of the white men. But all this friendliness was marred by an unfortunate occurrence.

10. The Boyd Massacre.—In 1809 a ship named the *Boyd* sailed from Sydney to go to England round Cape Horn. She had on board seventy white people, including some children of officers at Sydney who were on their way to England to be educated. As she was to call at New Zealand to get some kauri spars, five Maoris went with her, working their passage over. One of these Maoris, named Tarra, was directed during the voyage to do something which he refused to do. The captain caused him to be twice flogged. When the ship anchored in a bay a little to the north of the Bay of Islands, Tarra went ashore, and showed to his tribe his back all scarred with the lash. Revenge was agreed on. The captain was enticed ashore with a few men; and they were suddenly attacked and all killed. Then the Maoris quietly got alongside the ship, rushed on board and commenced the work of massacre among men, women and children, who were all unarmed. Some of the children fell and clasped the feet of Tarra, begging him to save them, but the young savage brained them without mercy. All were slain except a woman and two children who hid themselves during the heat of the massacre, and a boy who was spared because he had been kind to Tarra. All the bodies were taken ashore and eaten. One of the chiefs while curiously examining a barrel of gunpowder caused it to explode, blowing himself and a dozen others to pieces.

Te Pehi, the head chief of the Ngapuhi, was extremely vexed when he heard of this occurrence, and took some trouble to rescue the four survivors, but five whaling vessels gathered for revenge; they landed their crews, who shot thirty Maoris whether belonging to Tarra's tribe or not, and in their blind fury burnt Te Pehi's village, severely wounding the chief himself. This outrage stopped all friendly intercourse for a long time. The whalers shot the Maoris whenever they saw them, about a hundred being killed in the next three years, while the Maoris killed and ate any white people they could catch. Thus in 1816 the *Agnes*, an American brig, happened to be wrecked on their shores. They killed and ate everybody on board, except one man, who was tattooed and kept for a slave during twelve years.

11. The Missionaries.—In spite of all these atrocities a band of missionaries had the courage to settle in New Zealand and begin the work of civilising these Maori tribes. This enterprise was the work of a notable man named Samuel Marsden, who had in early life been a blacksmith in England, but had devoted himself with rare energy to the laborious task of passing the examinations needed to make him a clergyman. He was sent out to be the chaplain to the convicts at Sydney, and his zeal, his faith in the work he had to do, and his roughly eloquent style, made him successful where more cultured clergymen would have failed. For fourteen years he toiled to reform convicts, soldiers, and officers in Sydney; and when Governor King went home to England in 1807, after his term was expired, Marsden went with him on a visit to his friends. While in London, Marsden brought before the Mission Society the question of doing something to Christianise these fierce but intelligent people, and the society not only agreed, but employed two missionaries named Hall and King to undertake the work.

When Marsden, along with these two courageous men, started back to Sydney in the *Ann* convict ship, in 1809, there was on board, strangely enough, a Maori chief called Ruatara. This young fellow was a nephew of Hongi, the powerful head chief of the Ngapuhi tribe. Four years before, being anxious to see something of the wonders of civilised life, he had shipped as a sailor on board a whaler. He had twice been to Sydney and had voyaged up and down all the Pacific. At length, in 1809, he had gone to London, where he was lost in surprise at all he saw. The climate, however, tried him severely, and he was sick and miserable on the voyage back to Sydney. Marsden was kind to him and gave him a home in his own house. Ruatara had many troubles and dangers to meet, through many months, before he was at last settled among his own people.

THE REV. SAMUEL MARSDEN, "THE APOSTLE OF NEW ZEALAND".

Meantime, the new Governor of Sydney refused to allow the missionaries to go to New Zealand. The massacre of the sixty-six people of the *Boyd* had roused a feeling of horror, and it seemed a wicked waste of life to try to live among savages so fierce. The missionaries were therefore employed in Sydney. In 1813 Governor Macquarie directed that every vessel leaving for New Zealand should give bonds to the extent of a thousand pounds to guarantee that the white men should not carry off the natives or interfere with their sacred places. Then the trouble between the two races quieted down a little, and in 1814 the missionaries thought they might at least make further inquiries. A brig called the *Active* of 100 tons was bought; and on board it went Hall with another missionary called Kendall (grandfather of the poet) who had lately come out. They reached the Bay of Islands, taking with them abundance of presents. They saw Ruatara, and persuaded him with his uncle, Hongi, and other chiefs to go to Sydney in the *Active*, and there discuss the question of a mission station. They went, and Hongi guaranteed the protection of his tribe, the Ngapuhi, if the missionaries would settle in their territory.

12. The Mission Station.—It was in November, 1814, that the *Active* sailed with the mission colony, consisting of Kendall, King, and Hall, their wives and five children and a number of mechanics; in all twenty-five Europeans, together with eight Maoris. They took three horses, a bull, two cows, and other live stock, and after a quick passage anchored near the north of the North Island. Marsden was with them as a visitor, to see the place fairly started. He was troubled on landing to find that the Ngapuhi were at war with their near neighbours, the Wangaroans, and he saw that little progress would be made till these tribes were reconciled. Marsden fearlessly entered with only one companion into the heart of the hostile tribe; met Tarra, the instigator of the *Boyd* massacre, and slept that night in the very midst of the Wangaroans. Wrapt up in his greatcoat, he lay close by Tarra, surrounded by the sleeping forms of men and women who, only a few years before, had gathered to the horrid feast. Surprised at this friendly trust, the Wangaroans were fascinated, and subsequently were led by him like children. They were soon induced to rub noses with the chiefs of Ngapuhi as a sign of reconciliation, and were then all invited on board the *Active*, where a merry breakfast brought old enemies together in friendly intercourse.

The missionaries with twelve axes bought 200 acres of land on the shore of the Bay of Islands. Half an acre was soon enclosed by a fence; a few rough houses were built and a pole set up, upon which floated a white flag with a cross and a dove and the words

"Good tidings"; Ruatara made a pulpit out of an old canoe, covered it with cloth, and put seats round it. There, on Christmas Day, 1814, Marsden preached the first sermon in New Zealand to a crowded Maori audience, who understood not one word of what was said, but who, perhaps, were benefited by the general impressiveness of the scene.

In the following February, Marsden returned to Sydney, thinking the mission in a fair way of success. But all was not to be so harmonious as he dreamt; the liberated convicts, who formed the bulk of the crews of sealing and whaling vessels, treated the natives with coarseness and arrogance; the Maoris were quick to revenge themselves, and the murders, thefts, and quarrels along all the shore did more harm than the handful of missionaries could do good. Three or four times they wished to leave, and as often did Marsden return and persuade them to stay. Their lives at least were safe; for Hongi, the Ngapuhi chief, found that they were useful in the way of bringing trade about, but he was dissatisfied because they would not allow guns and powder to be sold by the white men to him and his people.

13. Tribal Wars.—Hongi saw that the tribe which possessed most guns was sure to get the upper hand of all the others. He therefore contrived in another way to secure these wonderful weapons. For in 1820 when Kendall went home to England for a trip Hongi went with him, and saw with constant wonder the marvels of the great city. The sight of the fine English regiments, the arsenals, the theatres, the big elephant at Exeter Change Menagerie, all impressed deeply the Maori from New Zealand forests. He stayed for a while at Cambridge, assisting a professor to compile a dictionary of the Maori language, and going to church regularly all the time. Then he had an audience from George IV., who gave him many presents, and among others a complete suit of ancient armour. For a whole season, Hongi was a sort of lion among London society. People crowded to see a chief who had eaten dozens of men, and so many presents were given him that when he came back to Sydney he was a rich man. He sold everything, however, except his suit of armour, and with the money he bought 300 muskets and plenty of powder, which he took with him to New Zealand. Having reached his home he informed his tribe of the career of conquest he proposed; with these muskets he was going to destroy every enemy. "There is but one king in England," he said; "there shall be only one among the Maoris." He soon had a force of a thousand warriors, whom he embarked on board a fleet of canoes, and took to the southern shores of the Hauraki Gulf, where the Ngatimaru lived, ancient enemies of the Ngapuhi, who, however, felt secure in their numbers and in the strength of their great pah Totara. But Hongi captured the pah, and slew five hundred of the unfortunate inmates. The Ngatimaru tribe then retreated south into the valley of the Waikato River, and summoned their men and all their friends; a total of over three thousand were arrayed on that fatal battle-field. Hongi with his muskets gained a complete victory. He shot the hostile chief with his own gun, and tearing out his eyes, swallowed them on the field of battle. Over a thousand were killed, and Hongi and his men feasted on the spot for some days till three hundred bodies had been eaten. The victors then returned, bearing in their canoes another thousand captives, of whom many were slain and cooked to provide a share of the horrid feast to the women of the tribe.

In his bloodthirsty wars Hongi showed great skill and energy. During the two following years he defeated, slaughtered, and ate large numbers of the surrounding tribes, and when a number of these unfortunate people withdrew to a pah of enormous strength, nearly surrounded by a bend of the Waikato River, he dragged his canoes over to that river, ascended it, dashed at the steep cliffs, the ditches and palisades, and once more the muskets won the day. A thousand fell in the fight; then the women and children were slaughtered in heaps. The strong tribe of the Arawa further south had their chief pah on an island in the middle of Lake Rotorua. Hongi with great labour carried his canoes over to the lake. The spear-armed Maoris could do nothing in defence while he shot at them from the lake; and when he assaulted the island, though they came down to the water's edge to repel him, again there was victory for the muskets. Thus did Hongi conquer till the whole North Island owned his ascendancy. But in 1827 his career came to an end, for having quarrelled with his former friends, the tribe of which Tarra was chief, he killed them all but twenty, but in the fight was himself shot through the lungs; for that tribe had now many muskets also, and a ball fired when the massacre was nearly over passed through Hongi's chest, leaving a hole which, though temporarily healed, caused his death a few months later. Pomaré succeeded him as chief of the Ngapuhi, and made that tribe still the terror of the island. At one pah Pomaré killed 400 men; and he had his own way for a time in all his fights. But the other tribes now began to see that they could not possibly save themselves except by getting muskets also, and as they offered ten times their value for them in pork and flax and other produce, English vessels brought them over in plenty. The remnant of the Waikato tribe having become well armed and well exercised in shooting under Te Whero Whero, they laid an ambush for Pomaré and killed him with almost the whole of the 500 men who were with him. The other tribes joined Te Whero Whero, and in successive battles ruined the Ngapuhi. Te Whero Whero held the leadership for a time, during which he almost exterminated the Taranaki tribe. He was practically lord of all the North Island till he met his match in Rauparaha, the most determined and wily of all the Maori leaders. He was the chief of a tribe living in the south of the North Island, and he gathered a wild fighting band out of the ruined tribes of his own and the surrounding districts. Many battles were fought between him and Te Whero Whero, in which sometimes as many as a thousand muskets were in use on each side. Rauparaha was at length overcome, and with difficulty escaped across the strait to the South Island, while Te Whero Whero massacred and enslaved all over the North Island, cooking as many as 200 bodies after a single fight. And yet the evil was in a way its own cure, for, through strenuous endeavours, by this time every tribe had a certain proportion of its men well armed with muskets; and thus no single tribe ever afterwards got the same cruel ascendancy that was obtained first by the Ngapuhi and then by the Waikato tribe. But fights and ambushes, slaughters, the eating of prisoners and all the horrid scenes of Maori war went on from week to week all over the North Island.

CHAPTER XXIV.

NEW ZEALAND COLONISED.

1. Kororarika.—All this fighting of the Maori tribes made them more dependent on the trade they had with white men. They could neither make guns nor powder for themselves, and the tribe that could purchase none of the white man's weapons was sure to be slaughtered and eaten by other tribes. Hence white men were more eagerly welcomed, and in course of time nearly two hundred of them were living Maori fashion with the tribes. But it was at the Bay of Islands that the chief trading was carried on. For it was there that the kauri timber grew; it was there that the pigs were most plentiful and the cargoes of flax most easily obtained; and when a man named Turner set up a grog-shop on the shores of the bay all the whaling ships made this their usual place for resting and refitting. Behind the beach the hills rise steeply, and on these hills a number of white men built themselves homes securely fenced, and defended, sometimes even by a cannon or two. But down on the little green flat next to the beach, rude houses were more numerous. In the year 1838 there were about 500 persons resident in the little town, which was now called Kororarika, but at times there were nearly double that number of people resident in it for months together. A wild and reckless place it was, for sailors reckoned themselves there to be beyond the reach of English law.

At one time as many as thirty-six ships lay off the town of Kororarika, and in a single year 150 ships visited the bay: generally staying a month or more at anchor. The little church and the Catholic mission station up on the hill did less good to the natives than these rough sailors did harm, and at length the more respectable white men could stand the disorder no longer. They formed an association to maintain decency. They seized, tried, fined or sometimes locked up for a time the worst offenders, and twice they stripped the ruffians naked, gave them a coat of tar, stuck them all over with white down from a native plant, and when they were thus decorated, expelled them from the town, with a promise of the same treatment if ever they were seen back in it.

2. Hokianga.—Long before this the capacities of New Zealand and the chances of making wealth there became well known in England, and in 1825 an association was formed to colonise the country. It sent out an agent, who reported that Hokianga, a deep estuary on the west coast, just opposite to Kororarika, and only thirty miles away from it, was a charming place for a settlement. The agent bought a square mile of land from the Maoris and also two little islands in the harbour. The company fitted out a ship the *Rosanna*, and sixty colonists sailed out in her to form the pioneers of the new colony. They landed, and liked the look of the place, but they were timid by reason of the tales they had heard of Maori ferocity. Now at this time the Ngapuhis were at war with the Arawas, and the latter were getting up a war dance, which the settlers were just in time to see. Five or six hundred men stood in four long rows, stamping in time to a chant of their leader. It was night, a fire lit up their quivering limbs and their rolling eyes; they joined in a chorus, and when they came to particular words they hissed like a thousand serpents; they went through the performance of killing their enemies, cutting up their bodies and eating them. The settlers fell into deep meditation and departed. Not half a dozen remained in New Zealand, the others went to Sydney, and so after an expense of £20,000 this association, which had been formed for the kindly purpose of putting people in lands less crowded than their own, failed and was disbanded.

3. Settled Government.—Between 1825 and 1835 the Maoris of the North Island were in a miserable state. Wars and massacres and cannibal feasts made the country wretched, and though the missionaries were respected they could not secure peace. But they persuaded the chiefs of some of the weaker tribes to appeal to England for protection against the conquering warriors who oppressed and destroyed their people. It was in 1831 that this petition was sent to King William, and about the same time the white men at Kororarika, terrified at the violence with which the Waikato men were ravaging the surrounding lands, asked the Governor at Sydney to interfere. The result was that although the English would not regularly take possession of New Zealand, they chose Mr. Busby, a gentleman well known in New South Wales, to be the Resident there, his business being, so far as possible, to keep order. How he was to keep order without men or force to make his commands obeyed it is hard to see; but he was expected to do whatever could be done by persuasion, and to send for a British war-ship if ever he thought it was needed.

The first war-ship that thus came over did more harm than good. Its visit was caused by a disastrous wreck. The whaling barque *Harriet*, under the command of a man named Guard, a low fellow who had formerly been a convict, was trading among the islands when she was wrecked off the coast of Taranaki. The Maoris attacked the stranded ship, but the crew stayed on her and fired into the assailants, and it was not till after quite a siege, in which twelve seamen were killed, that the rest fled from the wreck, leaving Mrs. Guard and her two children in the hands of the Taranaki tribe. Guard and twelve seamen, however, though they escaped for a time were caught by a neighbouring tribe, to whom he promised a cask of gunpowder if they would help him to reach an English ship. This they did, and Guard reached Sydney, where he begged Sir Richard Bourke to send a vessel for the rescue of his wife and children. Bourke sent the *Alligator*, with a company of soldiers, who landed and demanded the captive seamen. These were given up, but the captain of the ship supported Guard in breaking his promise and refusing to give the powder, under the plea that it was a bad thing for natives. The *Alligator* then went round to Taranaki for the woman and children. The chief of the tribe came down to the beach and said they would be given up for a ransom. The white men seized him, dragged him into their boat to be a hostage, but he jumped out of the boat and was speared with bayonets. He was taken to the ship nearly dead. Then the natives gave up the woman and one child in return for their chief. After some parley a native came down to the beach with the other child on his shoulders. He said he would give it up if a proper ransom was paid. The English said they would give no ransom, and when the man turned to go away again, they shot him through the back, quite dead. The child was recovered, but Mrs. Guard and the children testified that this native had been a good friend to them when in captivity. Nevertheless, his head was cut off and tumbled about on the beach. The *Alligator* then bombarded the native pah, destroyed all its houses to the number of 200, with all the provisions they contained, killing from twenty to thirty men in the process. This scarcely agreed with the letter which Mr. Busby had just received, in which he was directed to express to the Maori chiefs the regret which the King of England felt at the injuries committed by white men against Maoris.

4. Captain Hobson.—But there were many difficulties in securing justice between fickle savages and white men who were in general so ruffianly as those who then dwelt in New Zealand. The atrocities of the *Harriet* episode did some good, however, for along with other circumstances they stirred up the English Government to make some inquiries into the manner in which Englishmen treated the natives of uncivilised countries. These inquiries showed much injustice and sometimes wanton cruelty, and when a petition came from the respectable people of Kororarika, asking that some check should be put upon the licence of the low white men who frequented that port, the English Government resolved to annex New Zealand if the Maoris were willing to be received into the British Empire. For that purpose they chose Captain Hobson, a worthy and upright sea-captain, who in his ship of war, the *Rattlesnake*, had seen much of Australia and New Zealand. It was he who had taken Sir Richard Bourke to Port Phillip in 1837, and Hobson's Bay was named in his honour. After that he had been sent by Bourke to the Bay of Islands to inquire into the condition of things there, and when he had gone home to England he had given evidence as to the disorder which prevailed in New Zealand. He was sent in a war-ship, the *Druid*, with instructions to keep the white men in order, and to ask the natives if they would like to become subjects of Queen Victoria and live under her protection. If they agreed to do so, he was to form New Zealand into an English colony and he was to be its Lieutenant-Governor under the general control of the Governor of New South Wales.

Hobson reached Sydney at the end of 1839 and conferred

with Governor Gipps, who helped him to draw up proclamations and regulations for the work to be done. On leaving Sydney, Hobson took with him a treasurer and a collector of customs for the new colony, a sergeant of police and four mounted troopers of the New South Wales force, together with a police magistrate to try offenders, and two clerks to assist in the work of government. It was the 29th of January, 1840, when he landed at the Bay of Islands. Next day, on the beach, he read several proclamations, one of which asserted that all British subjects, even though resident in New Zealand, were still bound to obey British laws; and another declared that as white men were tricking the Maoris into selling vast tracts of land for goods of little value, all such bargains made after that date would be illegal, while all made before that date would be inquired into before being allowed. It was declared that if the Maoris in future wished to sell their land the Governor would buy it and pay a fair price for it. All white men who wished for land could then buy from the Governor. Three days later the respectable white men of Kororarika waited on Captain Hobson to congratulate him on his arrival and to promise him their obedience and assistance.

5. Treaty of Waitangi.—Meantime Hobson had asked the missionaries to send word round to all the neighbouring chiefs that he would like to see them, and on the 5th of February, 1840, a famous meeting took place on the shore of the Bay of Islands near the mouth of the pretty river Waitangi. There on a little platform on a chair of state sat the new Governor, with the officers of the ship in their uniform, and a guard of mariners and sailors; while beside the platform stood the leading white men of Kororarika. Flags fluttered all round the spot. At noon, when Hobson took his seat, there were over five hundred Maoris, of whom fifty were chiefs, in front of the platform. Then one of the missionaries rose and in the Maori tongue explained what the Queen of England proposed. First, that the Maoris, of their own accord, should allow their country to be joined to the British Empire. Second, that the Queen would protect them in their right to their land and all their property, and see that no white men interfered with them in it, but that if they chose to sell any of their land, then the Governor would buy it from them. Third, that the Queen would extend to the Maoris, if they so desired, all the rights and privileges of British subjects and the protection of British law.

When these proposals had been fully explained the Maoris were asked to say what they thought of them. Twenty-six chiefs spoke in favour of accepting, and so bringing about peace and order in the land. Six spoke against them, declaring that thus would the Maoris be made slaves. The natives seemed very undecided, when Waka Nene arose and in an eloquent address showed the miseries of the land now that fire-arms had been introduced, and begged his countrymen to place themselves under the rule of a queen who was able and willing to make the country quiet and happy. The Maoris were greatly excited, and Hobson therefore gave them a day to think over the matter. There was much discussion all night long among the neighbouring pahs and villages; but the next day when the Maoris gathered, forty-six chiefs put their marks to the parchment now always known as the treaty of Waitangi.

This treaty was taken by missionaries and officers from tribe to tribe, and in the course of two or three months over five hundred chiefs had signed it. On the 21st May, Hobson proclaimed that the islands of New Zealand were duly added to the British Empire, and that he would assume the rule of the new colony as Lieutenant-Governor. Meantime houses had been built at Kororarika for the Governor and his officers; a customhouse had been set up, and taxes were levied on all goods landed, so as to provide a revenue with which to pay these and other Government expenses.

6. Auckland.—But the people at Kororarika had bought from the natives all the level land in the place, and thinking their town would soon be a great city, and the capital of an important colony, they would not sell it except at very high prices. Now Captain Hobson had seen at the head of the Hauraki Gulf a place which seemed to him to be more suitable for the capital of the future colony. To this lovely spot he changed his residence. He bought from the natives about thirty thousand acres, and on an arm of the gulf, where the Waitemata harbour spreads its shining waters, he caused a town to be sur-

AUCKLAND FROM THE WHARF.

veyed and streets to be laid out. In April, 1841, after he had reserved sufficient land for Government offices, parks and other public purposes, he caused the rest to be offered in allotments for sale by auction. There was a general belief that now, when the islands were formally annexed to the British Empire, New Zealand would be a most prosperous colony, and that land in its capital would go up rapidly in value. Many speculators came over from Sydney. The bidding was brisk, and the allotments were sold at the rate of about six hundred pounds per acre. A few months later a sale was held of lands in the suburbs and of farming lands a little way out from the town. This was again successful. Houses began to spring up, most of them slender in structure, but with a few of solid appearance. Next year ships arrived from England with 560 immigrants, who rapidly settled on the land, and before long a thriving colony was formed. The little town was very pretty, with green hills behind the branching harbour that lay in front, dotted with volcanic islets. The whole district was green; and the figures of Maoris in the grassy streets, their canoes bringing in vegetables to market, their pahs seen far off on the neighbouring hills, gave the scene a charming touch of the romantic. A company of six soldiers with four officers came from Sydney to defend the settlers, and barracks were built for them. The name chosen for the city was Auckland, after a gentleman named Eden, who had taken for half a century a deep interest in colonising experiments, and who had been raised to the peerage with the title of Lord Auckland.

7. New Zealand Company.—Meantime another part of New Zealand had been colonised under very different circumstances. The English association, which in 1825 attempted to form a settlement at Hokianga and failed, had consisted of very influential men. They had not given up their plans altogether, and in 1837 they formed a new association called the New Zealand Company. That restless theorist Edward Gibbon Wakefield, who had already sent out the settlers who had just founded Adelaide, joined this association, and impressed the members with his own idea already described on page 67. It was arranged that a colony should be sent out to New Zealand on the plan of a complete little community. There were to be gentlemen and clergymen and teachers; so many farmers, so many carpenters, so many blacksmiths; every trade was to be represented so that everybody would have something to do, and there would be none too many of any one kind. A bill was brought before Parliament for the purpose of establishing a colony after this fashion, and at first Parliament was inclined to favour the bill. But the missionaries in New Zealand were hostile to the proposal. They were steadily converting the Maoris to Christianity. They hoped to turn them into quiet, industrious and prosperous people, if white men did not come and take away their land from them. Parliament, therefore, refused to pass the bill. But the company had gone too far to retreat. It had already arranged with many settlers to take them and their families out to New Zealand, and had begun to sell land at so much an acre, nobody knew where except that it was to be in New Zealand. They therefore quietly purchased and fitted out a vessel named the *Tory* to go to New Zealand and make arrangements. The party was under the charge of Colonel Wakefield, brother of Edward Gibbon Wakefield; and he took with him surveyors to lay out the land, farming experts to judge of the soil, and a scientific man to report on the natural products. This vessel sailed away quietly in May, 1839, hoping to reach New Zealand unnoticed. The English Government heard of it however, informed the company that its action was illegal, and immediately afterwards sent off Captain Hobson in the *Druid*, as has been already described, to take possession on behalf of the British nation. The New Zealand Company then apologised; said that they would direct their agents who had gone out to New Zealand to obey the Governor in all things, and promised that the new settlement should abide by the law.

8. Wellington.—Meantime the *Tory* was ploughing the deep on her way to New Zealand. Her passengers first saw the new country on the west coast of the South Island. They were then very much disappointed, for the shore was high and wild, the mountains were close behind it, and their lofty sides were gloomy and savage. The whole scene was grand, but did not promise much land that would be suitable for farming. They turned into Cook Strait, and anchored in Queen Charlotte Sound, a lovely harbour, but surrounded by high hills clothed in dark and heavy forests. When they landed, they were amazed at the depth and richness of the black soil and the immense size to which the trees grew. Such a soil could grow all sorts of produce in rich abundance, but it would cost forty pounds an acre to clear it for ploughing. Boats were got out, however, and parties rowed up into all the branches of the beautiful harbour, but without seeing any sufficient extent of level or open land. Then they crossed the strait, and sailing in by a narrow entrance, viewed all the wide expanse of Port Nicholson. It was a great harbour with a little wooded island in its middle; it opened out into quiet arms all fringed with shelly beaches, and behind these rose range after range of majestic mountains. The trouble was that here too the land which was fairly level was too limited in extent to satisfy the colony's needs; for already in England the company had sold 100,000 acres of farming land, and the purchasers would soon be on their way to occupy it. After examining the shores with care they chose the beach of the east side as the site for their town. Behind it stretched the beautiful valley of the Hutt River, enclosed by mountains, but with broad grassy meadows lying between. Here they started to build a town which they called Britannia, and they made friends with the Maoris of the district. A Pakeha Maori named Barrett acted as interpreter. The natives went on board the *Tory*, were shown 239 muskets, 300 blankets, 160 tomahawks and axes, 276 shirts, together with a quantity of looking-glasses, scissors, razors, jackets, pots, and scores of other things, with eighty-one kegs of gunpowder, two casks of cartridges and more than a ton of tobacco. They were asked if they would sell all the land that could be seen from the ship in return for these things. They agreed, signed some papers and took the goods on shore, where they at once began to use the muskets in a grand fight among themselves for the division of the property. It was soon discovered that the site of the town was too much exposed to westerly gales, and the majority of the settlers crossed Port Nicholson to a narrow strip of grassy land between a pretty beach and some steep hills. Here was founded the town called Wellington, after the famous duke.

By this time the settlers were arriving thick and fast. The first came in the *Aurora*, which reached the settlement on 22nd January, 1840; other ships came at short intervals, till there were twelve at anchor in Port Nicholson. The settlers were pleased with the country; they landed in good spirits and set to work to make themselves houses. All was activity—surveyors, carpenters, bricklayers, blacksmiths, every one busy, and rapidly a smart little town of some hundred houses rose behind the beach. The Maoris came and helped in the work, getting three or four shillings a day for their services, and proving themselves very handy in many ways. All were in sanguine spirits, when word came from Governor Hobson at Auckland that, in accordance with his proclamation, all purchases of land from the natives were illegal, he having come to protect the Maoris from imposition.

9. The Land Question.—Now Colonel Wakefield had fancied that he had bought 20,000,000 acres for less than £9,000 worth of goods, and he was assigning it as fast as he could to people who had paid £1 an acre to the company in England. Here was a sad fix. The Governor sent down his chief officer, Mr. Shortland, who rode across the island with the mounted police, and told the settlers not to fancy the land theirs, as he would ere long have to turn them off. Disputes arose, for it seemed absurd that fifty-eight Maori chiefs should sell the land on which many thousands of people dwelt, the majority of these people never having so much as heard of the bargain. The settlers talked of starting for South America and forming a colony in Chili, but more kept on coming, so that they had not ships enough to take them across. And, besides, they had paid a pound an acre to the company and demanded their land. Colonel Wakefield went off to Auckland to talk the matter over with Governor Hobson, who left the difficulty to be settled by his superior, Governor Gipps, at Sydney.

Wakefield then went to Sydney to see Governor Gipps, who said that the whole thing was irregular, but that he would allow the settlers to occupy the land, supposing that every Maori who had a proper claim to any part of it got due compensation, and if twenty acres of the central part of Wellington were reserved for public buildings. These conditions Wakefield agreed to, and, very glad to have got out of a serious difficulty, he returned with the good tidings. Shortly afterwards Governor Hobson himself visited Wellington, but was very coldly received by the settlers there.

In the next two years 350 ships arrived at Wellington, bringing out over 4,000 settlers. Of these about 1,000 went up into the valleys and made farms; but 3,000 stayed in and around Wellington, which then grew to be a substantial little town, with four good piers, about 200 houses of wood or brick and about 250 houses of more slender construction. More than 200 Maoris could be seen in its streets clad in the European clothes given as payment for the land. In all there were about 700 Maoris in the district, and for their use the company set apart 11,000 acres of farm lands, and 110 acres in the town. Roads were being made into the fertile valleys, where eight or ten thousand acres were occupied as farms and being rapidly cleared and tilled. Parties were organised to go exploring across the mountains. They brought back word that inland the soil was splendid, sometimes covered with forests, sometimes with meadows of long grass or New Zealand flax, but always watered by beautiful rivers and under a lovely climate. The Maoris were everywhere friendly throughout their journey.

10. Taranaki.—In the beginning of the year 1840, an emigration society had been formed in the south-west of England to enable the farm labourers and miners of Cornwall, Devon, and Dorset to settle in less crowded lands. The Earl of Devon was its president, and Plymouth its headquarters. They chose New Zealand for the site of their colony, and understanding that the New Zealand Company had bought half of the North Island they gave that company £10,000 for the right to select 60,000 acres of it. It was in March, 1841, that the pioneers of this new colony arrived at Wellington under the guidance of Mr. Carrington, a surveyor in the ship *William Bryant*. The exploring party had just come back, and its report of the Taranaki land was very tempting. Immediately after receiving that report Colonel Wakefield had gone off to purchase it. He found a few natives left there, the remnant of the tribes whom Te Whero Whero had either destroyed or carried into slavery. These few people had taken refuge up in the awful solitudes of the giant Mount Egmont, but had come back to dwell, a sorrow-stricken handful, in the homes of their fathers. Barrett was left to arrange a bargain with them, and in return for a quantity of goods they sold all the land along sixty miles of coast with a depth of fifteen miles inland. This was the land which

Wakefield recommended for the new settlers, and he lent them a ship to take them round. There they landed, and in spite of their disappointment at the want of a safe harbour, they set to work and built up their little town, which they called New Plymouth.

In September of the same year the main body of settlers arrived for this new colony, and were landed at Taranaki, when they immediately scattered out over the country, as fast as Carrington could survey it for them. But there was now a difficulty. For Te Whero Whero and his tribe had released many hundreds of the Taranaki natives who had been carried off as slaves. Whether it was because they had now become Christians or because the slaves were more in number than they could use, it was not easy to determine; but at any rate, in that very month of September when hundreds of white men were arriving to occupy the land, hundreds of Maoris were coming back to re-occupy it. They begged the settlers not to fell their big trees, but were very mild in their conduct. They chose places not yet claimed by the white men, and there fenced in the land on which to grow their sweet potatoes.

Meanwhile there was another complication. By Maori custom a warrior had the ownership of the lands he conquered. Governor Hobson therefore regarded Te Whero Whero as the owner of the Taranaki land, and gave him £400 for his right to it. Hobson declared that the Auckland Government was the owner of this land, and that all settlers must buy it from him. Eventually the trouble was cleared up for the time being, when Hobson allowed the company to keep ten miles of coast running back five or six miles, the rest to belong to the Government, which would set aside a certain part for the use of the Maoris. In December, 1842, a settler claimed a piece of land which a Maori had fenced in; he pulled down the fence; the Maoris put it up again. The settler assisted by an officer pulled it down once more. A young chief who brandished a tomahawk and threatened mischief was arrested, and carried into New Plymouth where a magistrate liberated him, and declared the action of the settler illegal. Matters for a time kept in this unfriendly state, ominously hinting the desperate war that was to follow.

11. Wanganui.—Meanwhile the settlers in the Wellington

district were finding that by crossing difficult mountains they could get sufficient level land for their purpose, and at the close of 1840 two hundred of them sailed 150 miles north to where the river Wanganui falls into Cook Strait. The land was rich and the district beautiful. Colonel Wakefield supposed that he had bought the whole of it, though the natives afterwards proved that they sold only a part on the north side of the river. Here, about four miles from the mouth of the stream, the settlers formed a little town which they called Petre, but which is now known as Wanganui. The natives were numerous; on the river banks their villages were frequent, and up on the hills, that rose all around like an amphitheatre, the palisades of their fortified pahs were easily visible. But the fine black soil of the district, in places grassy, in places with patches of fine timber, proved very attractive to the settlers, and soon there came half a dozen ships with more colonists direct from England. The natives were friendly to white men, and gave them a cordial welcome. Down the river came their canoes laden with pigs, potatoes, melons, and gourds for sale in the market of the little town. All was good-will until the Maoris found that the white men had come not merely to settle among them, but to appropriate all the best of the land. Then their tempers grew sour and the prospect steadily grew more unpleasant.

12. Nelson.—The emigration spirit was at this time strong in England; for it was in the year 1840 to 1841 that free settlers chiefly colonised both Victoria and South Australia. New Zealand was as much a favourite as any, and when the New Zealand Company proposed in 1841 to form a new colony somewhere in that country to be called Nelson, nearly 100,000 acres were sold at thirty shillings an acre to men who did not know even in which island of New Zealand the land was to be situated. In April of the same year the pioneers of the new settlement started in the ships *Whitby* and *Will Watch*, with about eighty settlers, their wives, families and servants. Captain Arthur Wakefield was the leader, and he took the ships to Wellington, where they waited while he went out to search for a suitable site. He chose a place at the head of Tasman Bay, where, in a green hollow fringed by a beautiful beach and embosomed deep in majestic hills, the settlers soon gathered in the pretty little town of Nelson. The soil was black earth resting on great boulders; out of it grew low bushes easily cleared away, and here and there stood a few clumps of trees to give a grateful shade. The place was shut in by the hills so as to be completely sheltered from the boisterous gales of Cook Strait, and altogether it was a place of dreamy loveliness. Its possession was claimed by Rauparaha, the warrior, on the ground of conquest. With him and other chiefs the settlers had a conference, the result of which was that a certain specified area round the head of the bay was purchased. But the white men regarded themselves as having the right of superior beings to go where they wished and do with the land what they wished. Finding a seam of good coal at a place outside their purchase they did not in any way scruple to send a vessel to carry it off, in spite of the protests of the Maoris.

13. Death of Governor Hobson.—These things hinted at troubles which were to come, but in 1842 all things looked promising for the colonies of New Zealand. There were altogether about 12,000 white persons, most of them being men who wore blue shirts and lived on pork and potatoes. Auckland the capital had 3,000 but, Wellington was the largest town with 4,000 people. Next to that came Nelson with 2,500; New Plymouth and Wanganui were much smaller but yet thriving places. They had no less than nine newspapers, most of them little primitive sheets, but wonderful in communities so young. In October, 1841, Dr. George Selwyn was appointed to be Bishop of New Zealand; and he left England with a number of clergymen who settled in Auckland, Wellington, Nelson, and New Plymouth. Churches began to spring up, and schools not only for white children, but also for Maoris. An immense change for the better had appeared among the Maoris. The last case of cannibalism took place about this time; and though they still fought among one another, it was not with the same awful bloodshed that had characterised the previous twenty years.

On the 16th November, 1840, the Queen declared New Zealand an independent colony. Hobson was then no longer Lieutenant-Governor merely, and subject to the Governor at Sydney. He was Governor Hobson, and of equal rank with all the other Governors. He now had a Legislative Council to assist him in making for New Zealand such laws as might be needed in her peculiar circumstances. In that council the Chief Justice, the Colonial Secretary, the Surveyor-General, the Attorney-General and the Protector of the Maoris had seats. But Hobson did not long enjoy his new dignity. He had had a difficult task to perform, and his duty had led him into conflict with many people who wished to purchase their land from the natives at ridiculous prices. In the midst of his worries he had several strokes of paralysis, of which the last killed him in September, 1842 ; and he was buried in the cemetery at Auckland. He had lived, however, to see New Zealand colonised, and had died much liked by the Maoris, without seeing any of that bitter struggle between the two races which was soon to shed so much blood and waste so much treasure.

CHAPTER XXV.

WHITE MEN AND MAORIS.

1. Governor Fitzroy.—When Governor Hobson died, his place was taken by his friend Lieutenant Shortland until a new Governor could be sent out. The English people were at this time very anxious to see that the natives of new lands which they colonised should be fairly treated, and for that purpose they chose Captain Fitzroy to be the new Governor. Up to this time he had been the captain of a ship and had made himself famous in surveying and mapping little known shores in his ship the *Beagle*, in which he had visited New Zealand on a trip round the world, and he was therefore called to give evidence as to its condition before the Committee of the House of Lords in 1838. He was well known to have shown much consideration to native tribes, and his strong wish to deal justly by them had often been shown. This was the main reason for his appointment. He landed in November, 1843, and found the colony in a state of great depression, the public treasury being not only empty but in debt. For many officials had been appointed, judges, magistrates, policemen, customs receivers and so on ; and to pay the salaries of these every one had relied on the continued sale of land.

But in 1841 there had come out the first Land Commissioner, William Spain, who began to inquire into the disputes about land which had arisen between white men and Maoris. Out of every ten acres the white men said they had bought he allowed them to keep only one. This was but fair to the Maoris, who had been induced very often to make most foolish bargains; but the settlers ceased to buy land when they were not certain of keeping it. Hence the land sales stopped; the Governor owed £20,000 more than he could pay, and so he was confronted with troubles from his very first arrival.

2. Wairau Massacre.—Just before he came an incident had happened which deepened the trouble of the colony. At the north of the South Island, not far from Nelson, there was a fine valley watered by the stream Wairau, which Colonel Wakefield claimed, alleging that it was part of the land he had bought with the Nelson district. Rauparaha and his son-in-law, Rangihaeata, claimed it by right of conquest, and they had a couple of hundred stout warriors at their back, all well armed with muskets. Mr. Spain sent word that he was coming to settle the dispute, but, in spite of that, Captain Wakefield sent surveyors to measure out the land for occupation by the settlers. The surveyors were turned off by Rauparaha, who carried their instruments and other property carefully off the land and then burnt the huts they had put up. The Maoris did no violence, and were courteous though determined. The surveyors returned to Nelson, and Captain Wakefield induced the local magistrates to issue a warrant for the arrest of Rauparaha and Rangihaeata. To execute this warrant Mr. Thompson, the police magistrate, himself went in a small vessel, and with him went Captain Wakefield, seven other gentlemen, and forty labourers, in all a party of forty-nine, of whom thirty-five were armed with guns.

When they landed at the mouth of the Wairau River, Piraha, a Christian native, met them and begged them not to go on, as Rauparaha was ready to fight, but they paid no attention, and after marching eight miles up the pretty valley they saw the Maoris about 100 in number standing behind the stream, which though only waist-deep had a rushing current of chilly water. Rauparaha said: "Here am I. What do you want with me?"

Mr. Thompson said he must go to Nelson; and an irritating conversation ensued. Rangihaeata drew up his tall form, his curly black hair setting off a face of eagle sharpness, and from his eye there gleamed an angry light. Behind him stood his wife, the daughter of Rauparaha, and near them this latter chief himself, short and broad, but strong and wiry-looking, a man with a cunning face, yet much dignity of manner. When the handcuffs were produced by Mr. Thompson, Rauparaha warned him not to be so foolish. The magistrates gave the order to fix bayonets and advance; as the white men were crossing the stream a shot was fired by one of them. It struck dead the wife of Rangihaeata. Thereupon the Maoris fired a volley and the white men hesitated on the brink of the water; a second volley and a third told upon them with deadly effect, and the labourers, who carried arms but had neither martial spirit nor experience, turned and fled.

Five of the gentlemen with four of the labourers stood their ground, and when the Maoris crossed they surrendered. Rauparaha called out to spare them; but Rangihaeata, mad at the loss of a wife he loved, brained them with his tomahawk one after another, while the young men hunted the labourers through the trees and slew such as they overtook. Twenty-seven white men reached the shore and were carried quickly in the boats to the brig, five of them badly wounded. Twenty-two lay dead alongside of five natives whom the white men had slain.

Rauparaha feared the vengeance of the white man. He had few resources in the South Island, while the Nelson settlers could send 500 armed men against him. He crossed in his own war canoes, over a stormy strait in wild weather; weary and wet with spray, he landed in the south of the North Island, roused his countrymen by his fervid oratory, to which he gave a fine effect by jingling before them the handcuffs with which he was to have been led a prisoner to Nelson. A day or two after the massacre, a Wesleyan clergyman went out from Nelson to Wairau and reverently buried those ghastly bodies with the cloven skulls. Not one had been mangled, far less had there been any cannibalism.

3. Effects of Wairau Massacre.—The Maoris were clearly less ferocious than they had been, and more than half of

them had become fervid Christians after a fashion, but in some respects they were getting their eyes opened. The missionaries had told them that the white men were coming for their benefit; yet now they began to see that the white men were soon to be the lords of the soil, and that the natives must sink back into the position of servants. If a white man visited a Maori village he was received as a man of distinction and entertained. If a Maori chief went to a white man's town, he was allowed to wander in the street; or if at all accosted it was with the condescension of a superior race to a race of servants. The Maori blood was firing up. The story of Wairau made them change their mind about the white man's courage. The whalers had been hearts of daring; these new-comers had run and bawled for their lives. The natives were anxious also as to the result which would happen when all the lands near the shore should have been occupied by white men, and they themselves hemmed up in the interior.

A special interest was given to these feelings when in 1844 Te Whero Whero gave a great feast, only two miles out of Auckland, partly as a welcome to Governor Fitzroy, and partly as a demonstration in regard to the land question. He displayed a lavish bounty; 11,000 baskets of potatoes and 9,000 sharks, with great stores of other provisions, were distributed. But when the settlers saw a war dance of 1,600 men, all well armed with muskets, and drilled with wonderful precision, they felt that their lives were at the mercy of the native tribes. Not one-fourth of that number of armed men with any training for battle could have been sent forth from the settlement for its own defence. This gave a significance to the Wairau massacre that created quite a panic. Fresh settlers ceased to come; many that were there already now left. Those who had taken up farms far out in the country abandoned them and withdrew to the towns.

4. Honi Heke.—And yet the great majority of the Maoris seem to have had no unfriendly purpose. When Governor Fitzroy went down to see Rauparaha he had no more than twelve white men with him, when he entered an assemblage of 500 Maoris. He said he had come to inquire about the sad quarrel at Wairau, and Rauparaha told him his story while others supported it by their evidence. Fitzroy stated that the Maoris had been very wrong to kill those who had surrendered, but as the white men had fired first he would take no vengeance for their death. Indeed, at Wellington and Nelson, Fitzroy openly said that the magistrates were wholly misguided in trying to arrest the native chief; and at Nelson he rebuked all those who had been concerned in the affair. This gave great offence to the white men. They asked if the blood of their friends and relatives was thus to be shed and no sort of penalty to be exacted for the slaughter. Many of the magistrates resigned, and a deep feeling of irritation was shown towards the Governor, some of the settlers petitioning the English Government to recall him.

In the August of 1844 a young chief named Honi Heke, who dwelt at the Bay of Islands, on account of a private quarrel with a rough whaler, entered the town of Kororarika with a band of armed followers. He plundered a few shops and cut down a flagstaff on which the Union Jack floated from a steep hill behind the town. There were then not more than ninety soldiers in New Zealand, and when Heke threatened to burn Kororarika, and do the same to Auckland, there was too good reason to fear that he might be as good as his word, for he had 200 well-armed men at his back, and a comrade of his, named Kawiti, had nearly as many. A chief named Waka-Nene with his men kept Heke in check, while Fitzroy sent to Sydney and received 160 soldiers with two cannon. These landed at the Bay of Islands, but Waka-Nene begged the Governor not to hurry into hostilities. He arranged for a friendly meeting. Fitzroy met nine principal chiefs, who apologised and made Heke send also a written apology. Fitzroy said he would redress some wrongs the natives said they suffered, and having obtained from Heke ten muskets by way of fine and having again set up the flagstaff he returned to Auckland.

But before the year was ended Heke approached the town once more with 100 armed men. He insulted it from the hills, cut down the flagstaff again, and then withdrew to the forests. Fitzroy published a proclamation offering £100 for his capture, and Heke replied by offering £100 for the head of Fitzroy. The Governor now caused a new flagstaff to be set up, all sheathed with iron at the bottom, and with a strong wooden house attached to it, in which a score of soldiers were always to keep guard. A block-house or small wooden fortress was set up at a little distance down the hill towards Kororarika. Nevertheless, Heke said he would come and cut down the flagstaff again. Then the inhabitants of Kororarika began to drill in order to give him a warm reception if he came. Lieutenant Philpott, the commander of the *Hazard* ship of war, came ashore to drill them, and to mount one or two cannon. Yet Heke, lurking among the hills, contrived by a sudden dash to capture Lieutenant Philpott. However, after dealing courteously with him, he released him.

5. Kororarika Burnt.—On 11th March, 1845, at daylight, Heke with 200 men crept up to the flagstaff, surprised the men in the house attached, and when twenty men came out of the lower block-house to help their friends on the top of the hill, he attacked them and drove them down to the town in the hollow beside the shore. Close to the beach was a little hill, and on the top of this hill stood a house with a garden surrounded by a high fence. Behind this the soldiers and all the people of Kororarika took refuge. From the rocky high ground round about the Maoris fired down upon them, while the white men fired back, and the guns of the *Hazard*, which had come close in to the shore, kept up a constant roar. For three hours this lasted, ten white men being killed as well as a poor little child, while thirty-four of the natives were shot dead. The Maoris were preparing to retreat when, by some accident, the whole of the powder that the white men possessed was exploded. Then they had to save themselves. The women and children were carried out boat after boat to the three ships in the harbour. Then the men went off, and the Maoris, greatly surprised, crept cautiously down into the deserted town. They danced their war dance; sent off to their parents in the ships some white children who had been left behind, and then set fire to the town, destroying property to the value of £50,000.

Heke's fame now spread among the Maoris. When the settlers from Kororarika were landed at Auckland, homeless, desperate, and haggard, a panic set in, and some settlers sold their houses and land for a trifle, and departed. Others with more spirit enrolled themselves as volunteers. Three hundred men were armed and drilled. Fortifications were thrown up round the town, and sentries posted on all the roads leading to it. At Wellington and Nelson also men were drilled and stockades were built for defence.

6. First Maori War.—But Honi Heke was afraid of the soldiers, and when Colonel Hulme arrived from Sydney with several companies he withdrew to a strong pah of his, eighteen miles inland. Hulme landed at the nearest point of the coast, with a force of 400 men; these were joined by 400 friendly allies under Waka-Nene, whose wife led the tribe in a diabolic war dance, not a little startling to the British soldiers. The road that was to lead them to Honi Heke was only a track through a dense forest. Carts could not be taken, but each man carried biscuits for five days and thirty rounds of ammunition. Under four days of heavy rain they trudged along in the dripping pathway, all their biscuits wet and much of their powder ruined. At last on a little plain, between a lake and a wooded hill, they saw before them the pah of Honi Heke. Two great rows of tree trunks stuck upright formed a palisade round it. They were more than a foot thick, and twelve feet high, and they were so close that only a gun could be thrust between them. Behind these there was a ditch in which stood 250 Maoris, who could shoot through the palisades in security.

The British slept that night without tents round fires of kauri gum, but next morning all was astir for the attack. A rocket was sent whizzing over the palisades. It fell and burst among the Maoris, frightening them greatly, but succeeding discharges were failures, and the Maoris gathered courage to such an extent that a number under Kawiti came out to fight. The soldiers lowered their bayonets and charged, driving them back into the pah. During the night while the white men were smoking round their fires, the sound of the plaintive evening hymn rising in the still air from the pah suggested how strong was the hold that the new faith now had on the Maori mind. Next day Colonel Hulme, seeing that a place defended on all sides by such a strong palisade could not be captured without artillery, dug the graves of the fourteen soldiers killed, and marched back carrying with him thirty-nine wounded men.

222   HISTORY OF AUSTRALIA AND NEW ZEALAND.

There was dismay in Auckland when this news arrived. What could be said when 400 English soldiers retreated from 250

STRONGHOLD OF THE MAORIS AT RANGIRIRI.

savages? But, on the other hand, the Maoris had learnt a lesson They could not fight against English bayonets in the open, but while taking aim from behind palisades they were safe. Therefore they began in different places to strengthen their fortresses, and Honi Heke added new defences to his pah of Oheawai, which stood in the forest nineteen miles from the coast.

7. Oheawai.—More soldiers were sent from Sydney, and with them, to take the chief command, Colonel Despard, who had seen much fighting against hill tribes in India. He landed 630 men and six cannons; but these latter, being ship's cannons on wooden carriages with small wheels, stuck in the boggy forest roads. The men had to pull the guns, and they were assisted by 250 friendly Maoris. On the evening of 22nd June, 1845, they spread out before the pah during the gathering dusk. It was a strong place. In the midst of a deep and gloomy forest, a square had been cleared about a third of a mile in length and in breadth. Great trunks of trees had been set up in the earth, and they stood fifteen feet high; between their great stems, a foot or eighteen inches thick, there was just room enough left for firing a musket. Three rows of these gigantic palings, with a ditch five feet deep between the inner ones, made the fortress most dangerous to assault; and in the ground within hollows had been dug where men could sleep secure from shells and rockets. Two hundred and fifty warriors were there with plenty of muskets and powder.

On the second morning the British had got their guns planted within a hundred yards of the palisade, but the small balls they threw did little harm to such huge timber. The whole expedition would have had to retire had not a heavier gun come up. This threw shot thirty-two pounds in weight, and after twenty-six of these had struck the same place, a breach was seen of a yard or two in width. Colonel Despard ordered 200 men with ropes and hatchets and ladders to be ready for an assault at daybreak. In the still dawn of a wintry morning, the bugles rang out and the brave fellows gathered for the deadly duty. They rushed at the breach, and for ten minutes a wild scene ensued. The place was very narrow, and it was blocked by resolute Maoris, who shot down exactly half of the attacking party. Many of the soldiers forced their way through, but only to find a second and then a third palisade in front of them. Then they returned, losing men as they fled, and the whole British force fell back a little way into the forest. That night the groans and cries of the wounded, lying just outside the pah, were mingled with the wild shouts of the war dance within. Two days later the Maoris hoisted a flag of truce, and offered to let the white men carry off the dead and wounded. Thirty-four bodies lay at the fatal breach, and sixty-six men were found to have been wounded.

Sir George Grey.

A week later another load of cannon balls for the heavy gun was brought up, and the palisades were further broken down. A second assault would have been made, but during the night the Maoris tied up their dogs, and quietly dropping over the palisades at the rear of the pah, got far away into the forest before their retreat was known, for the howling of the dogs all night within the pah kept the officers from suspecting that the Maoris were escaping. The British destroyed the palisades, and carried off the stores of potatoes and other provisions which they found inside.

8. Governor Grey.—Fitzroy was preparing to chase Heke and Kawiti into their fastnesses, when he was recalled. The English Government thought he had not acted wisely in some ways and they blamed him for disobeying their instructions. They had more faith in that young officer, George Grey, who, after exploring in Western Australia, was now the Governor of South Australia. He arrived in November, 1845, to take charge of New Zealand; and at once went to Kororarika, where he found 700 soldiers waiting for orders. But he did not wish for fighting, if it could be avoided. He sent out a proclamation that Maoris who wished peace were to send in their submission by a certain day. If they did, he would see that the treaty of Waitangi was kept, and that justice was done to them.

Honi Heke sent two letters, but neither of them was satisfactory; and as more than a year passed without any signs of his submitting, Colonel Despard was directed to go after him. Heke was at a pah called Ikorangi; but Kawiti had 500 Maoris at a nearer pah called Ruapekapeka.

9. Ruapekapeka.—Despard took his men sixteen miles in boats up a river; then nine miles through the forest, and on the 31st December he had 1,173 soldiers with 450 friendly natives in a camp 800 yards from the pah. It was like the other pahs, but bigger and stronger, for behind the palisades there were earthen walls into which cannon balls would only plunge without doing any harm. Three heavy guns, however, were mounted, and when the Maoris sent up their flag, the first shot was so well aimed as to bring its flagstaff down amid the ringing cheers of the white men. All New Year's Day was spent in pouring in cannon balls by the hundred, but they did little harm. Next day the Maoris made a sally, but were driven back with the bayonet. Meantime, Heke came in one night with men to help his friend, and heavy firing on both sides was kept up for a week, after which two small breaches appeared near one of the corners of the palisades. The next day was Sunday, which the Maoris thought would be observed as a day of rest, but the soldiers, creeping cautiously up, pushed their way through the breaches; a number of the Maoris ran to arms and fired a volley or two, but before the main body could do anything several hundred soldiers were in the place. A stout fight took place, during which thirteen white men were killed. The Maoris, now no longer under cover, were no match for the soldiers, and they fled, leaving behind them all the provisions that were to have kept them for a whole season. This discouraged them, and Heke and Kawiti saw their men scatter out and join themselves to the quieter tribes for the sake of food. They therefore wrote to Grey asking peace, and promising to give no further trouble. Grey agreed, but left 200 soldiers at Kororarika in order to keep the Maoris of the district in check.

10. Rauparaha.—During the eighteen months while Heke's war was going on, troubles had been brewing at Wellington, where Rauparaha and Rangihaeata kept up an agitation. The latter declared his enmity; he plundered and sometimes killed the settlers; and when soldiers were sent round to keep him in order he surprised and killed some of them. But Rauparaha pretended to be friendly, though the Governor well knew he was the ringleader in the mischief. Grey quietly sent a ship, which by night landed 130 soldiers just in front of Rauparaha's house on the shore. They seized him sleeping in bed, and he was carried round to Auckland, where for some months he was kept a prisoner, though allowed to go about. Rangihaeata fled into the wildly wooded mountain ranges of the interior. Once or twice he made a stand, but was driven from his rocky positions, with the slaughter of men on both sides. At last he and his followers scattered out as fugitives into lonely and savage regions into which they could not be followed.

Thinking that good roads would do much to keep the country quiet, Grey offered half a crown a day to Maoris who would work at making roads. Quite a crowd gathered to the task, and for a while white men and Maoris toiled happily together, making good carriage roads into the heart of the country. But at Wanganui, in May, 1847, land disputes roused a tribe to bloodshed. They killed a white woman and her four little children; they attacked the town, and when the inhabitants withdrew to a stockade they had made, a fight took place which lasted for five hours, after which the Maoris burnt the town and retreated, carrying off all the cattle. Two months later, Governor Grey reached Wanganui, with 500 men. He chased the Maoris up the valley and fought them, gaining a decisive victory over them with the loss of two white men killed. He gave them no rest till the chiefs applied for peace, and early in the next year a meeting was held, and the principal chiefs of the district promised to obey the Queen's laws. The war had lasted five years, had cost a million pounds, and the lives of eighty-five white men, besides those of perhaps a hundred Maoris.

The English Government withdrew the larger part of the soldiers from New Zealand; but the colonists, to make themselves safe, enrolled a body they called the New Zealand Fencibles. They were all old soldiers who had retired from the British army, and who were offered little farms and a small payment. Five hundred came out from England on these terms, and were placed in four settlements round Auckland for the protection of that town. They were really farmers, who were paid to be ready to fight if need should arise. With their wives and children they made a population of 2,000 souls.

In this same year Rauparaha was allowed to go home. He was surprised at the permission and grateful for it; but he was an old man and died in the following year. In 1850 Honi Heke died, but Rangihaeata lingered on till 1856, giving no further trouble.

Governor Grey dealt fairly with the Maoris. He paid them for their lands. He hung such white men as murdered them. He set up schools to educate their children, and distributed ploughs and carts, harrows and horses, and even mills, so that they might grow and prepare for themselves better and more abundant food than they had ever known before.

CHAPTER XXVI.

NEW ZEALAND, 1843-1890.

1. Otago.—Meantime the New Zealand Company had not been idle, and E. G. Wakefield's busy brain was filled with fresh schemes. In 1849 an association had been formed at Glasgow in connection with the Free Church of Scotland, to send Scottish families out to New Zealand. Not knowing anything of the country, the new association asked the help of the New Zealand Company, which was readily given, as the new settlers proposed to buy land from the company. In 1844 an exploring party was sent out, and, after some inquiry, chose a place on the east coast of the South Island, called Otago. With the consent of the Governor 400,000 acres were there bought from the natives, and it seemed as if a new colony would soon be formed. But the

KNOX CHURCH, DUNEDIN.

news of the Wairau massacre and the unsettled state of the natives frightened intending settlers for a time. It was not till November, 1847, that the *John Wycliff* and the *Philip Lang* sailed from Greenock with the first company of settlers. They reached their new home in March, 1848, under the guidance of

Captain Cargill, an old soldier, who had been chosen as leader of the new settlement. At the head of a fine harbour, which they called Port Chalmers, they laid the foundations of a town, to which they gave the patriotic name of Dunedin, Gaelic for Edinburgh. It was in a fine district, troubled by few natives, and it steadily grew. Less than a year later, it had 745 inhabitants, who could boast of a good jetty, and a newspaper. The life of pioneers cannot be very easy, but these were of the right sort and prospered, and more would have joined them but for two circumstances. First came the news of the rich gold discoveries in California; and the most adventurous spirits hurried thither. Not only did this keep settlers from coming to New Zealand, but indeed a thousand of those she possessed left her shores for the goldfields. Then in this same year, 1848, a violent earthquake took place, which knocked down £15,000 worth of buildings in Wellington, and killed a man with his two children.

2. Canterbury.—Yet these unlucky accidents only delayed the progress of the colony by a year or two, and in the year 1850 a new settlement was formed. Seven years before this, Wakefield had conceived the idea of a settlement in connection with the Church of England. A number of leading men took up the notion, and among them was the famous Archbishop Whately. An association was formed which bought 20,000 acres of the New Zealand Company's land, to be selected later on. The settlers paid a high price for this land, but the greater part of the money so received was to be used for their own benefit, either in bringing out fresh settlers or in building churches and schools. A bishop and schoolmasters were to go out; a nobleman and other men of wealth bought land and prepared to take stock and servants out to the fine free lands of the south. Wakefield had enlisted in the new scheme a gentleman named John Robert Godley, who became very ardent, and under his direction three ships were filled with 600 settlers and their property, and left England on their long voyage to the Antipodes. They reached their destination, the east coast of the South Island, on 16th December, 1850, and gladly felt the soil of a lovely land under their feet. In their enthusiasm they sang the National Anthem, and scattered out to view their new homes. A high and rugged hill prevented their seeing inland till they climbed to its brow, and then they perceived long plains of fertile soil, watered by numerous streams of bright and rapid water. They resolved to found their city on the plains, making only a port upon the seashore. Governor Grey and his wife came over from Wellington to welcome them, and they found that much had been done to make them comfortable. Large sheds had been put up in which they could find shelter till they should build

CHRISTCHURCH CATHEDRAL.

their own homes. A pretty spot by a river named the Avon was chosen for the town, which was laid out in a square; and a church and schoolroom were built among the first erections. In keeping with the religious fervour that lay at the basis of the whole undertaking, the town was called Christchurch; while the name of Lyttelton was given to the seaport, a road being made between the two and over the hill.

During the next year 2,600 settlers arrived. Some of these

were young men of birth and fortune, who brought with them everything needed to transplant to New Zealand the luxuries of England. A large proportion of the settlers were labouring men of a superior class, who were brought out as servants at the expense of the wealthy settlers. There was a good deal of disappointment. Many of the labourers crossed over to Australia, where the gold discoveries offered every man a chance of fortune, and where wages were very high. The wealthiest people therefore had to do their own work, and few of them liked it. The result was that many left the settlement and never came back to it. But from Australia came relief. For some of the squatters who had been dislodged by the inroad of diggers to Victoria, hearing of the great grassy plains of Canterbury, with never a tree to be cleared from the natural pasturage, crossed with flocks of sheep, and bought land in the new settlement. In 1853 Canterbury had 5,000 people; it produced £40,000 worth of wool a year, and seventy vessels reached its seaport. For a place in its third year such progress was wonderful.

3. New Zealand Prosperous.

—The natives being at peace, and the price of land being reduced, settlers streamed steadily into New Zealand. In 1853 there were 31,000 white people in the colony, and they had bought from the natives 24,000,000 acres of land. They had a million of sheep, and their exports were over £300,000 in value. The Government was quite solvent again, having a revenue of £140,000 a year. A very large number of farms were by this time in full work, those in the North Island being chiefly used for crops, those in the South Island chiefly for sheep. But the New Zealand Company had disappeared. In 1850 it was a quarter of a million pounds in debt, and it was wound up, leaving its shareholders with heavy losses.

An important event in the history of New Zealand occurred on 30th June, 1852, when the English Parliament gave the colony power to make its own laws and manage its own affairs, practically without interference from London. A bill was passed providing that there should be six provinces, each with its own provincial council, consisting of not less than nine persons to be chosen to manage local affairs. There was also to be the General Assembly, consisting of a legislative council, appointed by the

Governor, and a House of Representatives consisting of forty members to be chosen by the colonists. The Governor, who was now Sir George Grey, did much to bring these new arrangements into force and to adapt them to the needs of the settlers. Having ruled well for eight years and brought the colony into a prosperous condition, and being required to set in order the affairs of Cape Colony, he left New Zealand on the last day of 1853, much regretted by the Maoris and also by the majority of the colonists.

THE MAORI KING.

Colonel Wynyard acted as Governor for the time being, and summoned the first Parliament of New Zealand to meet in May, 1854. He had much difficulty in getting the system of Cabinets of responsible Ministers to work smoothly. The colonists from different provinces had interests which lay in opposite directions, and political matters did not move easily. He was glad when the new Governor, Colonel Gore Browne, arrived in September, 1855. At that time New Zealand had 45,000 white settlers in it, and the discovery next year of rich goldfields in Otago attracted many more, and gave a great impetus to Dunedin. Everything promised a splendid future, when again the Maoris became troublesome.

4. The King Movement.—The Waikato tribe had always been averse to the selling of their land. They said truly enough that the money the white men gave for it was soon spent, but the land was gone for ever, and the settlers were fencing in

40,000 additional acres every year. They called a meeting on the banks of Lake Taupo to discuss the question. A large number of chiefs were present, and they agreed to form a Land League, all members of which undertook to sell no more land to white men. At this time also a new project was formed. The Maoris felt their weakness whilst divided up into so many tribes. Union would make them strong. They resolved to select one chief to be king of all the Maoris, and for that purpose they chose the redoubted Te Whero Whero, who hoisted the Maori flag. But he was old and inclined to die in peace, and, dying soon afterwards, was succeeded by his son, a young man of no ability. Many of the Maoris held aloof from these leagues; they were of tribes hostile to the Waikatos, or else they were glad to get the white man's money, and felt that they had still plenty of land for their own use. But in the heart of the North Island, some 4,000 or 5,000 Maori warriors nursed a wild project of driving the English out of the country. They gathered muskets and powder; they strengthened their pahs and filled them with potatoes and yams. Governor Browne took no steps to check them, and suffered several thousand muskets to be bought from English ships along the coasts.

5. Taranaki War.—Meantime a quarrel had been going forward which gave the Maoris a pretext for fighting. In 1859 Governor Browne had visited Taranaki, and announced that if any of the natives had land to sell he was ready to buy it. A Maori offered him 600 acres, proving that he was the owner of the land. The Governor gave him £200 for it; but the chief of the tribe to which this Maori belonged was one of the Land League, and refused to let the land be sold. The Governor after inquiry came to the conclusion that as the rightful owner of the land was willing to sell it, no one else had a claim to interfere. He sent surveyors up to measure the land. They were stopped by the chief. The Governor sent some soldiers to protect the surveyors. The whole of the Taranaki Maoris rose in arms, and swept the few soldiers down to the coast. They then ravaged the whole district, burning houses, crops, and fences; and all the settlers of Taranaki crowded for defence into the town of New Plymouth. Most of them were ruined, and many of them left for other colonies. Governor Browne now sent round from Auckland all the soldiers he had; but, in accordance with their agreement, the Waikato tribes sent warriors to assist the Taranaki tribe. Their Maori king having no great influence, these were placed under the command of Te Waharoa, a Maori chief of much skill and popularity. Many skirmishes took place, in which the natives, through their quickness and subtle plans, inflicted more injury than they received. But General Pratt having arrived from Sydney with fresh soldiers, and prepared to sap the pahs and blow them up, the Maoris became afraid, and Te Waharoa proposed that peace should be made, which was done in May, 1861.

6. Second Maori War.—

Governor Browne then called upon the Waikato tribes, who were then in arms, to make submission and take the oath of obedience to the Queen's laws. Very few did so; and when Sir Duncan Cameron arrived to take the chief command with more troops and big guns, he stated that he would invade the Waikato territory and punish those tribes for their disobedience.

But then came news that the English Government, being dissatisfied with the way in which matters were drifting into war, was going to send back Sir George Grey. He arrived in September, 1861, to take the place of Colonel Browne, and after a month or two summoned a great meeting of the Waikatos to hear him speak. They gathered and discussed the land question. Grey said that those who did not wish to sell their land could keep it by the treaty of Waitangi; but that no one must hinder another man from selling what was his own. The land for which Governor Browne had given £200 at Taranaki was still in the occupation of armed Maoris, and it must be given up. Grey reasoned with them, but they were obstinate. Bishop Selwyn went among them and exhorted them to peace, but made no impression.

Meanwhile General Cameron set his men at work to make roads, and during the year and a half while the Governor was trying to bring the Maoris to reason, he was making good military highways throughout the North Island.

In October, 1862, the Maoris held another great meeting among themselves to discuss their position. They had grown confident, and thought that the Governor's mildness arose from weakness. They resolved to fight. The Governor sent soldiers to take possession of the land at Taranaki. Te Waharoa sent word to the Taranaki Maoris to begin shooting, and he would soon be with them. He was as good as his word, and laid a trap for a body of English soldiers and killed ten of them.

The Waikatos sent an embassy to all the other tribes, urging them to join and drive the white men out of the country. Te Waharoa was chosen to command in a grand attack at Auckland, and for that purpose the Maoris in two columns moved stealthily through the forest down the Waikato valley towards the town, threatening to massacre every white man in it. But General Cameron was there in time to meet them. They fell back to a line of rifle pits they had formed, and from that shelter did much damage to the British troops. But at last the Maoris were dislodged and chased with bayonets up the Waikato, losing fifty of their men. They had stronger entrenchments farther up, where a thousand men were encamped with women to cook for them and to make cartridges. So strongly were they posted that Cameron waited for four months whilst guns and supplies were being brought up along the roads, which were now good and well made. By getting round to the side of their camp, and behind it, he made it necessary for them to fall back again, which they did.

7. Rangiriri.--They now made themselves very secure at a place called Rangiriri, where a narrow road was left between the Waikato River and a boggy lake. This space they had blocked with a fence of thick trees twenty feet high, and with two ditches running across the whole length. In the midst of this strong line they had set up a redoubt, a sort of square fortress, from the walls of which they could fire down upon the attackers in any direction. About 500 Maoris well armed took up their position in this stronghold. Cameron advanced against them with 770 men and two guns, each throwing shot of forty pounds weight. At the same time four gunboats with 500 soldiers were sent up the river to take the Maori position in flank. At half-past four on a July morning the British bugles sounded the attack, and the fight lasted until the darkness of night put an end to it. During that fierce day the British charged again and again, to be met by a murderous fire from behind the palisades and from the walls of

RANGIRIRI, FROM THE WAIKATO.

the redoubt. Forty-one soldiers had been killed and ninety-one wounded, the line of palisades had been captured, but the Maoris had all gathered safely within the redoubt. During the night the troops were quartered all round so as to prevent them from escaping, and a trench was cut to lead to a mine under the redoubt so that it could be blown up with gunpowder in the morning. The Maoris saw this project and could not prevent it. In the early dawn, after a night spent in war dances and hideous yelling, some of them burst out by the side towards the lake, and rushed past or jumped over the soldiers who were resting there. A heavy fire, poured into them from their rear, killed a great many of them. Seeing this, a large party of the Maoris, and among them Te Waharoa and the Maori king, stayed in the redoubt. But they knew that they were trapped, and next day they surrendered, in all 183 men with a few women. Sixty or seventy of the Maoris had been killed, but several hundreds escaped.

8. Orakau.—Meantime General Carey, who was next in command to General Cameron, had been chasing another large body of the Waikato tribe far up the river more than half way to its source in Lake Taupo. It was a wild and mountainous district, and the Maoris were sheltered at Orakau, a pah in a very strong position. Carey spent three days in running a mine under the walls, while his guns and mortars kept up a perfect storm of shot and shell. Then he offered to accept their surrender. They refused to give in. He begged them at least to let the women and children go and they would be allowed to pass out unhurt. They said that men and women would fight for ever and ever. Yet when the mines began to burst, and the guns poured in redoubled showers of death, they found they could hold the place no longer. They formed a column, and made a sudden rush to escape. So quick were they and so favourable the ground, that they would have escaped if the British had not had a body of 300 or 400 cavalry, who rode after them and sabred all who would not surrender. About 200 were killed, and although several hundreds escaped yet they were so dispersed that they made no further stand. They left their pahs, and though a series of skirmishes took place, yet the Waikato rebellion was ended, and Cameron had only to leave a sufficient number of military settlers along the Waikato Valley to make certain that peace and order would be maintained.

9. The Gate Pah.—There was a tribe at Tauranga, on the Bay of Plenty, with whom Governor Grey was displeased, for they had sent men, guns and food to help the Waikatos, and they showed a warlike disposition. He demanded their submission, and they refused it. He then sent General Cameron with 1,500 soldiers to deal with them. This force found the Tauranga tribe prepared to fight in a strong place called the Gate Pah, built on a ridge with a swamp at each side. They had 500 men in it, all well armed. Cameron had three heavy guns placed in position, and during the night 700 soldiers passed round one of the swamps to get at the rear of the Maoris. In the morning a terrific fire was opened, and for two hours the place was swept by shot and shell, but the Maoris had dug underground shelters for themselves, and were little injured. After that the guns were used to break a hole in the palisades, and at four o'clock there was a sufficient breach to admit an attacking party. Three hundred men were chosen, and put in front of the place. A rocket was sent up as a signal, and the attacking party dashed at the breach. As they entered it, not a Maori could be seen, but puffs of smoke all along the earthen bank showed where they were concealed. The assailants were a dense crowd, on whom every shot told. All the officers were killed. More men kept crowding in, only to drop before the murderous fire. Suddenly a panic seized the men. A rush was made to get out of the breach again, and while the soldiers were running away volley after volley was fired into the crowd. General Cameron did not renew the attack, for evening was falling. There came on a dark wet night; and although surrounded on all hands, the Maoris contrived to slip gently past the sentries, leaving some wounded men behind them.

10. Te Ranga.—The Maoris fell back a few miles and chose a strong position at Te Ranga for a new pah. They had only dug the ditches and made some rifle pits when the British were upon them. The troops carried the position with a rush, the Maoris standing up against the bayonets with the coolest courage. A hand-to-hand fight forced the natives out of the ditches, and then they turned and fled. The horse soldiers pursued and killed many. Altogether 123 of the Maoris were killed and a large number captured, while the English lost ten men killed.

11. Wereroa.—After this action, though skirmishes were frequent, the Maoris made no determined stand, and on the English side affairs were carried on in a slow fashion. General Cameron had under him 10,000 regular soldiers, and nearly 10,000 colonial volunteers. He had nearly a dozen vessels of different sorts, either on the coasts or up the river, and he had an abundance of heavy guns. There arose quarrels between him and the Governor, who thought that with less than 1,000 Maoris under arms more progress ought to have been made. General Cameron resigned and departed in the middle of 1865. The Governor wished him before he went to attack a pah called Wereroa, but the general said he required 2,000 more men to do it, and refused. Yet Sir George Grey, taking himself the command of the colonial forces, captured the fort without losing a man. The bulk of the Maoris escaped, and kept up for a time a guerilla warfare in forests and on mountain sides; but at last the Tauranga tribes, or the miserable remnant that was left, surrendered to the Governor. Grey, in admiration of their generous and often noble conduct and their straightforward mode of fighting, allowed all the prisoners to go free; and though he punished them by confiscating a quarter of their land, he did his best to settle them on the other three-fourths in peace and with such advantages as British help could secure them. So there came quietness round the Bay of Plenty.

12. The Hau Hau Religion.—Meantime new trouble was brewing in the Taranaki district. There the soldiers were skirmishing with the Maoris, but had them well in control, when a pair of mad or crafty native priests set the tribes in wild commotion, by declaring that the Angel Gabriel had told them in a vision that at the end of the year 1864 all white men would be driven out of New Zealand, that he himself would defend the Maoris, and that the Virgin Mary would be always with them; that the religion of the white men was false, and that legions of angels would come and teach the Maoris a better religion. In the meantime all good Maoris who shouted the word Hau Hau as they went into battle would be victorious, and angels would protect their lives. A body of these fanatics, deeply impressed with the belief in these and many other follies, tried their fortunes against the soldiers at Taranaki, but with small success. Forty of them, in spite of shouting their Hau Hau, fell before the muskets and guns of the white men. Then 300 of them made an effort in another direction, and, moving down the river Wanganui, threatened the little town at its mouth. Wanganui was defended by 300 soldiers; but all the out settlers up the valley were leaving their farms and hurrying in for shelter, when 300 men of the Wanganui tribe, who liked the white men and were friendly with them, offered to fight the Hau Haus. The challenge was accepted; and about 200 of the fanatics landed on a little island called Moutoa, in the middle of the river. Though surrounded by a pretty margin of white pebbles, it was covered with ferns and thick scrub. Through this at daybreak the combatants crept towards each other, the Hau Haus gesticulating and making queer sounds. At last they fell to work, and volley after volley was discharged at only ten yards distance. The friendly natives, having seen three of their chiefs fall, turned and fled. Many had plunged into the river, when one of their chiefs made a stand at the end of the island, and gathering twenty men around him poured in a volley and killed the Hau Hau leader. This surprised the fanatics and they hesitated; then a second volley and a charge routed them. Back came the friendly Maoris who had fled, and chased their enemies into the stream, wherein a heavy slaughter took place. About seventy of the Hau Haus were slain. The twelve who fell on the friendly side were buried in Wanganui with military honours, and a handsome monument now marks the place where their bones rest.

13. Conclusion of Maori Wars.—In 1866 General Chute came to take command of the troops, in place of General Cameron. A vigorous campaign crushed the Hau Haus after much skirmishing in different parts of the Wellington district. But the chief trouble arose from another source. The 183 prisoners taken at Rangiriri, together with some others taken afterwards, were detained on board a hulk near Auckland. Sir George Grey wished to deal in a kindly fashion with them, and proposed to release them if they gave their word not to give further trouble. The Ministers of his Cabinet were against this proposal, but agreed that he should send them to an island near Auckland to live there without any guards. They gave their promise, but broke it and all but four escaped, Te Waharoa being among them. They chose the top of a circular hill thirty-five miles from Auckland and there fortified themselves in a pah called Omaha. But they did no harm to any one, and as they soon quietly dispersed they were not meddled with.

A wild outburst of Hau Hau fanaticism on the east coast of the Bay of Plenty stirred up the fires of discord again, when a worthy old Church of England missionary named Mr. Volkner was seized, and, after some savage rites had been performed, was hanged on a willow tree as a victim. More fighting followed, in which a large share was taken by a Maori chief named Ropata, who, clad in European uniform and with the title of Major Ropata, fought stoutly against the Hau Haus, and captured several pahs.

14. Te Kooti.—When the last of these pahs was captured an English officer declared that one of the friendly chiefs named Te Kooti was playing false and acting as a spy. Thinking to do as Governor Grey had done with Rauparaha, this officer seized the chief, who, without trial of any sort, was sent off to the Chatham Islands, a lonely group 300 miles away, which New Zealand was now using as a penal establishment for prisoners. This conduct was quite unfair, as Te Kooti, so far as can now be known, was not a spy, and was friendly to the English.

Nearly 300 Maoris were on the Chatham Islands, most of them Hau Hau prisoners. They were told that if they behaved well they would be allowed to return in two years. When two years were past and no signs of their liberation appeared, Te Kooti planned a bold escape. An armed schooner, the *Rifleman*, having come in with provisions the Maoris suddenly overpowered the twelve soldiers who formed their guard, and seized the vessel. One soldier was killed whilst fighting, but all the rest were treated gently. The whole of the Maoris went on board and then the crew were told that unless they agreed to sail the vessel back to New Zealand they would all be killed. Day and night Maori guards patrolled the deck during the voyage, and one of them with loaded gun and drawn sword always stood over the helmsman and compelled him to steer them home. They reached the shores of New Zealand a little north of Hawke Bay, and landed, taking with them all the provisions out of the vessel, but treating the crew in a kindly way. A ship was sent round with soldiers who attacked the runaways, but they were too few, and too hastily prepared, so that Te Kooti easily defeated them. Three times was he attacked by different bodies of troops, and three times did he drive off his assailants. Cutting a path for himself through the forests, he forced his way a hundred miles inland to a place of security. But his people had no farms, and no means of raising food in these wild mountain regions, and the provisions they had taken from the *Rifleman* were used in a few months.

15. Poverty Bay Massacre.—Then, roused to madness by hunger, of which some of them had died, they crept cautiously back to the Poverty Bay district. Falling at night upon the little village, they slaughtered men, women, and children, as well as all the quiet Maoris they could catch. The dawn woke coldly on a silent village, wherein fifty or sixty bodies lay gashed and mangled in their beds, or at their doors, or upon their garden paths. An old man and a boy escaped by hiding. After taking all the provisions out of the place, Te Kooti set fire to the houses and retreated to the hills, where, on the top of a peak 2,000 feet high, he had made a pah called Ngatapa, which was defended on every side by precipices and deep gorges. There was only one narrow approach, and that had been fortified with immense care. The colonial troops under Colonel Whitmore, and bodies of friendly Maoris under Ropata, attacked him here. The work was very difficult, for after climbing those precipitous hills there were two palisades to be carried, one seven feet high and the other twelve. But science prevailed. After great exertions and appalling dangers the place was captured by Ropata, who climbed the cliffs and gained a corner of the palisades, killing a great number of Te Kooti's men in the action. During the night the rest escaped from the pah, sliding from the cliffs by means of ropes. But in the morning they were chased, and for two days the fugitives were brought back to the pah in twos and threes. Ropata took it for granted that they were all concerned in the massacre at Poverty Bay. Each of the captives as he arrived was stripped, taken to the edge of the cliff, shot dead, and his body thrown over. About a hundred and twenty were thus slaughtered. But

Te Kooti himself escaped, and for the next two years he lived the life of a hunted animal, chased through the gloomy forests by the relentless Ropata. He fought many fights: his twenty Hau Hau followers were often near to death from starvation; but at length wearied out he threw himself on the mercy of the white men, was pardoned, sunk into obscurity, and died in peace.

War was not really at an end till 1871; as up to that date occasional skirmishes took place. But there never was any fear of a general rising of the Maoris after 1866.

16. Progress of New Zealand.—These wars were confined to the North Island. Otago, Canterbury, and Nelson felt them only by way of increased taxes. Otherwise they were left in peace to pursue their quiet progress. They multiplied their population sixfold; they opened up the country with good roads; a railway was cut through the mountain to join Christchurch with its seaport, Lyttelton, by a tunnel half a mile long. A similar but easier railway was made to join Dunedin to Port Chalmers; gold was found in various parts, especially in Otago, and on the west coast round Hokitika. For a time New Zealand sent out gold

THE CARGILL FOUNTAIN, DUNEDIN.

every year to the value of two and a half million pounds, and this lucrative pursuit brought thousands of stout settlers to her shores.

In 1864 the New Zealand Parliament chose Wellington to be the capital of the colony, as being more central than Auckland. In 1868 an Act was passed to abolish the provinces, and to make New Zealand more completely a united colony. A great change began in this same year, when the first Maori chief was elected to be a member of the New Zealand Parliament. Before long there were six Maoris seated there, two of them being in the Upper House. These honourable concessions, together with a fairer treatment in regard to their land, did much to show the Maoris that their lives and liberties were respected by the white men. They had lost much land, but what was left was now of more use to them than the whole had formerly been. Their lives and their property were now safer than ever, and they learnt that to live as peaceful subjects of Queen Victoria was the happiest course they could follow. The Government built schools for them and sent teachers; it built churches for them and cared for them in many ways. Thus they became well satisfied, even if they sometimes remembered with regret the freer life of the olden times.

But Sir George Grey, who was the warm friend of the Maori, was no longer Governor. He had finished his work and his term of office had expired. Sir George Bowen came out to take his place. Grey after a trip to England returned to take up his residence in New Zealand, and a few years later allowed himself to be elected a member of its Parliament. Subsequently he became its Prime Minister, sinking his own personal pride in his desire to do good to the country.

From 1870 to 1877 the affairs of the country were chiefly directed by ministries in which Sir Julius Vogel was the principal figure. He started and carried out a bold policy of borrowing and spending the money so obtained in bringing out fresh settlers and in opening up the land by railways. This plan plunged the colony deeply into debt, but it changed the look of the place, and although it had its dangers and its drawbacks, it has done a great deal for the colony. At first the natives refused to let the railways pass through their districts, but in 1872 a great meeting of chiefs agreed that it would be good for all to have the country opened up. Some maintained a dull hostility till 1881, but all the same the railways were made, until at length 2,000 miles were open for traffic.

Between 1856 and 1880 nineteen different ministries managed the affairs of New Zealand, one after the other, the same Prime Minister however presiding over different ministries. The most notable of these have been, Sir William Fox, Edward W. Stafford, Major Atkinson, and Sir Julius Vogel.

NEW ZEALAND.

In 1880 the colony had increased to 500,000 white people, owning 12,000,000 sheep and exporting nearly £6,000,000 worth of goods. The Maoris were 44,000, but while the whites were rapidly increasing, the Maoris were somewhat decreasing. They had 112,000 sheep and nearly 50,000 cattle, with about 100,000 pigs.

The heavy expenditure of the borrowing years from 1870 to 1881 was followed by a time of depression from 1880 to 1890, during which Sir Robert Stout and Major Atkinson were Prime Ministers; but at the end of that period the colony began rapidly to recover. Its population approached 750,000, with 42,000 Maoris; its sheep were nearly 20,000,000 in number; and its farms produced 20,000,000 bushels of wheat and oats. It sent £4,000,000 worth of wool to England, and about £1,000,000 worth of frozen meat. The general history of the last twenty years may be summed up as consisting of immense progress in all material and social interests.

VICTORIA DEFENCE FLEET.

INDEX.

	PAGE
Abolition of Transportation	83
Active	196
Adelaide	70
Agricultural Co., N. S. W.	44
Albany	118, 136
Alexander, Mount	97
Alexandrina, Lake	53
Alfred, Prince	171
Alligator	202
Anti-Transportation	161
Arthur, Governor	36
Atkin, Judge-Advocate	30
Auckland	205
Australia, name given	2
Australian Bight	133
Ballarat	95
Bass	18, 20, 40
Bathurst	42
Batman	37, 58, 62
Baudin	23
Bentley	103
Bligh	29
Blue Mountains	40
Botany Bay	9, 11
Bourke	45, 64
Bowen, Lieutenant	32
Bowen, Sir George	129
Boyd	193
Brady	37
Brisbane, Governor	42
Brisbane River	120
Britannia	209
Browne, Colonel	162
Browne, Colonel Gere	232
Buccaneers' Archipelago	7
Buckley	63
Burke and Wills	143
Burra Mines	86
Busby	202
Caen, De	24
Caley's Repulse	40
Cameron, Sir Duncan	234
Canterbury	229
Carpenter, General	5
Castlemaine	97

	PAGE
Castlereagh	40
Chisholm, Mrs.	79
Christchurch	230
Clarke	20
Clarke, Rev. W. B.	91
Clunes	95
Collins, Governor	12, 32, 57
Convicts Prevention Act	99
Cook's Voyages	8, 118
Corner Inlet	21
Cotton Plantations	125
Cowper, Charles	170
Crawford	37
Crozet, Captain	190
Cumberland, vessel	24
Cunningham, Allan	49
Dalley	175
Dalrymple	22, 34
Dampier	6
Darling River	52
Darling, Sir Charles	178
Darling, Sir Ralph	43
Davey, Governor	34
Denison, Governor	108, 159
D'Entrecasteaux	11
Despard, Colonel	223
Du Cane	162
Du Fresne	190
Dunbar	110
Dunedin	229
Duyfhen	4
Edel	5
Endeavour	8, 188
Esmond	95
Eureka Stockade	104
Exhibitions—	
Sydney	174
Melbourne	182
Adelaide	168
Eyre, Edward	132
Fawkner	57, 62, 66
Fisher	70
Fitzroy, Governor	215
Fitzroy, Sir Charles	83
Flinders	18, 22, 24

	PAGE		PAGE
Forrest	154	King George's Sound	111, 118, 136
Foveaux, Colonel	31	Lalor	104, 105
Franklin, Sir John	38, 155	Lancey, Captain	62
Fremantle	112	Land Grants, W. A.	113
Furneaux	11	Land Laws, N. S. W.	76
Garden Island	112	Land League	238
Gate Pah	238	Land Question	46, 210
Gawler, Colonel	71, 75	Landsborough	152
Geelong	60	Lang, Dr.	80
Giles	154	La Perouse	11
Gipps, Governor	75	Latrobe	65, 80
Glenelg River	54	*Leeuwin*	4
Godley, John Robert	229	Legislative Assembly	108, 175
Gold, early rumours of	90	Legislative Council	44, 80, 108, 215
Gold in Queensland	123	Leichardt	140
Goldfields, aspect of	99	Licence Fee	101
Goldfields, rush to	93	Lonsdale	65
Gregory, A. C.	143	Lyttelton	230
Grey, Earl	82	Macarthur, John	28
Grey, Governor	75, 84, 224	M'Culloch	179
Grimes	56	M'Kinlay	152
Grose, Major	16	Macleay	52
Hacking, Port	20	Macquarie, Governor	38
Haines	176	Macquarie River	42, 49
Hargraves	91	Marion	11
Hartog, Dirk	4	Marsden, Samuel	194
Hau Hau	239	Melbourne	60, 65
Hawaiki	186	Merri Creek	60
Hawkesbury	16	Mitchell	54
Henty Bros.	61	Moreton Bay	10, 119
Hervey Bay	23	Murray, Lieutenant	23, 55
Hindmarsh, Governor	71	Murray River	52
Hobart Town	32	Nelson	213
Hobson, Governor	203, 214	New Hebrides	2
Hokianga	201	New Plymouth	212
Hongi	195	New South Wales Corps	26
Honi Heke	218	New South Wales named	10
Hotham, Sir Charles	103	New Zealand	9, 188
Howe, Cape	9	New Zealand Company	207
Howitt	151	New Zealand Fencibles	227
Hulme, Colonel	221	Norfolk Island	15, 35
Hume and Hovell	49	*Norfolk*, sloop	22
Humffray	104	Nuggets	98
Hunter, Captain	12, 16	Nuyts	5
Investigator, vessel	23	Oheawai	223
Jackson, Port	10, 12	Orakau	237
Johnstone, Major	28, 30	Otago	227
Kangaroo Island	23, 70	Ovens River	50, 101
Kapunda Mines	85	Oxley	48, 119
Keer-weer, Cape	4	Parkes, Sir H.	175
Kennedy, the explorer	141	Patriotic Six	159
Kennedy, a miner	103	Patterson, Colonel	16, 31, 34
Kererarika	200, 220	Peel, Mr.	116
King, Lieutenant	15, 25	Perth	113

INDEX.

	PAGE
Phillip, Governor	12
Polynesian Labour	126
Poole	137
Portland Bay	55
Port Chalmers	229
Port Phillip	55
Poverty Bay	242
Queen Charlotte Sound	190, 208
Queensland	123
Quiros, De	2
Railways in N. S. W.	171
Rangihaeata	216, 226
Rangiriri	235
Rauparaha	216, 226
Ruapekapeka	225
Ruatara	195
Rebecca, vessel	59
Redcliff Peninsula	120
Representative Government	80, 232
Risdon	32
Robe, Governor	88
Robertson, John	170
Rockhampton	124
Roebuck	7
Saltwater River	60
Sandhurst	97
Selwyn, Dr George	214
Separation of Port Phillip	79
Separation of Queensland	122
Settled Government	201
Shoalhaven River	21
Shortland, Lieutenant	17, 210, 215
Sirius, war-ship	12
Sorell, Governor	35
Soudan Expedition	175
South Australian Association	68
Spain, William	216
Spencer's Gulf	23
Stony Desert	139
Strzelecki	90
Stuart, M'Douall	137, 153
Sturt	15, 136
Supply, war-ship	12
Surville De	189
Sydney Cove	13
Tamar River	22
Taranaki	211, 233

	PAGE
Tarra	193
Tasman	5, 187
Tasmania named	162
Taylor	37
Te Kooti	241
Telegraph, overland	166
Te Pehi	192, 194
Te Ranga	238
Te Whero Whero	199, 212, 233
Todd, Charles	166
Tom Thumb, boat	18
Torrens' Real Property Act	164
Torrens, Colonel	70
Torres	3
Tribulation, Cape	10
Twofold Bay	21
University of Sydney	111
Vancouver	11
Van Diemen	5
Vern	105
Victoria	83, 175
Vlaming	112
Wairau	216
Waitangi	204
Wakefield, Edward Gibbon	67, 207, 227
Wakefield Colonel	208
Walker	152
Wanganui	212
Warburton	154
Weld, Governor	162
Wellington	208
Wentworth	40, 109
Wereroa	239
Western Port	21, 58
West Australia	111
Wilmot, Sir Eardley	158
Wilson's Promontory	21
Windsor	40
Wool-growing	28
Wynyord, Colonel	232
Yarra	59
York, Cape	4, 24, 142
Young, Sir Henry	89, 162
Young, Sir John	168
Zaachen	4

www.ingramcontent.com/pod-product-compliance
Lightning Source LLC
Chambersburg PA
CBHW021410230426
43666CB00006B/705